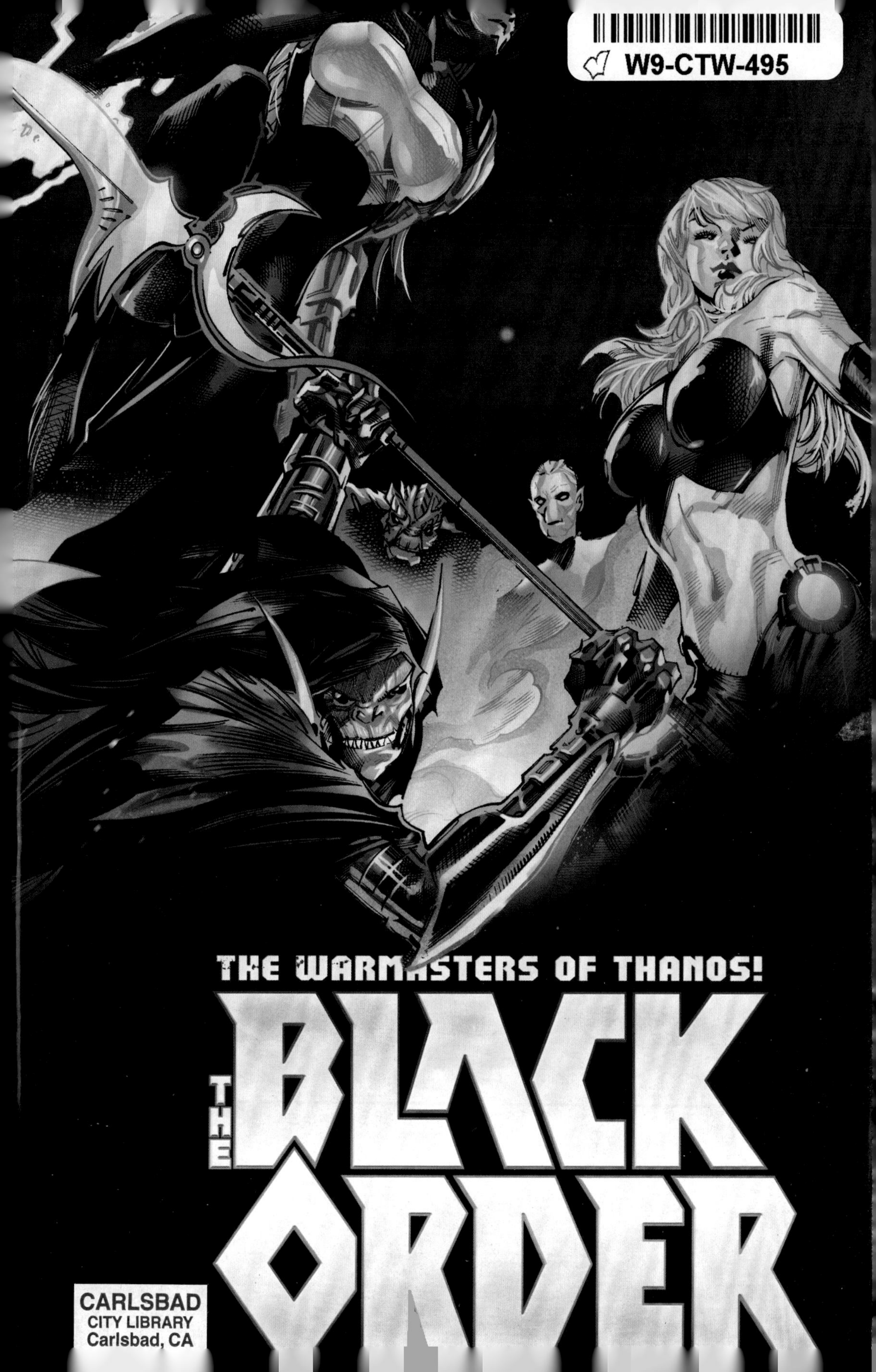

THE WARMASTERS OF THANOS!

THE BLACK ORDER

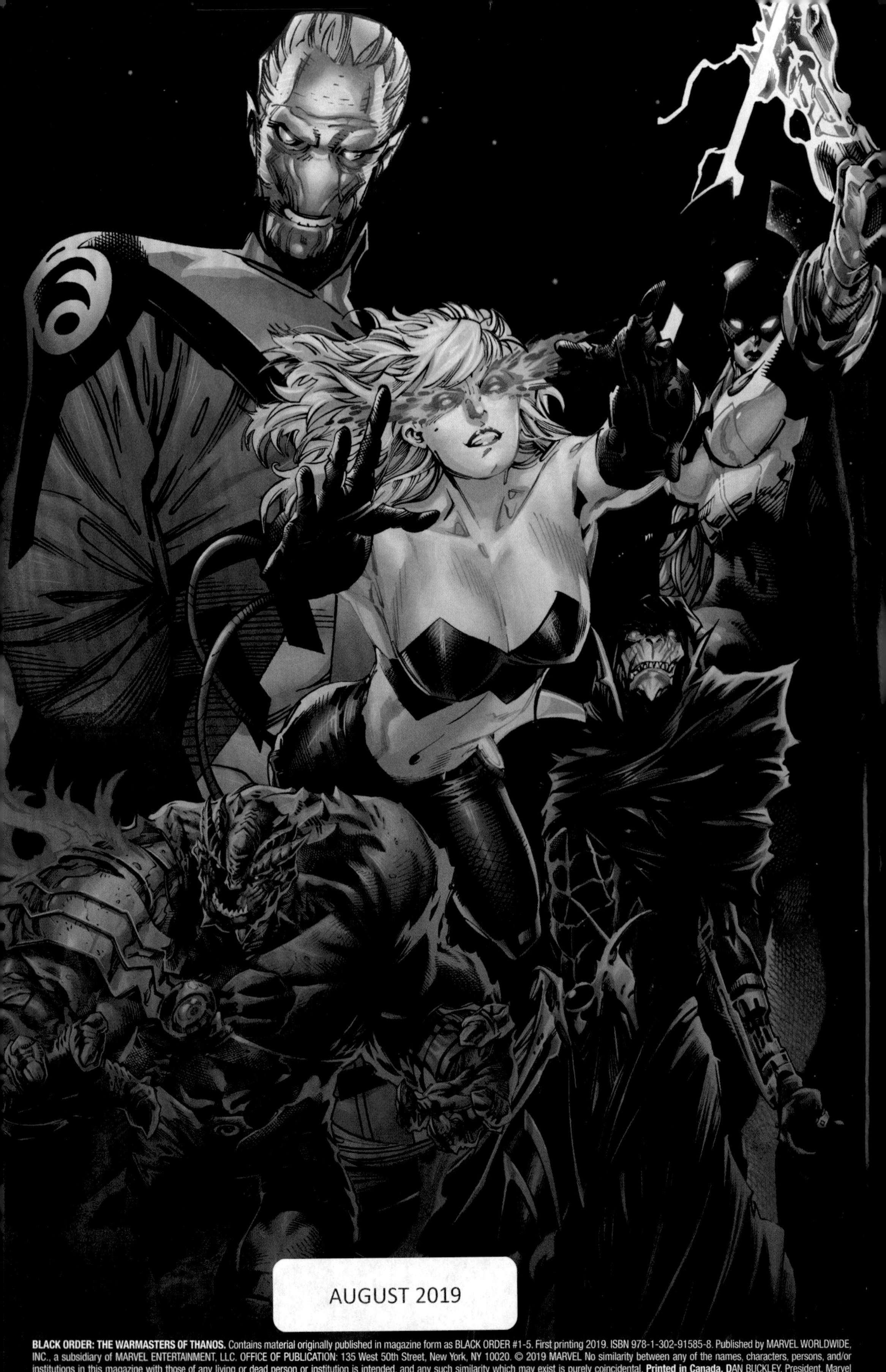

BLACK ORDER: THE WARMASTERS OF THANOS. Contains material originally published in magazine form as BLACK ORDER #1-5. First printing 2019. ISBN 978-1-302-91585-8. Published by MARVEL WORLDWIDE, INC., a subsidiary of MARVEL ENTERTAINMENT, LLC. OFFICE OF PUBLICATION: 135 West 50th Street, New York, NY 10020. © 2019 MARVEL No similarity between any of the names, characters, persons, and/or institutions in this magazine with those of any living or dead person or institution is intended, and any such similarity which may exist is purely coincidental. **Printed in Canada.** DAN BUCKLEY, President, Marvel Entertainment; JOHN NEE, Publisher; JOE QUESADA, Chief Creative Officer; TOM BREVOORT, SVP of Publishing; DAVID BOGART, Associate Publisher & SVP of Talent Affairs; DAVID GABRIEL, SVP of Sales & Marketing, Publishing; JEFF YOUNGQUIST, VP of Production & Special Projects; DAN CARR, Executive Director of Publishing Technology; ALEX MORALES, Director of Publishing Operations; DAN EDINGTON, Managing Editor; SUSAN CRESPI, Production Manager; STAN LEE, Chairman Emeritus. For information regarding advertising in Marvel Comics or on Marvel.com, please contact Vit DeBellis, Custom Solutions & Integrated Advertising Manager, at vdebellis@marvel.com. For Marvel subscription inquiries, please call 888-511-5480. **Manufactured between 2/15/2019 and 3/19/2019 by SOLISCO PRINTERS, SCOTT, QC, CANADA.**

THE WARMASTERS OF THANOS!

THE BLACK ORDER

DEREK LANDY
WRITER

PHILIP TAN (#1-4),
HARVEY TOLIBAO (#2)
& **CARLOS MAGNO** (#5)
PENCILERS

MARC DEERING (#1-4),
GUILLERMO ORTEGO (#1, #4),
LE BEAU UNDERWOOD (#1-4),
HARVEY TOLIBAO (#2), **ANDY OWENS** (#3),
VICTOR OLAZABA (#3), **RAFAEL FONTERIZ** (#3)
& **SCOTT HANNA** (#4-5)
INKERS

JAY DAVID RAMOS (#1-5),
DONO SÁNCHEZ-ALMARA (#2, #5),
RACHELLE ROSENBERG (#3)
& **ISRAEL SILVA** (#3)
COLORISTS

PHILIP TAN &
PETER STEIGERWALD (#1-2);
PHILIP TAN, MARC DEERING &
ARIF PRIANTO (#3); AND **INHYUK LEE** (#4-5)
COVER ART

VC's CLAYTON COWLES
LETTERER

ALANNA SMITH
ASSOCIATE EDITOR

TOM BREVOORT
EDITOR

COLLECTION EDITOR **JENNIFER GRÜNWALD** · ASSISTANT EDITOR **CAITLIN O'CONNELL** · ASSOCIATE MANAGING EDITOR **KATERI WOODY**
EDITOR, SPECIAL PROJECTS **MARK D. BEAZLEY** · VP PRODUCTION & SPECIAL PROJECTS **JEFF YOUNGQUIST**
SVP PRINT, SALES & MARKETING **DAVID GABRIEL** · BOOK DESIGNER **SALENA MAHINA** WITH **CARLOS LAO**

EDITOR IN CHIEF **C.B. CEBULSKI** · CHIEF CREATIVE OFFICER **JOE QUESADA**
PRESIDENT **DAN BUCKLEY** · EXECUTIVE PRODUCER **ALAN FINE**

1

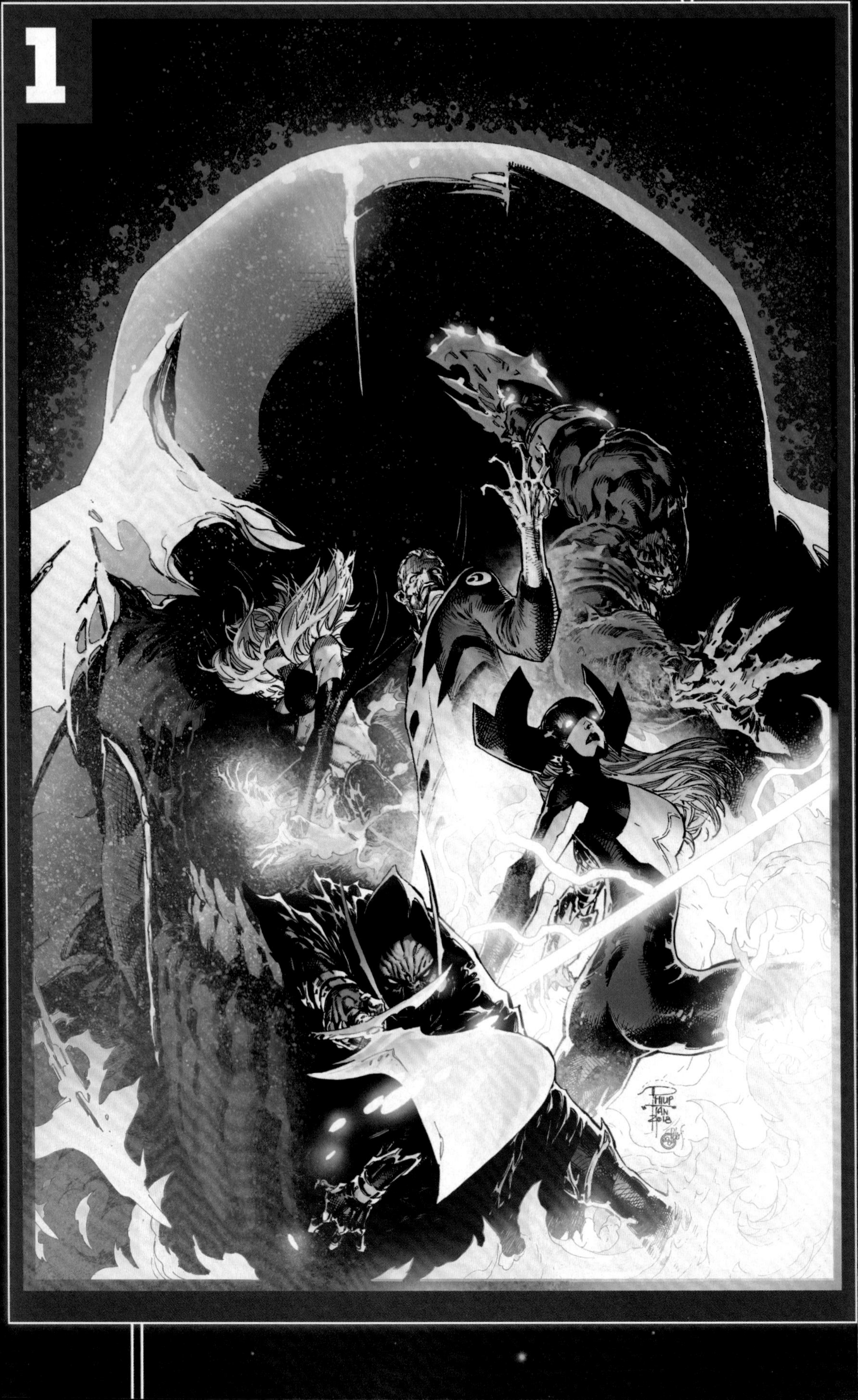
PHILIP TAN 2018

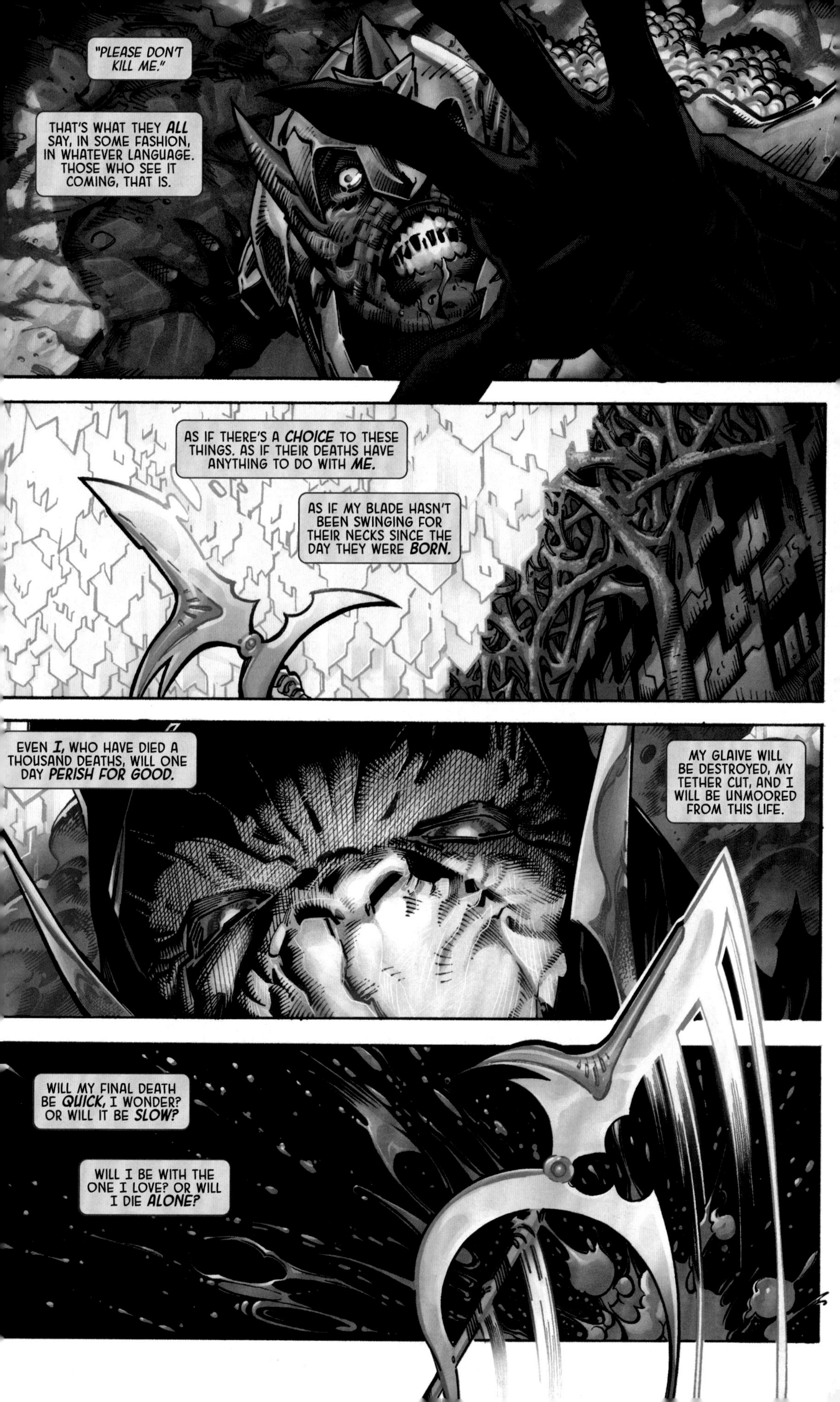
"PLEASE DON'T KILL ME."
THAT'S WHAT THEY ALL SAY, IN SOME FASHION, IN WHATEVER LANGUAGE. THOSE WHO SEE IT COMING, THAT IS.
AS IF THERE'S A CHOICE TO THESE THINGS. AS IF THEIR DEATHS HAVE ANYTHING TO DO WITH ME.
AS IF MY BLADE HASN'T BEEN SWINGING FOR THEIR NECKS SINCE THE DAY THEY WERE BORN.
EVEN I, WHO HAVE DIED A THOUSAND DEATHS, WILL ONE DAY PERISH FOR GOOD.
MY GLAIVE WILL BE DESTROYED, MY TETHER CUT, AND I WILL BE UNMOORED FROM THIS LIFE.
WILL MY FINAL DEATH BE QUICK, I WONDER? OR WILL IT BE SLOW?
WILL I BE WITH THE ONE I LOVE? OR WILL I DIE ALONE?

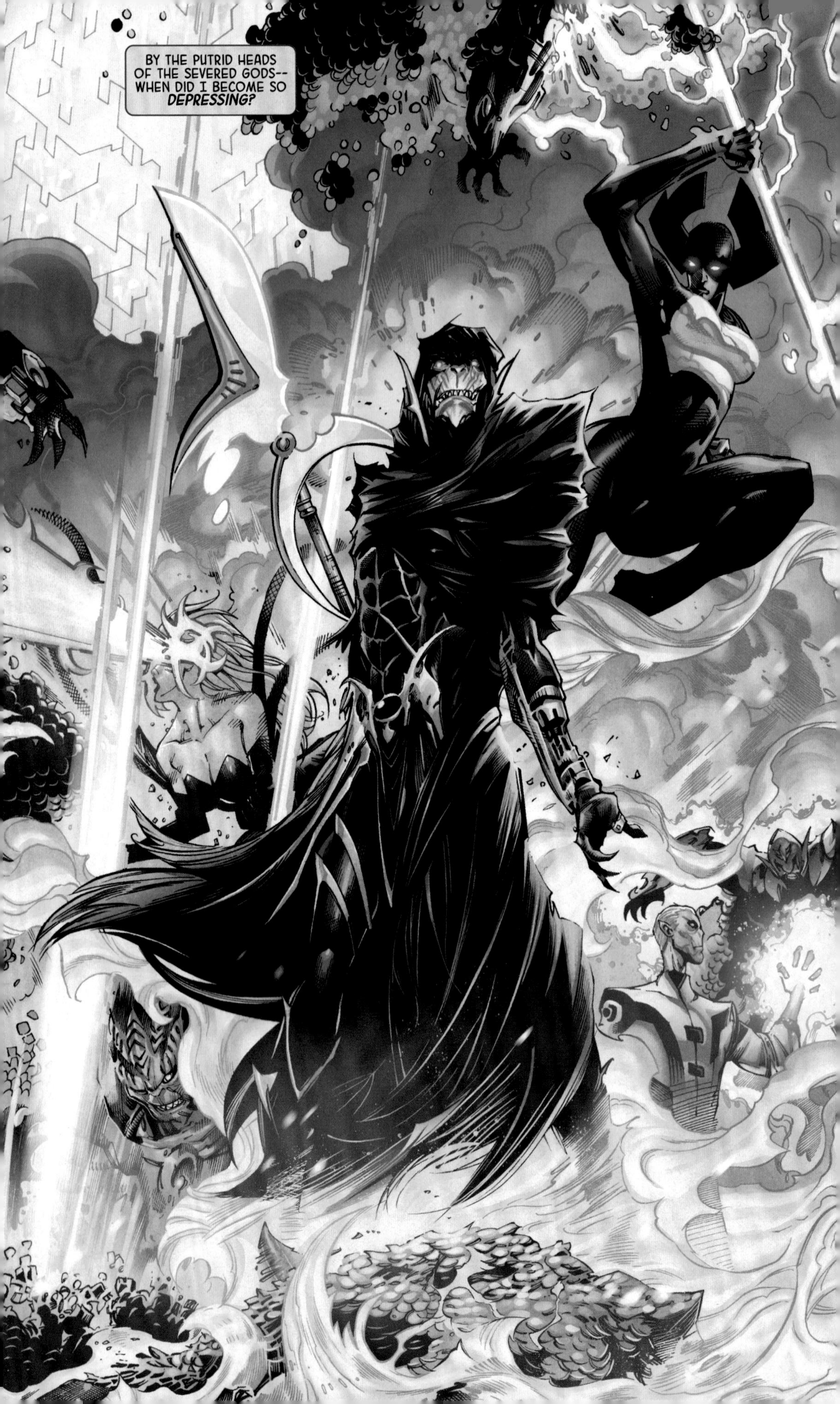
BY THE PUTRID HEADS OF THE SEVERED GODS-- WHEN DID I BECOME SO *DEPRESSING?*

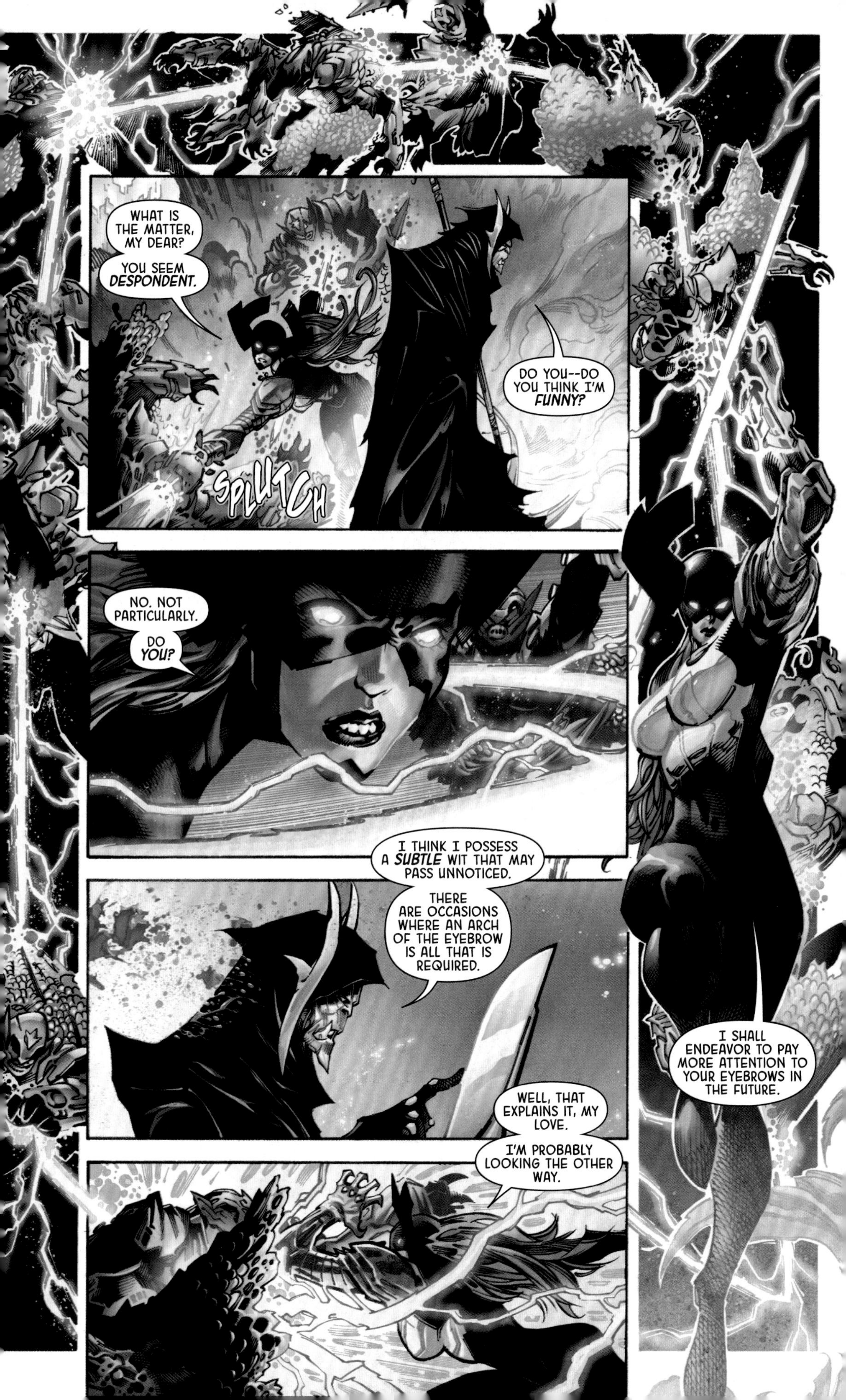
WHAT IS THE MATTER, MY DEAR?
YOU SEEM DESPONDENT.
DO YOU--DO YOU THINK I'M FUNNY?
SPLUTCH
NO. NOT PARTICULARLY.
DO YOU?
I THINK I POSSESS A SUBTLE WIT THAT MAY PASS UNNOTICED.
THERE ARE OCCASIONS WHERE AN ARCH OF THE EYEBROW IS ALL THAT IS REQUIRED.
I SHALL ENDEAVOR TO PAY MORE ATTENTION TO YOUR EYEBROWS IN THE FUTURE.
WELL, THAT EXPLAINS IT, MY LOVE.
I'M PROBABLY LOOKING THE OTHER WAY.

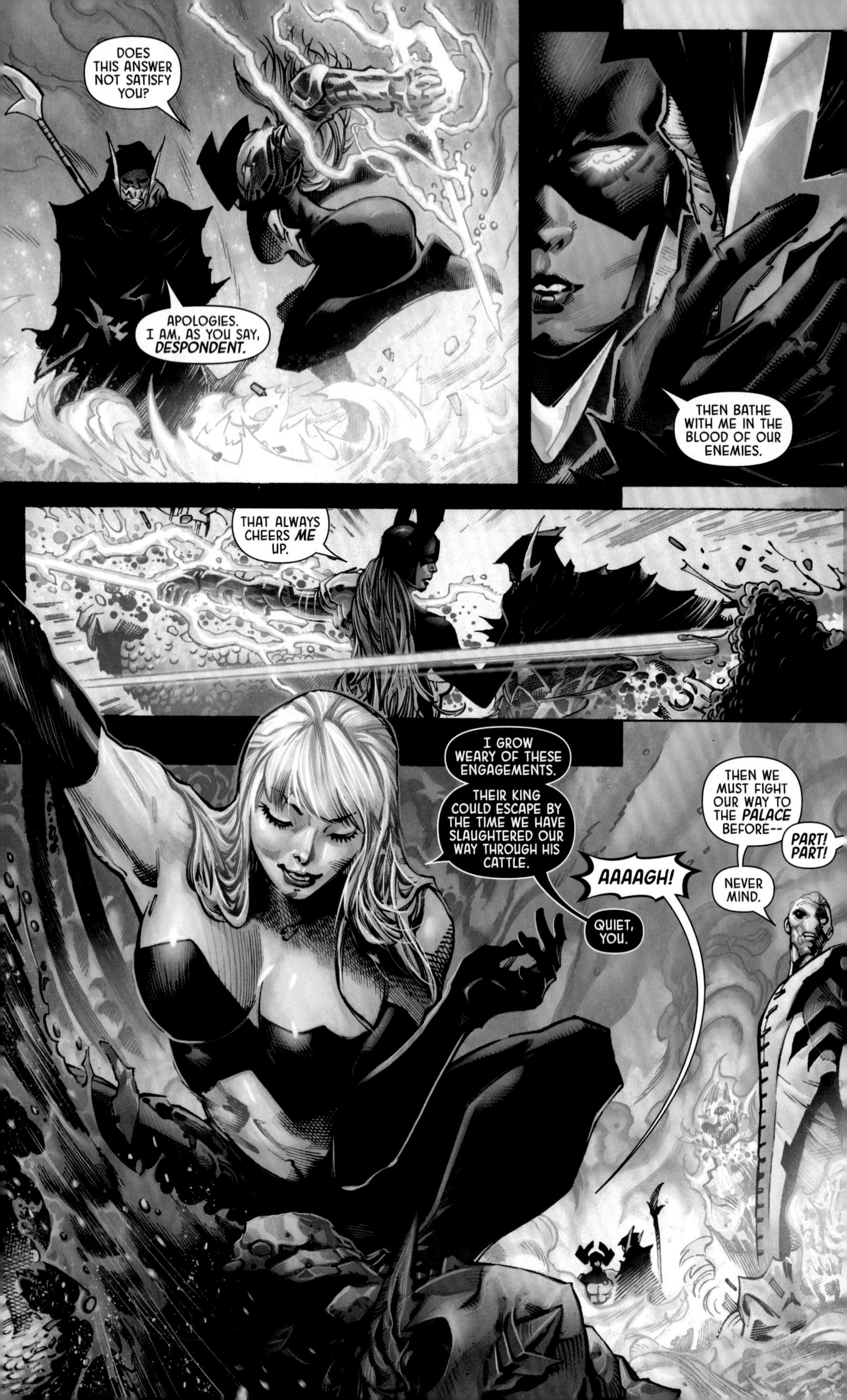
DOES THIS ANSWER NOT SATISFY YOU?
APOLOGIES. I AM, AS YOU SAY, DESPONDENT.
THEN BATHE WITH ME IN THE BLOOD OF OUR ENEMIES.
THAT ALWAYS CHEERS ME UP.
I GROW WEARY OF THESE ENGAGEMENTS.
THEIR KING COULD ESCAPE BY THE TIME WE HAVE SLAUGHTERED OUR WAY THROUGH HIS CATTLE.
AAAAGH!
QUIET, YOU.
THEN WE MUST FIGHT OUR WAY TO THE PALACE BEFORE--
PART! PART!
NEVER MIND.

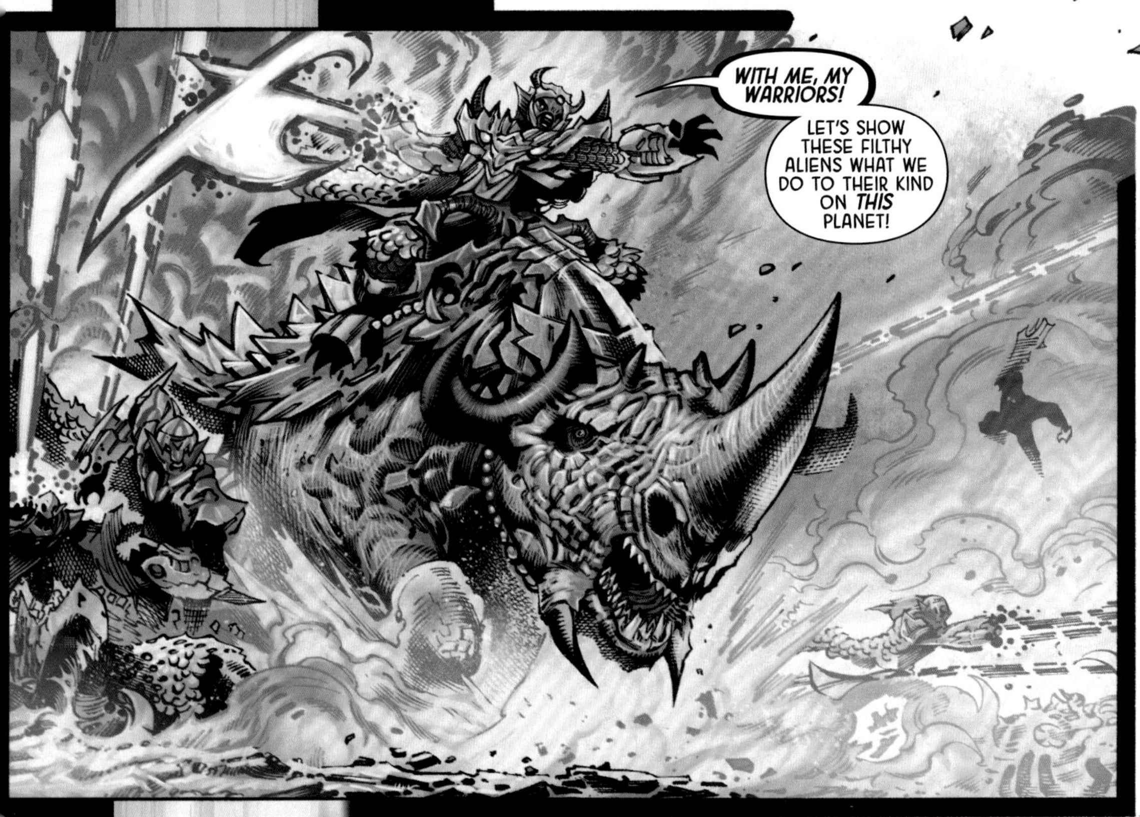
WITH ME, MY WARRIORS!
LET'S SHOW THESE FILTHY ALIENS WHAT WE DO TO THEIR KIND ON THIS PLANET!

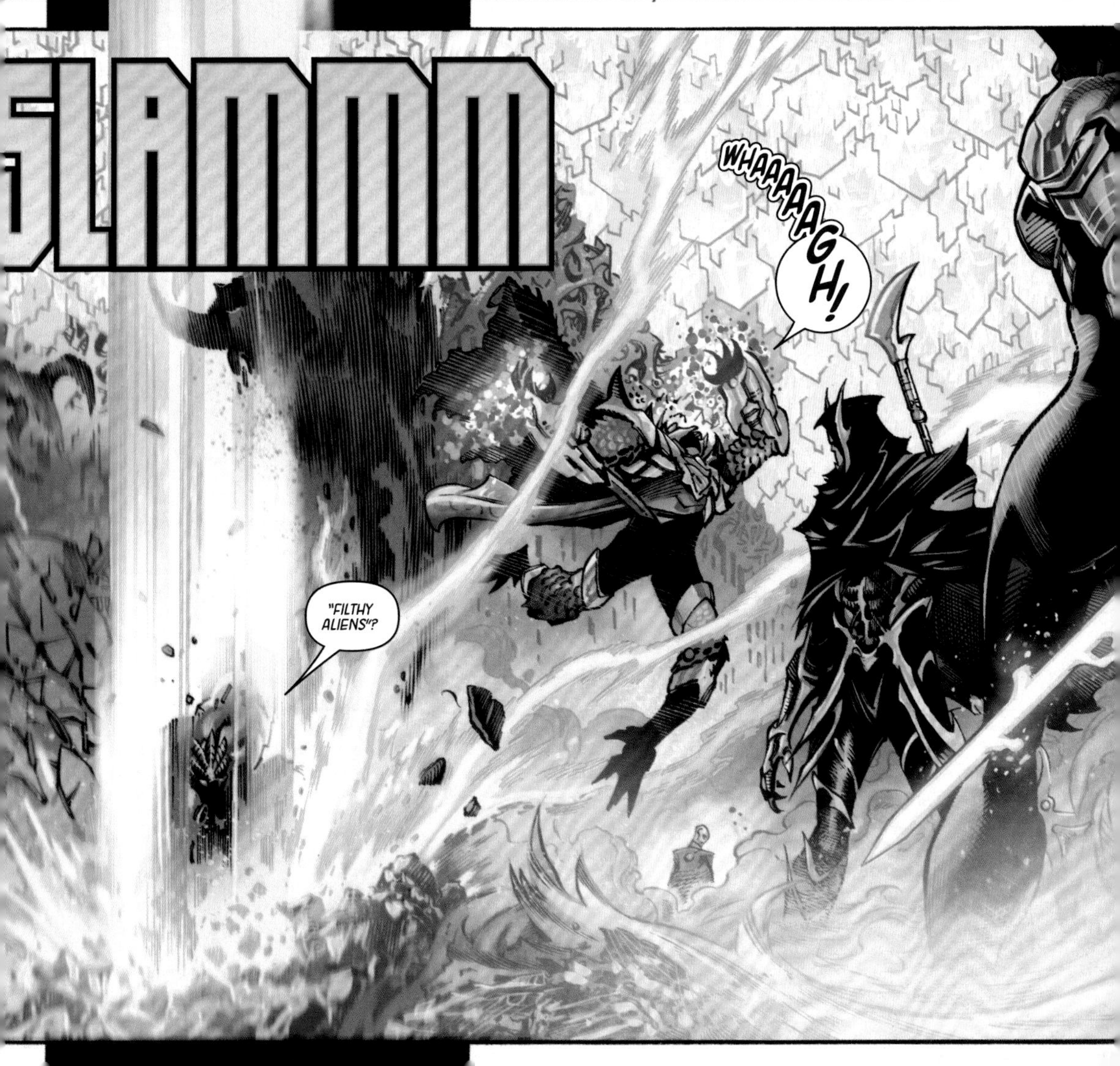
SLAMMM
WHAAAAAAGH!
"FILTHY ALIENS"?

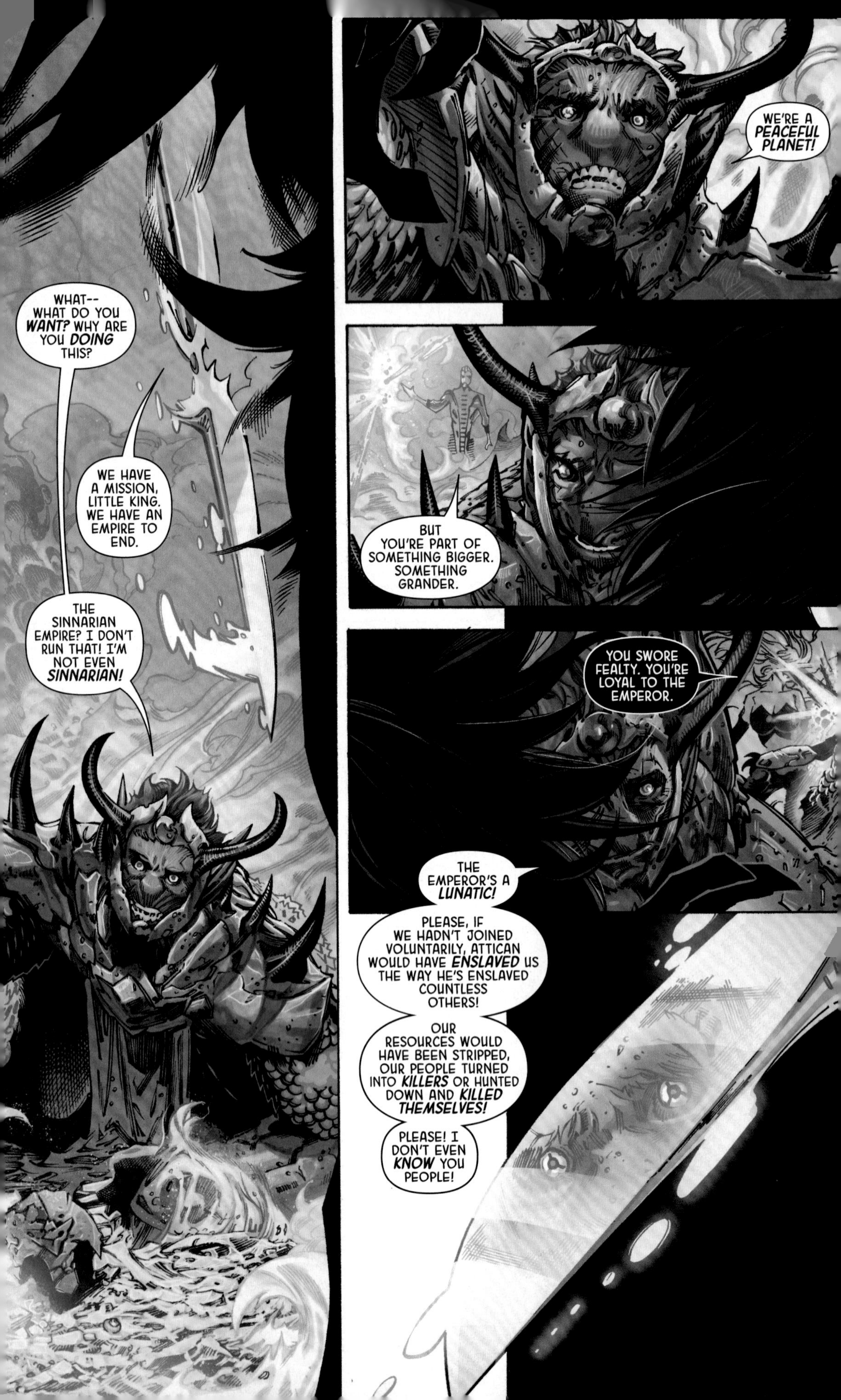
WHAT-- WHAT DO YOU WANT? WHY ARE YOU DOING THIS?
WE HAVE A MISSION, LITTLE KING. WE HAVE AN EMPIRE TO END.
THE SINNARIAN EMPIRE? I DON'T RUN THAT! I'M NOT EVEN SINNARIAN!
WE'RE A PEACEFUL PLANET!
BUT YOU'RE PART OF SOMETHING BIGGER. SOMETHING GRANDER.
YOU SWORE FEALTY. YOU'RE LOYAL TO THE EMPEROR.
THE EMPEROR'S A LUNATIC!
PLEASE, IF WE HADN'T JOINED VOLUNTARILY, ATTICAN WOULD HAVE ENSLAVED US THE WAY HE'S ENSLAVED COUNTLESS OTHERS!
OUR RESOURCES WOULD HAVE BEEN STRIPPED, OUR PEOPLE TURNED INTO KILLERS OR HUNTED DOWN AND KILLED THEMSELVES!
PLEASE! I DON'T EVEN KNOW YOU PEOPLE!

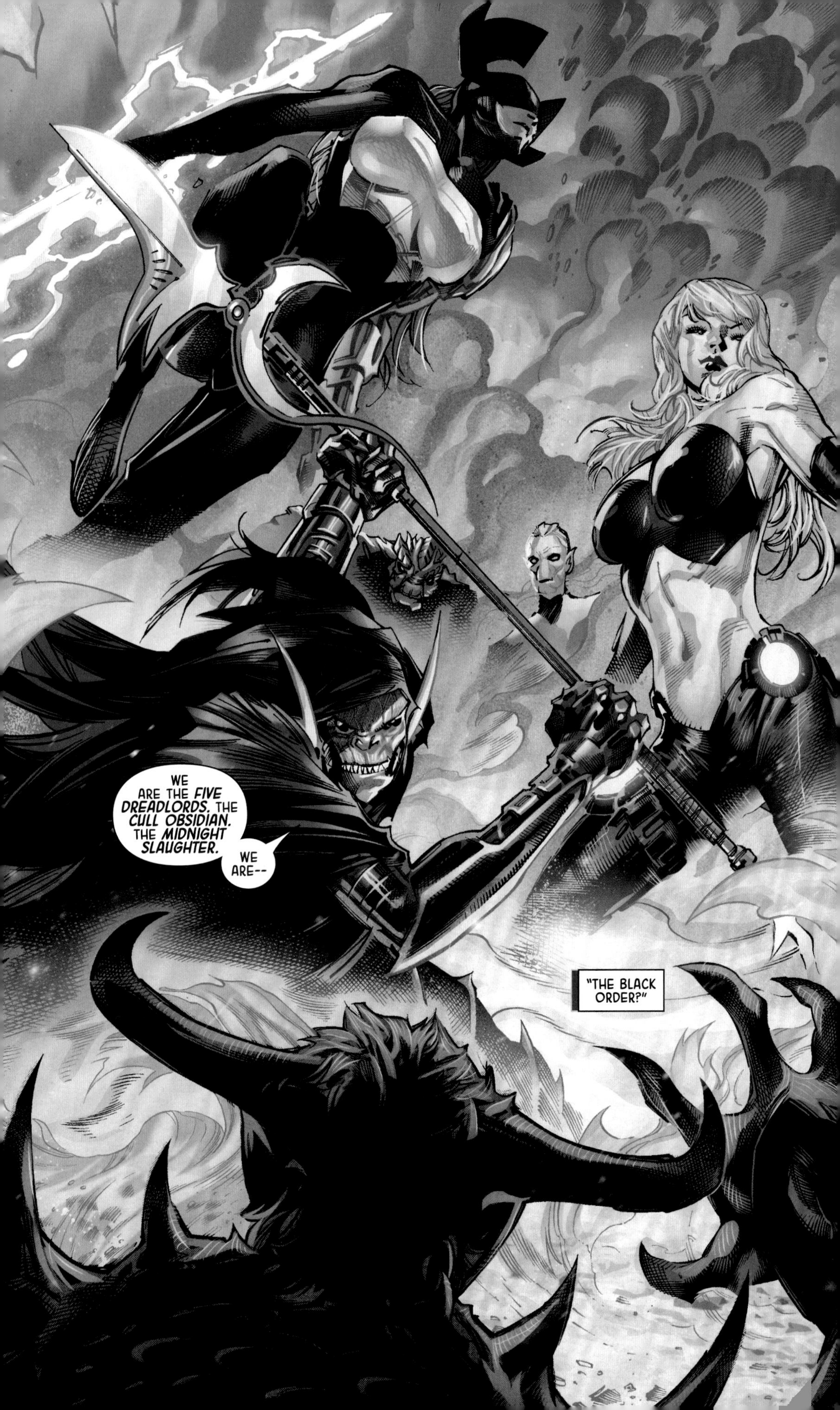
WE ARE THE FIVE DREADLORDS. THE CULL OBSIDIAN. THE MIDNIGHT SLAUGHTER.
WE ARE--
"THE BLACK ORDER?"

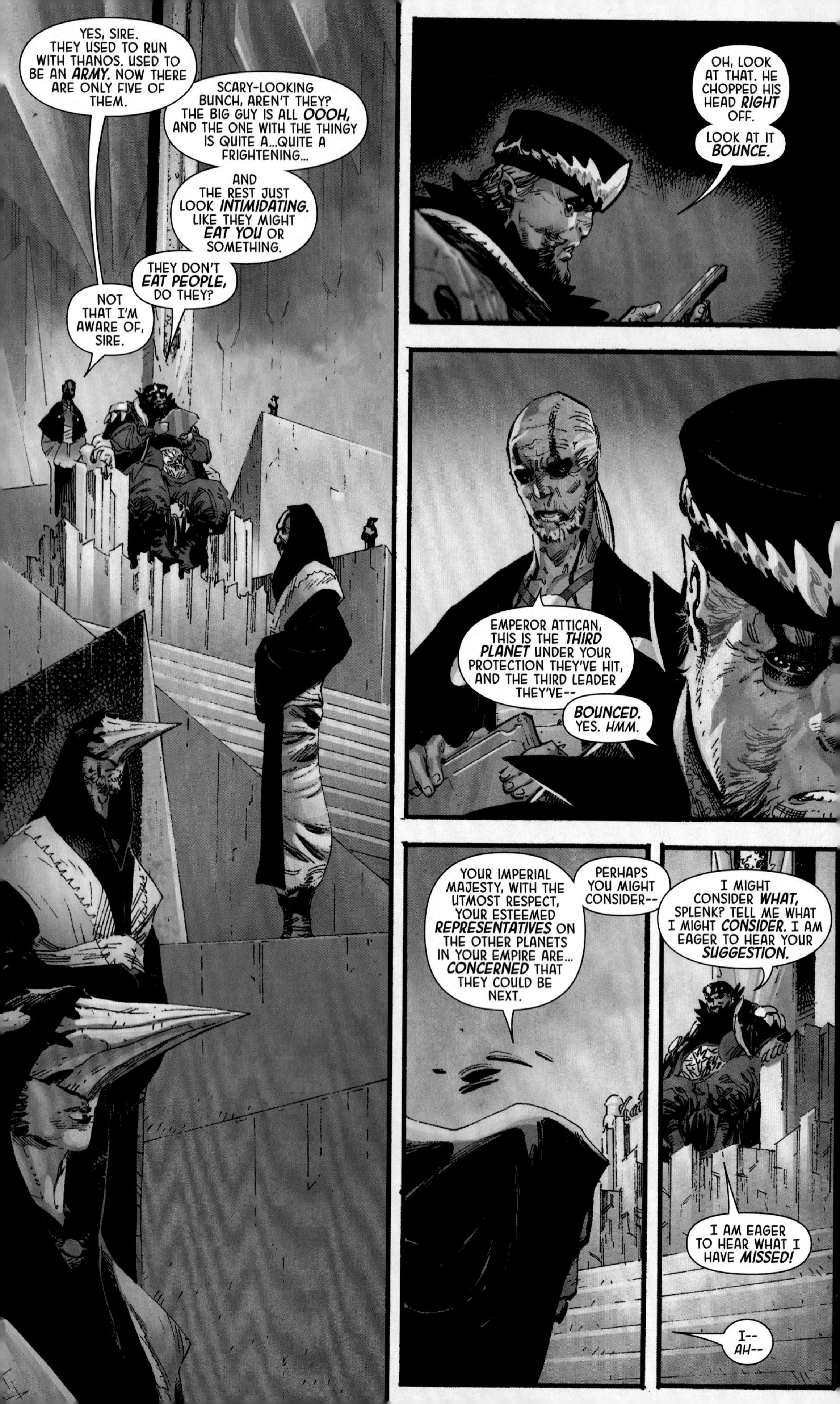

YES, SIRE. THEY USED TO RUN WITH THANOS. USED TO BE AN ARMY. NOW THERE ARE ONLY FIVE OF THEM.
SCARY-LOOKING BUNCH, AREN'T THEY? THE BIG GUY IS ALL OOOH, AND THE ONE WITH THE THINGY IS QUITE A...QUITE A FRIGHTENING...
AND THE REST JUST LOOK INTIMIDATING. LIKE THEY MIGHT EAT YOU OR SOMETHING.
THEY DON'T EAT PEOPLE, DO THEY?
NOT THAT I'M AWARE OF, SIRE.
OH, LOOK AT THAT. HE CHOPPED HIS HEAD RIGHT OFF.
LOOK AT IT BOUNCE.
EMPEROR ATTICAN, THIS IS THE THIRD PLANET UNDER YOUR PROTECTION THEY'VE HIT, AND THE THIRD LEADER THEY'VE--
BOUNCED. YES. HMM.
YOUR IMPERIAL MAJESTY, WITH THE UTMOST RESPECT, YOUR ESTEEMED REPRESENTATIVES ON THE OTHER PLANETS IN YOUR EMPIRE ARE... CONCERNED THAT THEY COULD BE NEXT.
PERHAPS YOU MIGHT CONSIDER--
I MIGHT CONSIDER WHAT, SPLENK? TELL ME WHAT I MIGHT CONSIDER. I AM EAGER TO HEAR YOUR SUGGESTION.
I AM EAGER TO HEAR WHAT I HAVE MISSED!
I-- AH--

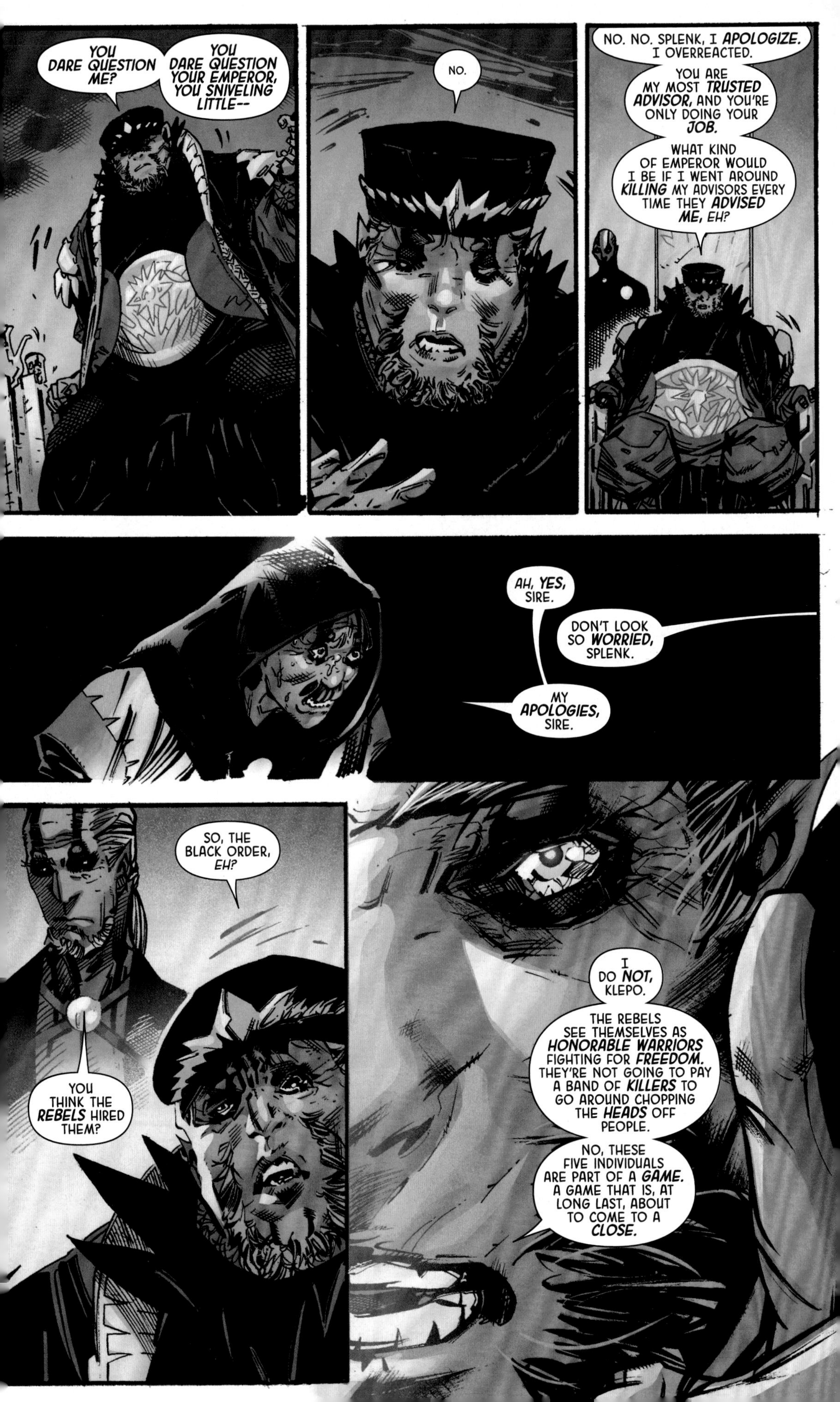
YOU DARE QUESTION ME?
YOU DARE QUESTION YOUR EMPEROR, YOU SNIVELING LITTLE--
NO.
NO. NO. SPLENK, I APOLOGIZE. I OVERREACTED.
YOU ARE MY MOST TRUSTED ADVISOR, AND YOU'RE ONLY DOING YOUR JOB.
WHAT KIND OF EMPEROR WOULD I BE IF I WENT AROUND KILLING MY ADVISORS EVERY TIME THEY ADVISED ME, EH?
AH, YES, SIRE.
DON'T LOOK SO WORRIED, SPLENK.
MY APOLOGIES, SIRE.
SO, THE BLACK ORDER, EH?
YOU THINK THE REBELS HIRED THEM?
I DO NOT, KLEPO.
THE REBELS SEE THEMSELVES AS HONORABLE WARRIORS FIGHTING FOR FREEDOM. THEY'RE NOT GOING TO PAY A BAND OF KILLERS TO GO AROUND CHOPPING THE HEADS OFF PEOPLE.
NO, THESE FIVE INDIVIDUALS ARE PART OF A GAME. A GAME THAT IS, AT LONG LAST, ABOUT TO COME TO A CLOSE.

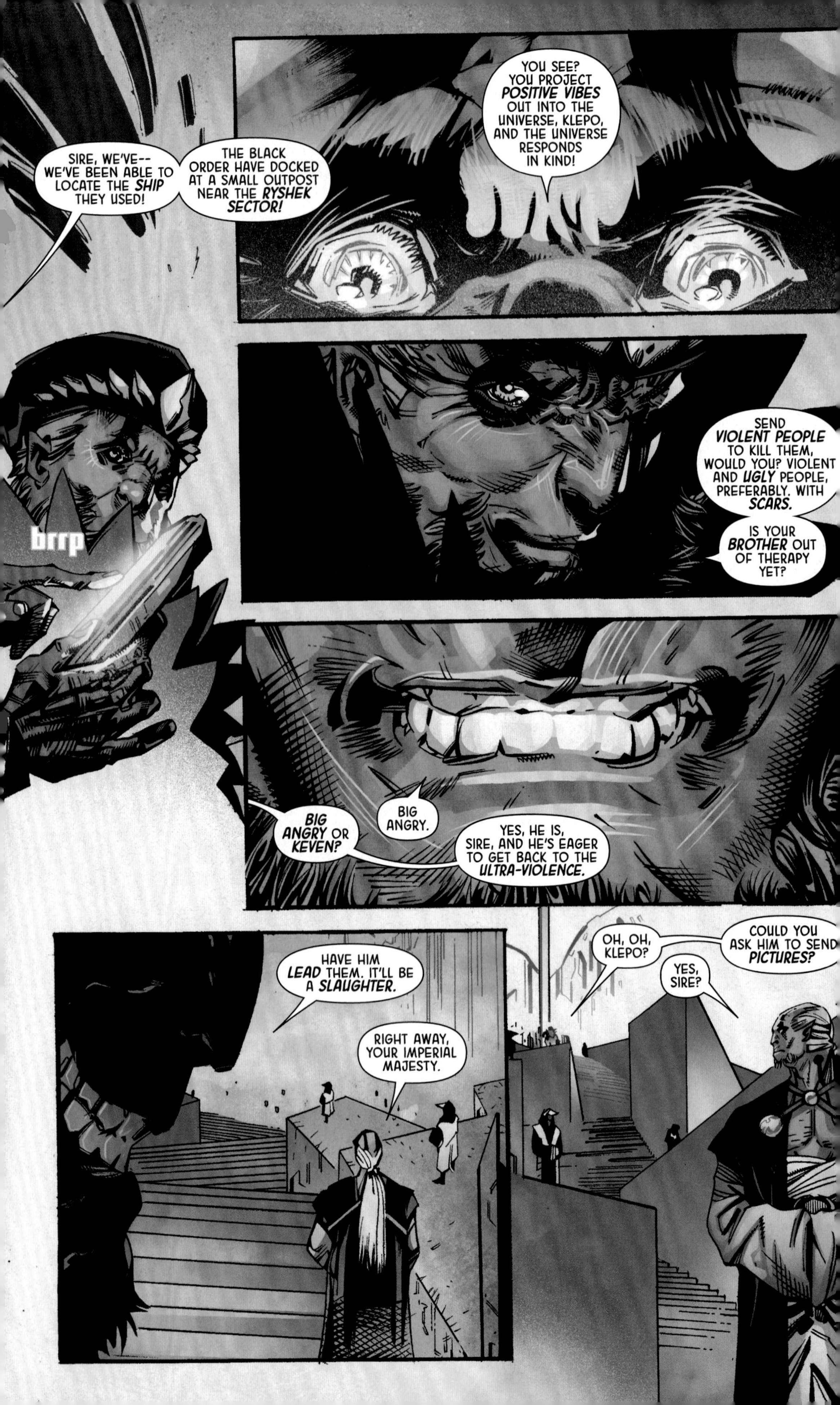
SIRE, WE'VE-- WE'VE BEEN ABLE TO LOCATE THE SHIP THEY USED!
THE BLACK ORDER HAVE DOCKED AT A SMALL OUTPOST NEAR THE RYSHEK SECTOR!
YOU SEE? YOU PROJECT POSITIVE VIBES OUT INTO THE UNIVERSE, KLEPO, AND THE UNIVERSE RESPONDS IN KIND!
brrp
SEND VIOLENT PEOPLE TO KILL THEM, WOULD YOU? VIOLENT AND UGLY PEOPLE, PREFERABLY. WITH SCARS.
IS YOUR BROTHER OUT OF THERAPY YET?
BIG ANGRY OR KEVEN?
BIG ANGRY.
YES, HE IS, SIRE, AND HE'S EAGER TO GET BACK TO THE ULTRA-VIOLENCE.
HAVE HIM LEAD THEM. IT'LL BE A SLAUGHTER.
RIGHT AWAY, YOUR IMPERIAL MAJESTY.
OH, OH, KLEPO?
YES, SIRE?
COULD YOU ASK HIM TO SEND PICTURES?

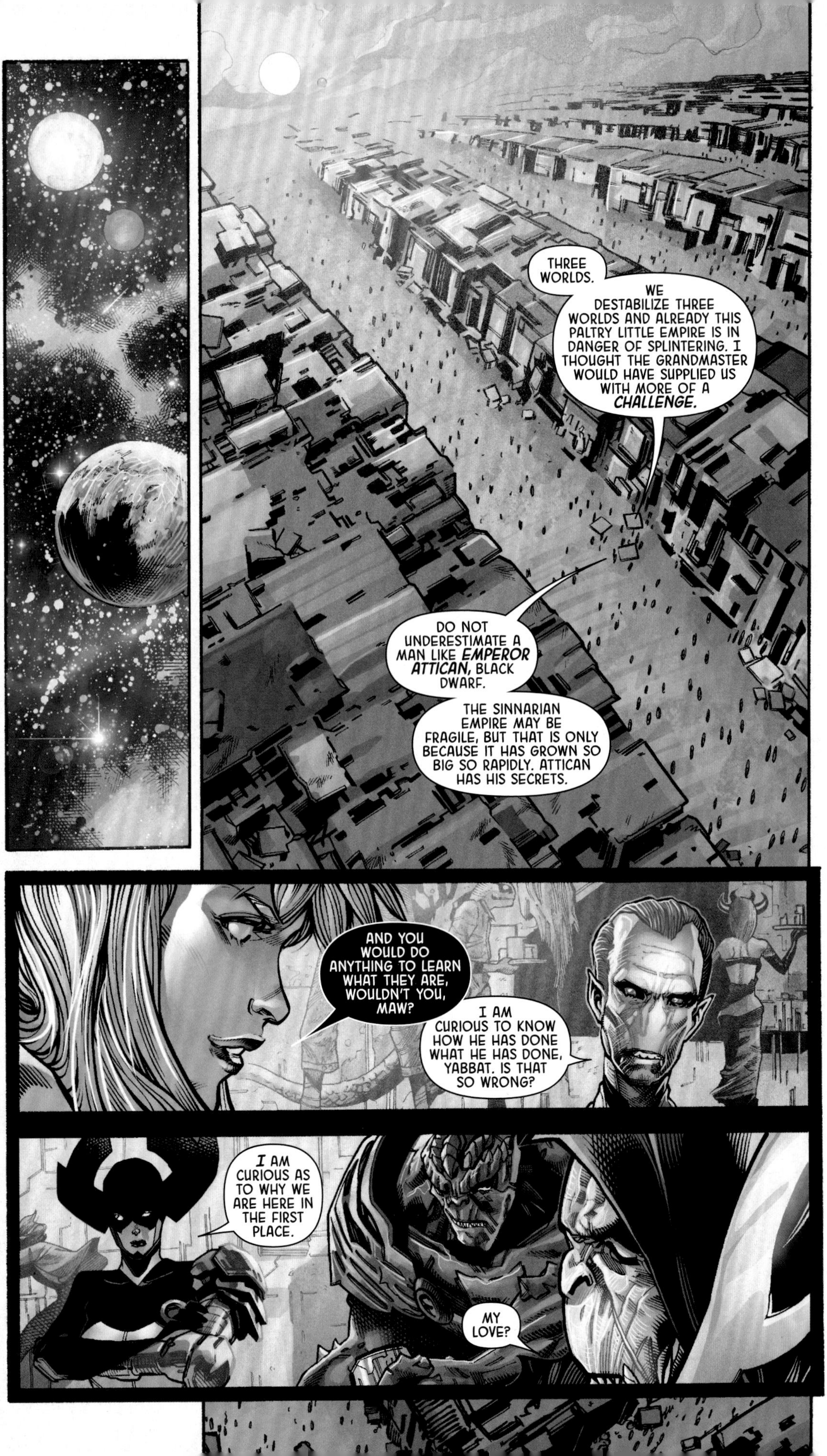
THREE WORLDS.
WE DESTABILIZE THREE WORLDS AND ALREADY THIS PALTRY LITTLE EMPIRE IS IN DANGER OF SPLINTERING. I THOUGHT THE GRANDMASTER WOULD HAVE SUPPLIED US WITH MORE OF A *CHALLENGE.*
DO NOT UNDERESTIMATE A MAN LIKE *EMPEROR ATTICAN,* BLACK DWARF.
THE SINNARIAN EMPIRE MAY BE FRAGILE, BUT THAT IS ONLY BECAUSE IT HAS GROWN SO BIG SO RAPIDLY. ATTICAN HAS HIS SECRETS.
AND YOU WOULD DO ANYTHING TO LEARN WHAT THEY ARE, WOULDN'T YOU, MAW?
I AM CURIOUS TO KNOW HOW HE HAS DONE WHAT HE HAS DONE, YABBAT. IS THAT SO WRONG?
I AM CURIOUS AS TO WHY WE ARE HERE IN THE FIRST PLACE.
MY LOVE?

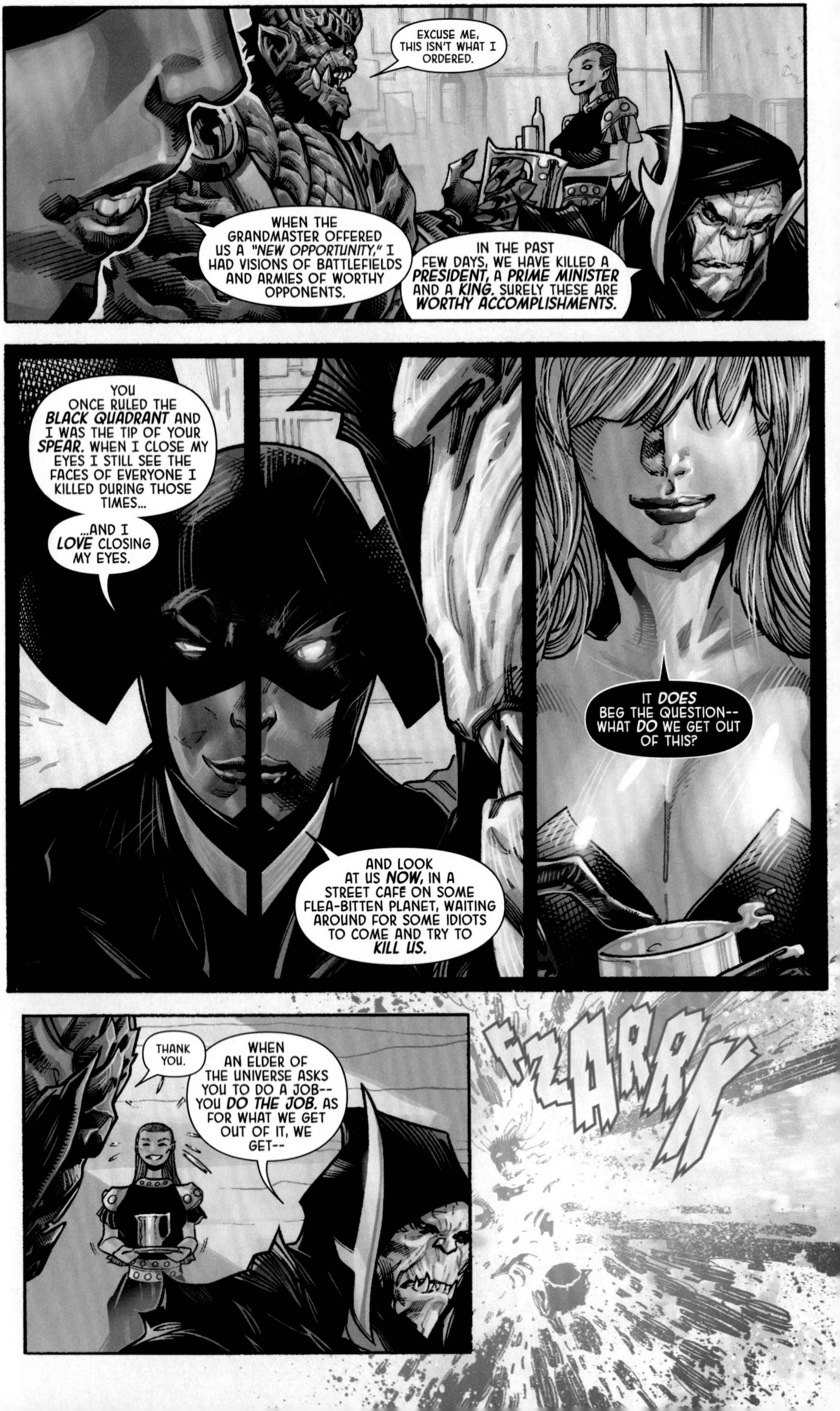
EXCUSE ME, THIS ISN'T WHAT I ORDERED.
WHEN THE GRANDMASTER OFFERED US A "NEW OPPORTUNITY," I HAD VISIONS OF BATTLEFIELDS AND ARMIES OF WORTHY OPPONENTS.
IN THE PAST FEW DAYS, WE HAVE KILLED A PRESIDENT, A PRIME MINISTER AND A KING. SURELY THESE ARE WORTHY ACCOMPLISHMENTS.
YOU ONCE RULED THE BLACK QUADRANT AND I WAS THE TIP OF YOUR SPEAR. WHEN I CLOSE MY EYES I STILL SEE THE FACES OF EVERYONE I KILLED DURING THOSE TIMES...
...AND I LOVE CLOSING MY EYES.
AND LOOK AT US NOW, IN A STREET CAFÉ ON SOME FLEA-BITTEN PLANET, WAITING AROUND FOR SOME IDIOTS TO COME AND TRY TO KILL US.
IT DOES BEG THE QUESTION-- WHAT DO WE GET OUT OF THIS?
THANK YOU.
WHEN AN ELDER OF THE UNIVERSE ASKS YOU TO DO A JOB-- YOU DO THE JOB. AS FOR WHAT WE GET OUT OF IT, WE GET--

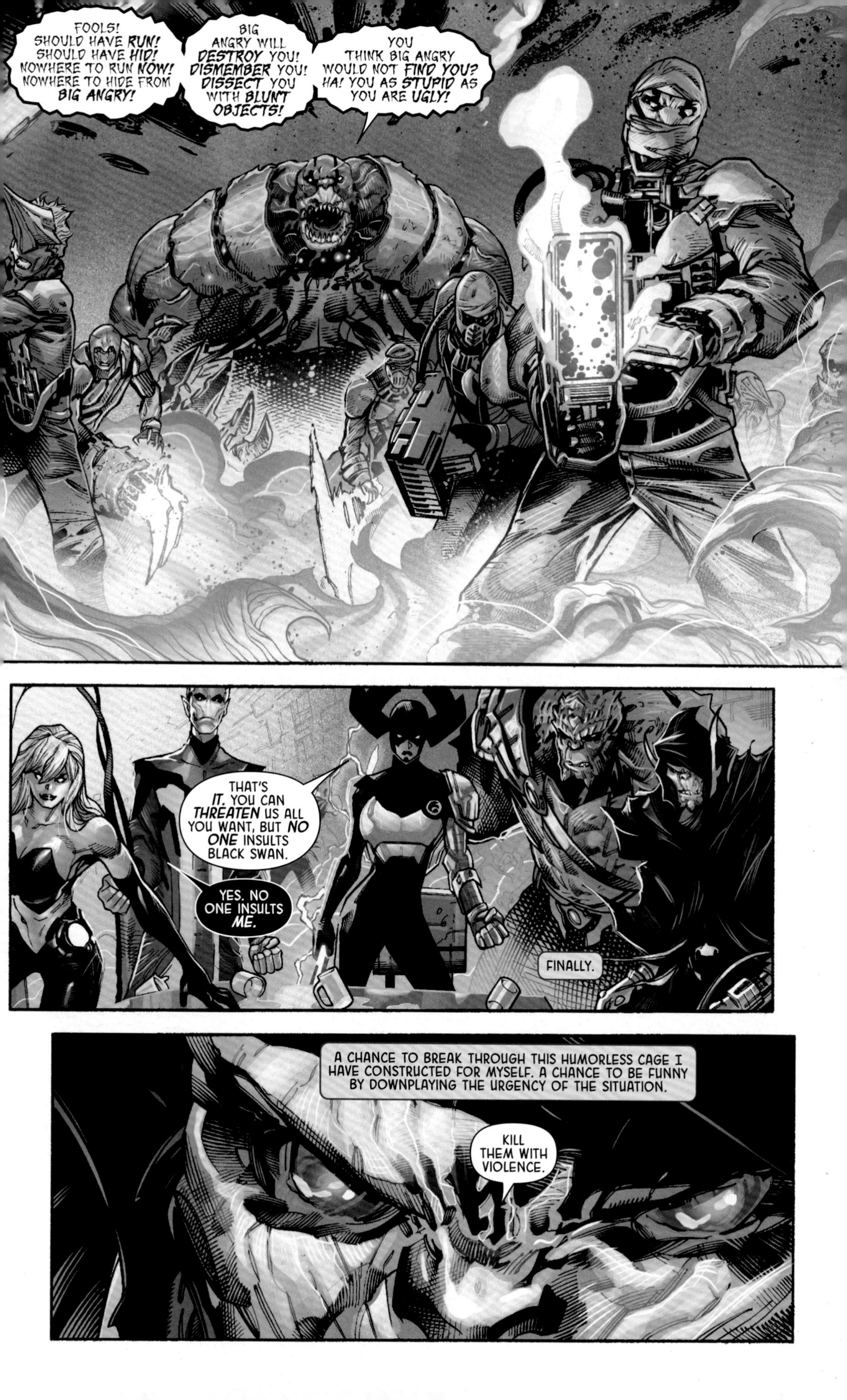
FOOLS! SHOULD HAVE RUN! SHOULD HAVE HID! NOWHERE TO RUN NOW! NOWHERE TO HIDE FROM BIG ANGRY!
BIG ANGRY WILL DESTROY YOU! DISMEMBER YOU! DISSECT YOU WITH BLUNT OBJECTS!
YOU THINK BIG ANGRY WOULD NOT FIND YOU? HA! YOU AS STUPID AS YOU ARE UGLY!
THAT'S IT. YOU CAN THREATEN US ALL YOU WANT, BUT NO ONE INSULTS BLACK SWAN.
YES. NO ONE INSULTS ME.
FINALLY.
A CHANCE TO BREAK THROUGH THIS HUMORLESS CAGE I HAVE CONSTRUCTED FOR MYSELF. A CHANCE TO BE FUNNY BY DOWNPLAYING THE URGENCY OF THE SITUATION.
KILL THEM WITH VIOLENCE.

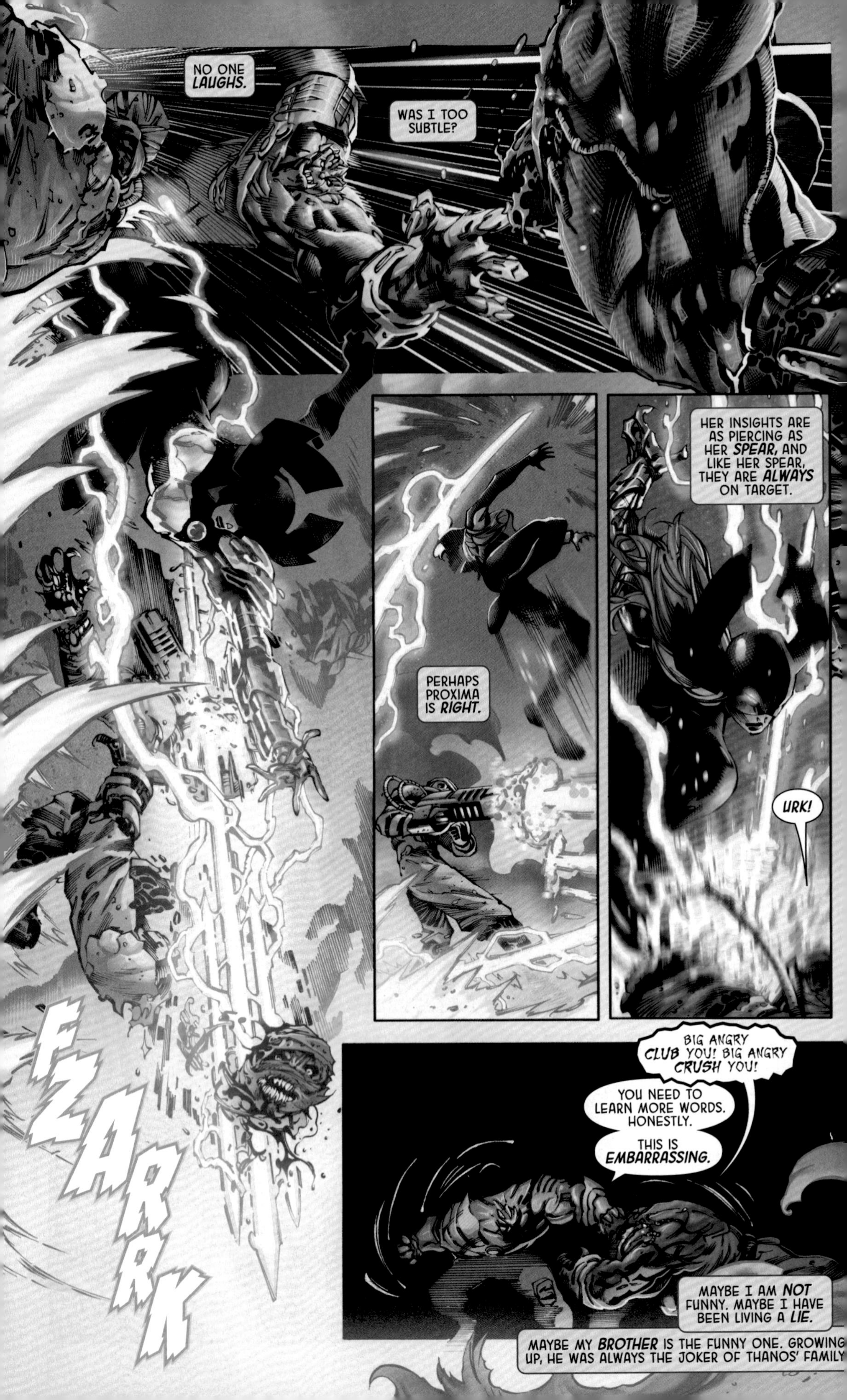
NO ONE LAUGHS.
WAS I TOO SUBTLE?
HER INSIGHTS ARE AS PIERCING AS HER SPEAR, AND LIKE HER SPEAR, THEY ARE ALWAYS ON TARGET.
PERHAPS PROXIMA IS RIGHT.
URK!
FZARRK
BIG ANGRY CLUB YOU! BIG ANGRY CRUSH YOU!
YOU NEED TO LEARN MORE WORDS. HONESTLY.
THIS IS EMBARRASSING.
MAYBE I AM NOT FUNNY. MAYBE I HAVE BEEN LIVING A LIE.
MAYBE MY BROTHER IS THE FUNNY ONE. GROWING UP, HE WAS ALWAYS THE JOKER OF THANOS' FAMILY

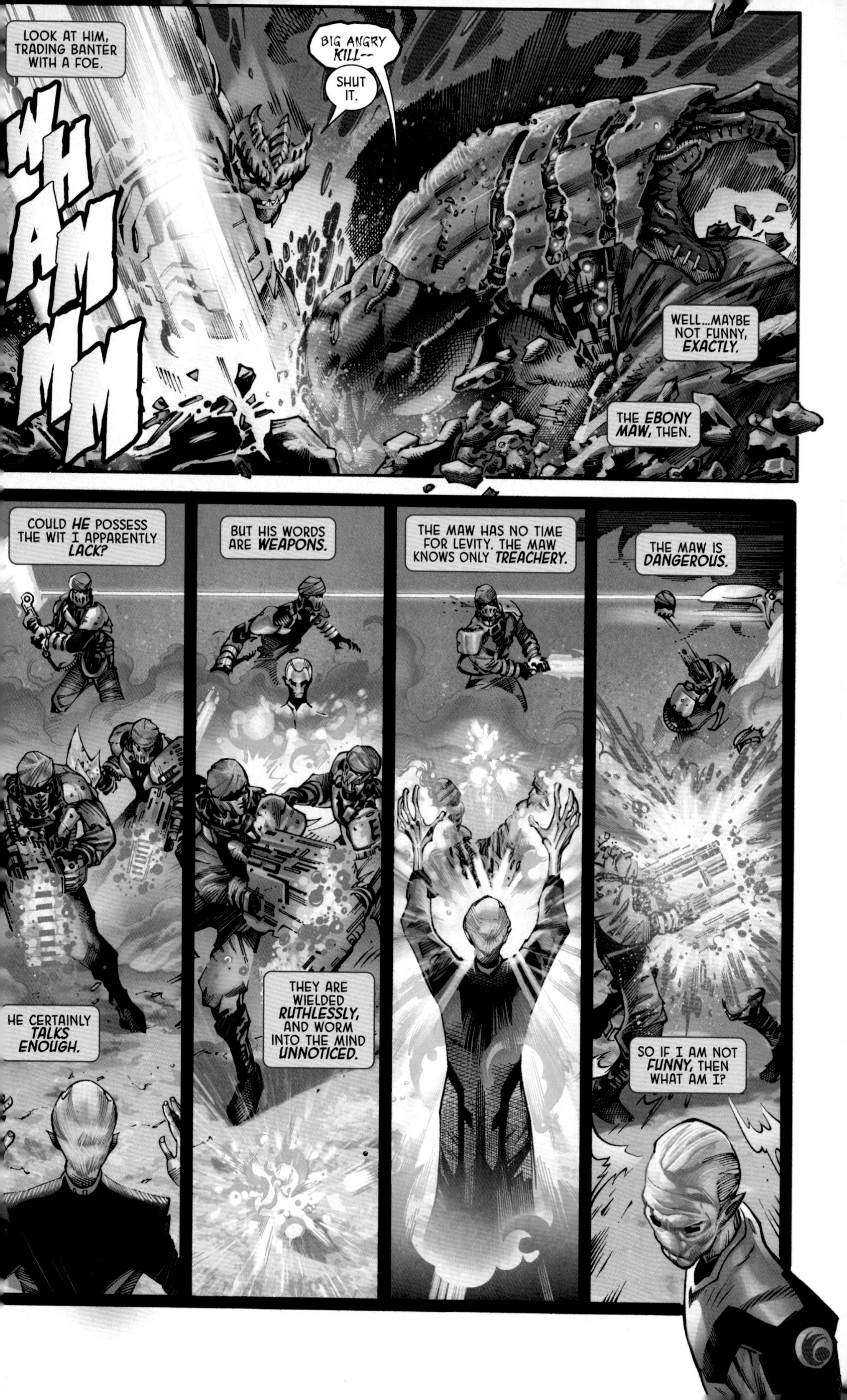
LOOK AT HIM, TRADING BANTER WITH A FOE.
BIG ANGRY KILL--
SHUT IT.
WHHAMMM
WELL...MAYBE NOT FUNNY, EXACTLY.
THE EBONY MAW, THEN.
COULD HE POSSESS THE WIT I APPARENTLY LACK?
HE CERTAINLY TALKS ENOUGH.
BUT HIS WORDS ARE WEAPONS.
THEY ARE WIELDED RUTHLESSLY, AND WORM INTO THE MIND UNNOTICED.
THE MAW HAS NO TIME FOR LEVITY. THE MAW KNOWS ONLY TREACHERY.
THE MAW IS DANGEROUS.
SO IF I AM NOT FUNNY, THEN WHAT AM I?

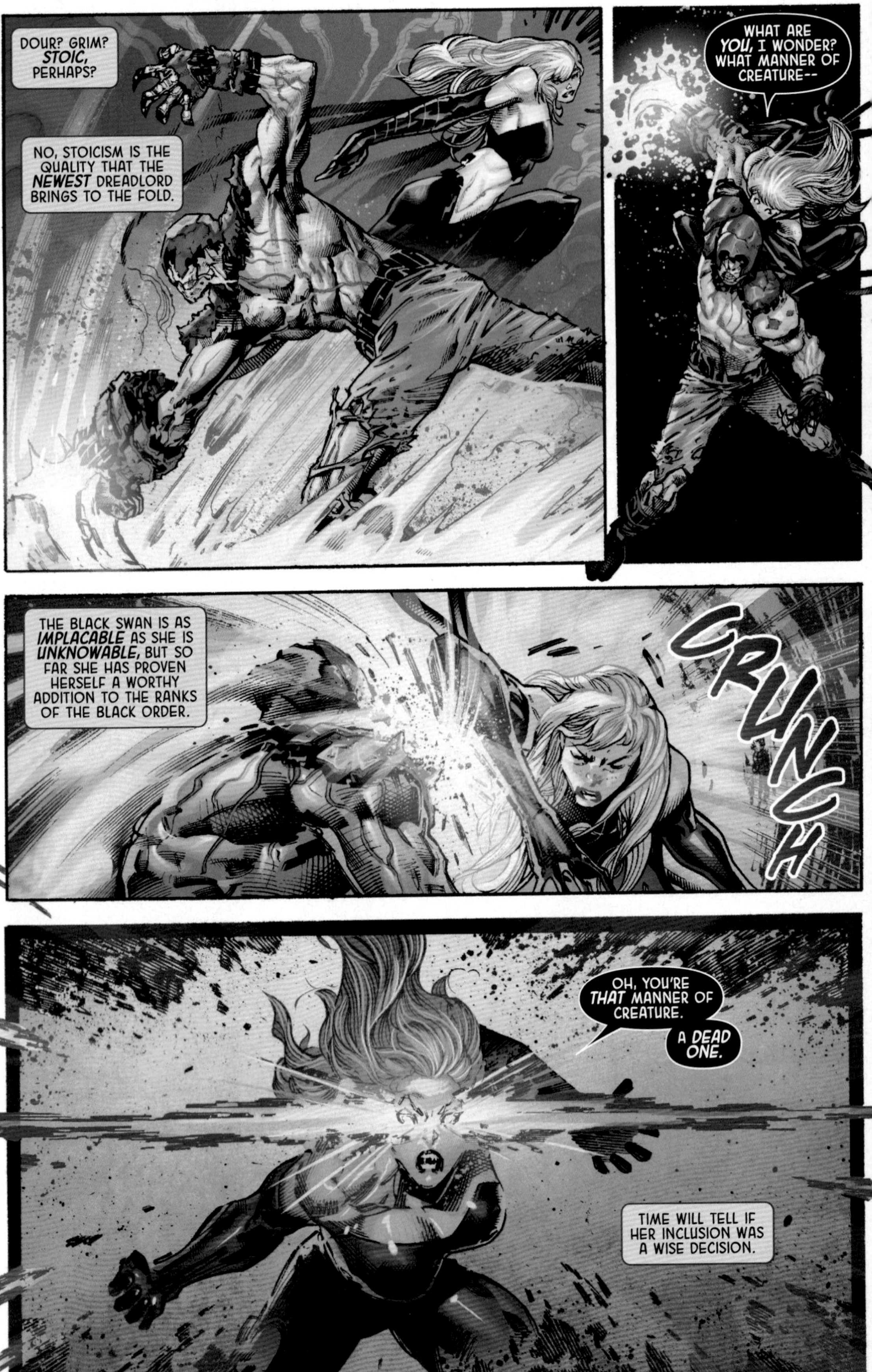
DOUR? GRIM? STOIC, PERHAPS?
NO, STOICISM IS THE QUALITY THAT THE NEWEST DREADLORD BRINGS TO THE FOLD.
WHAT ARE YOU, I WONDER? WHAT MANNER OF CREATURE--
THE BLACK SWAN IS AS IMPLACABLE AS SHE IS UNKNOWABLE, BUT SO FAR SHE HAS PROVEN HERSELF A WORTHY ADDITION TO THE RANKS OF THE BLACK ORDER.
CRUNCH
OH, YOU'RE THAT MANNER OF CREATURE.
A DEAD ONE.
TIME WILL TELL IF HER INCLUSION WAS A WISE DECISION.

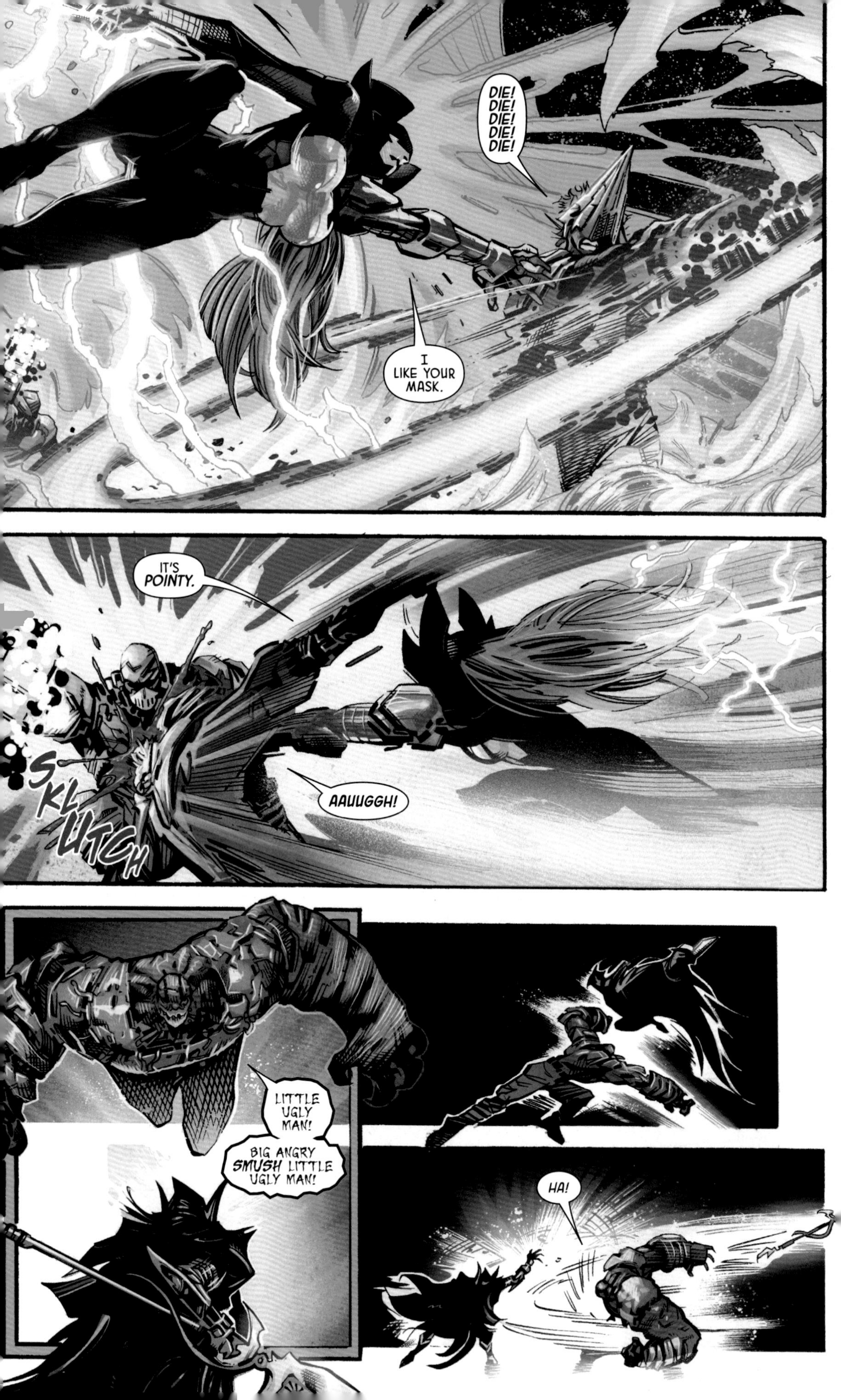

DIE! DIE! DIE! DIE! DIE!
I LIKE YOUR MASK.
IT'S POINTY.
SKLUTCH
AAUUGGH!
LITTLE UGLY MAN!
BIG ANGRY SMUSH LITTLE UGLY MAN!
HA!

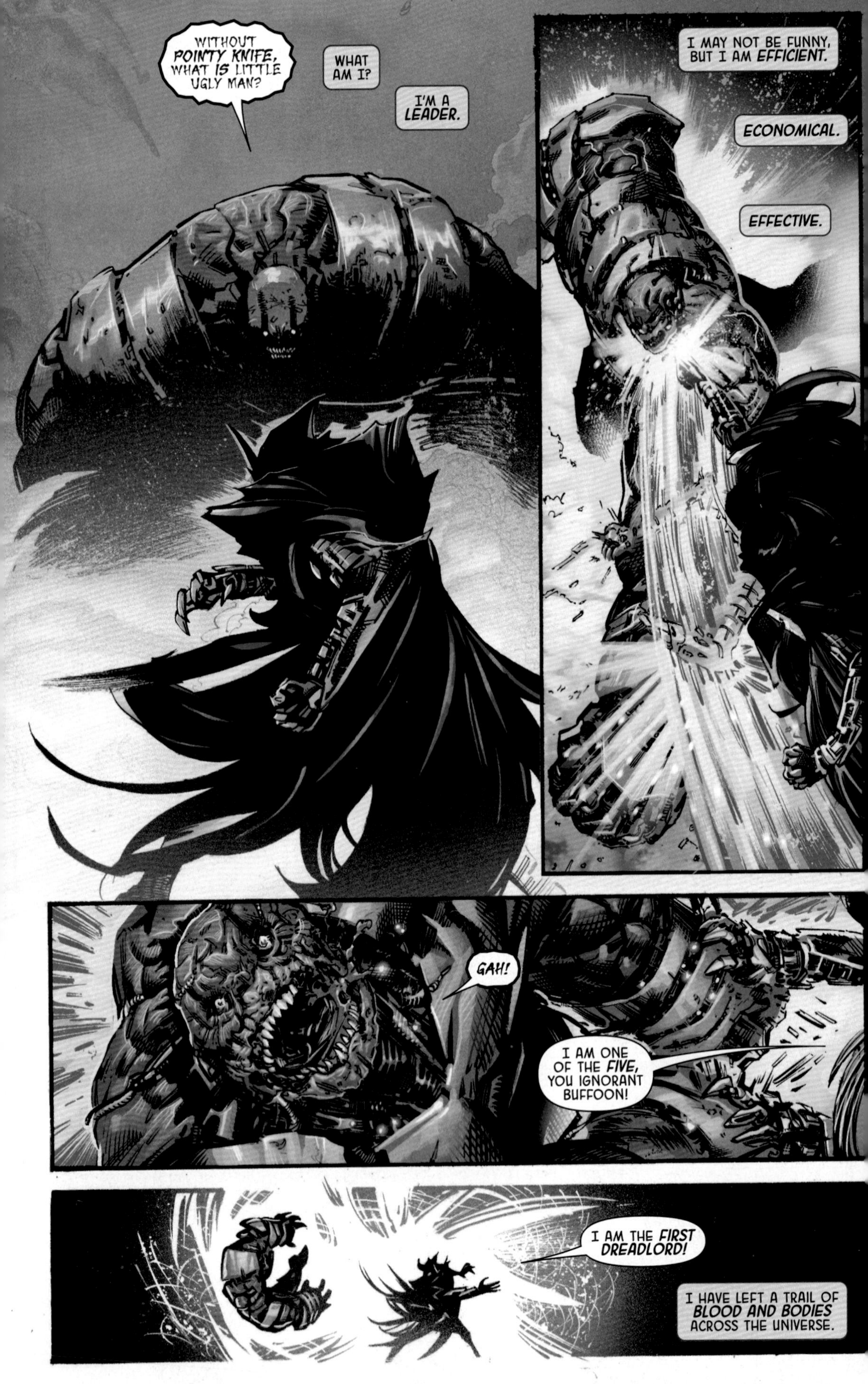
WITHOUT POINTY KNIFE, WHAT IS LITTLE UGLY MAN?
WHAT AM I?
I'M A LEADER.
I MAY NOT BE FUNNY, BUT I AM EFFICIENT.
ECONOMICAL.
EFFECTIVE.
GAH!
I AM ONE OF THE FIVE, YOU IGNORANT BUFFOON!
I AM THE FIRST DREADLORD!
I HAVE LEFT A TRAIL OF BLOOD AND BODIES ACROSS THE UNIVERSE.

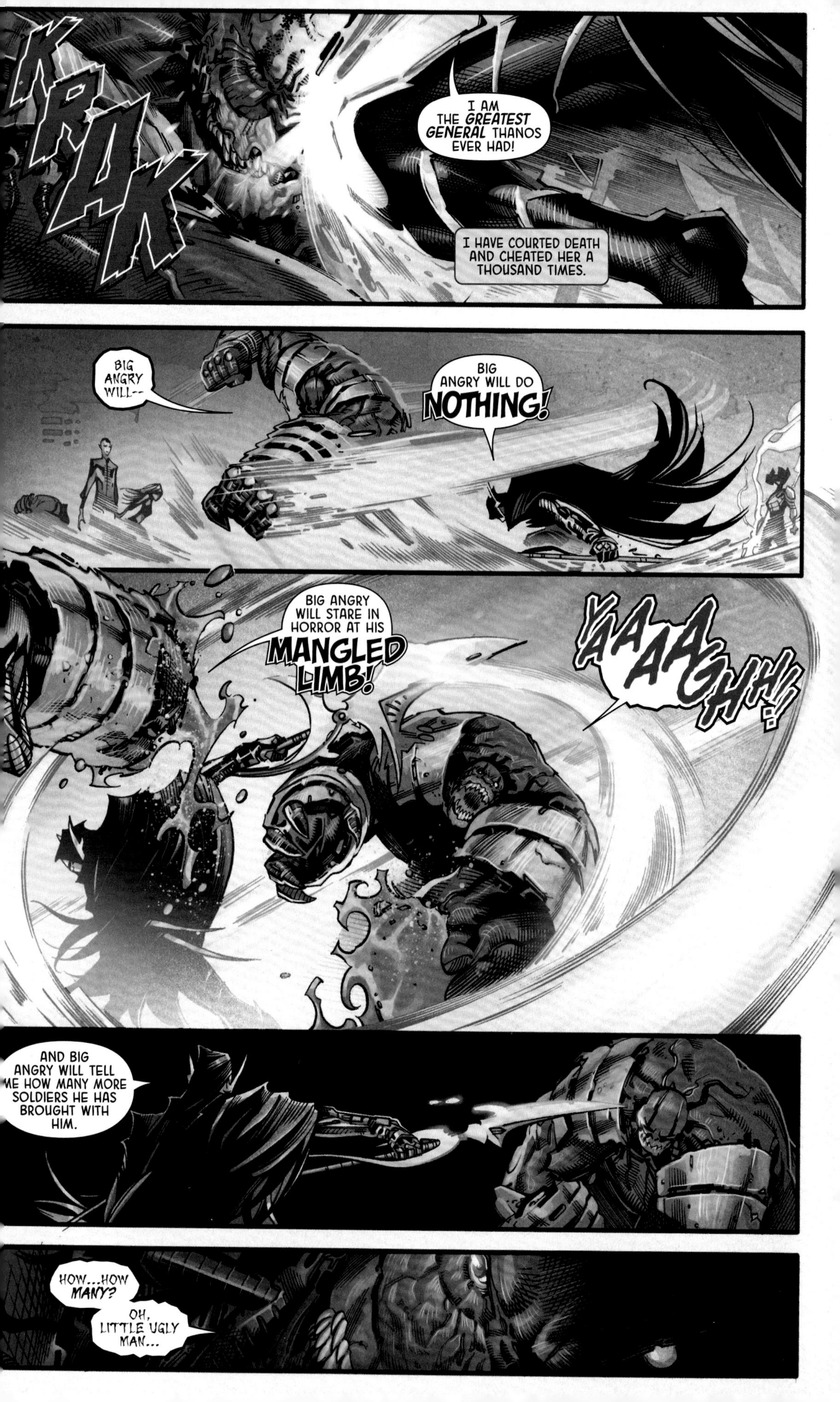

KRAK
I AM THE GREATEST GENERAL THANOS EVER HAD!
I HAVE COURTED DEATH AND CHEATED HER A THOUSAND TIMES.
BIG ANGRY WILL--
BIG ANGRY WILL DO NOTHING!
BIG ANGRY WILL STARE IN HORROR AT HIS MANGLED LIMB!
YAAAAGHH!!
AND BIG ANGRY WILL TELL ME HOW MANY MORE SOLDIERS HE HAS BROUGHT WITH HIM.
HOW...HOW MANY?
OH, LITTLE UGLY MAN...

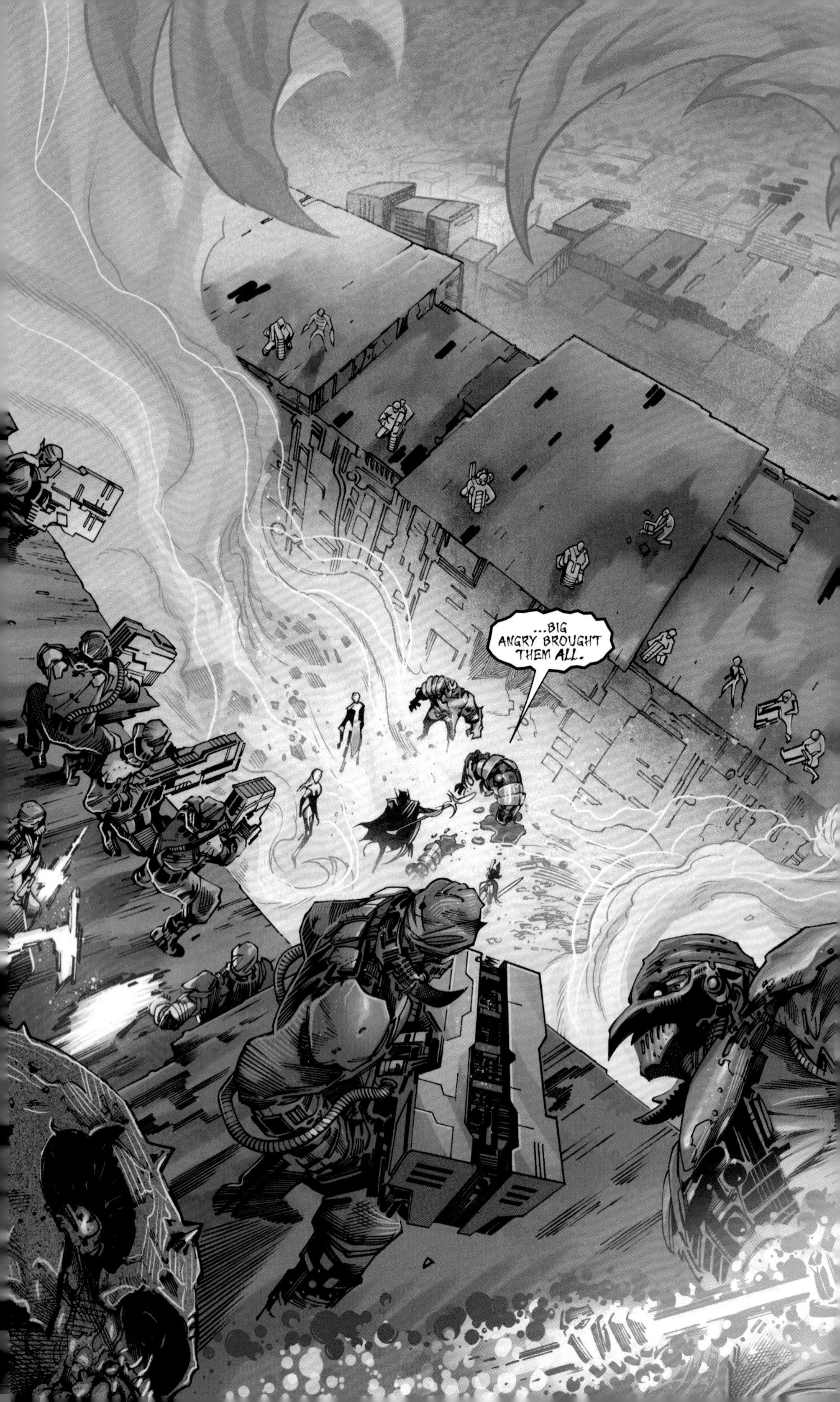
...BIG ANGRY BROUGHT THEM ALL.

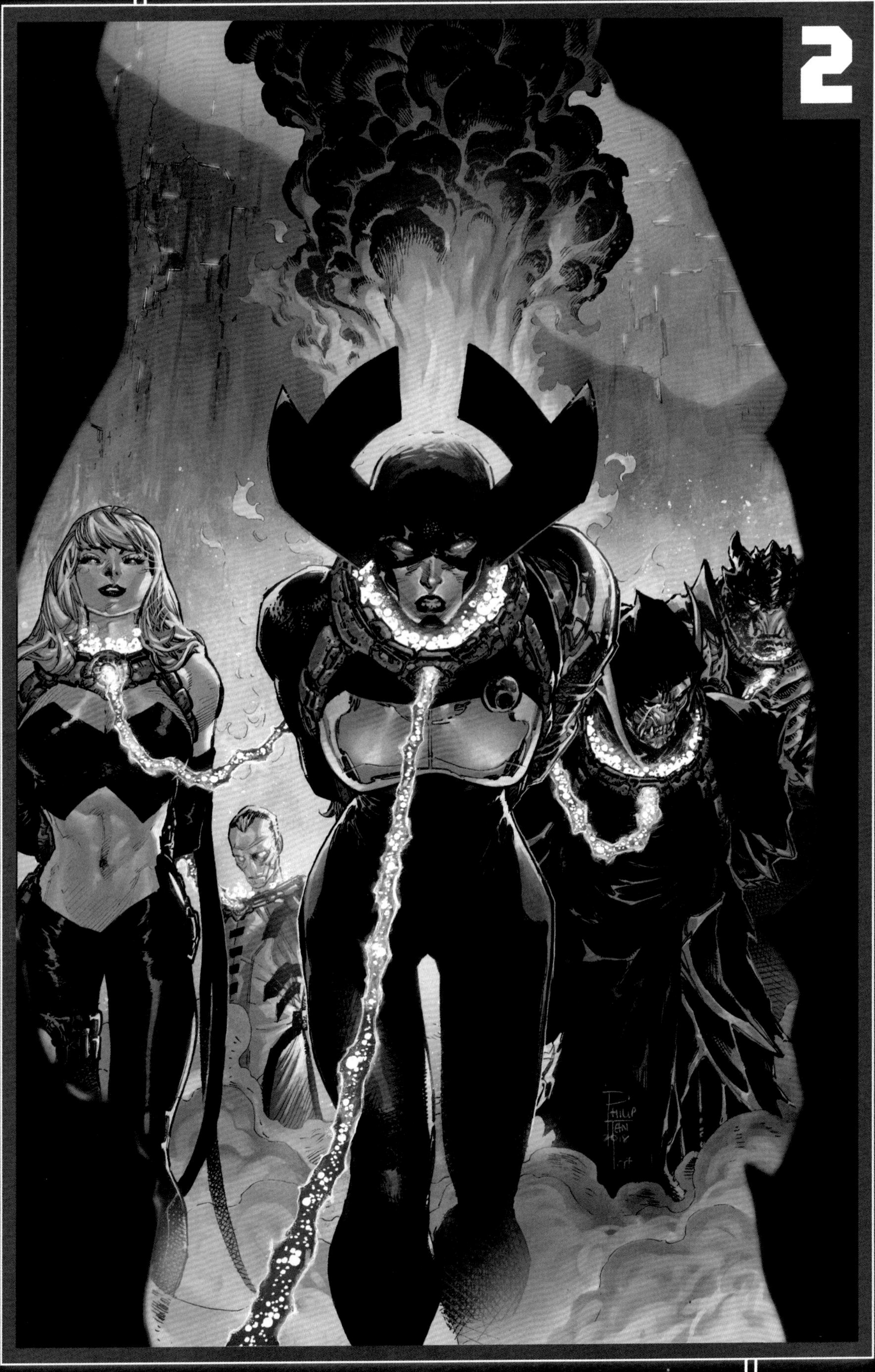
2

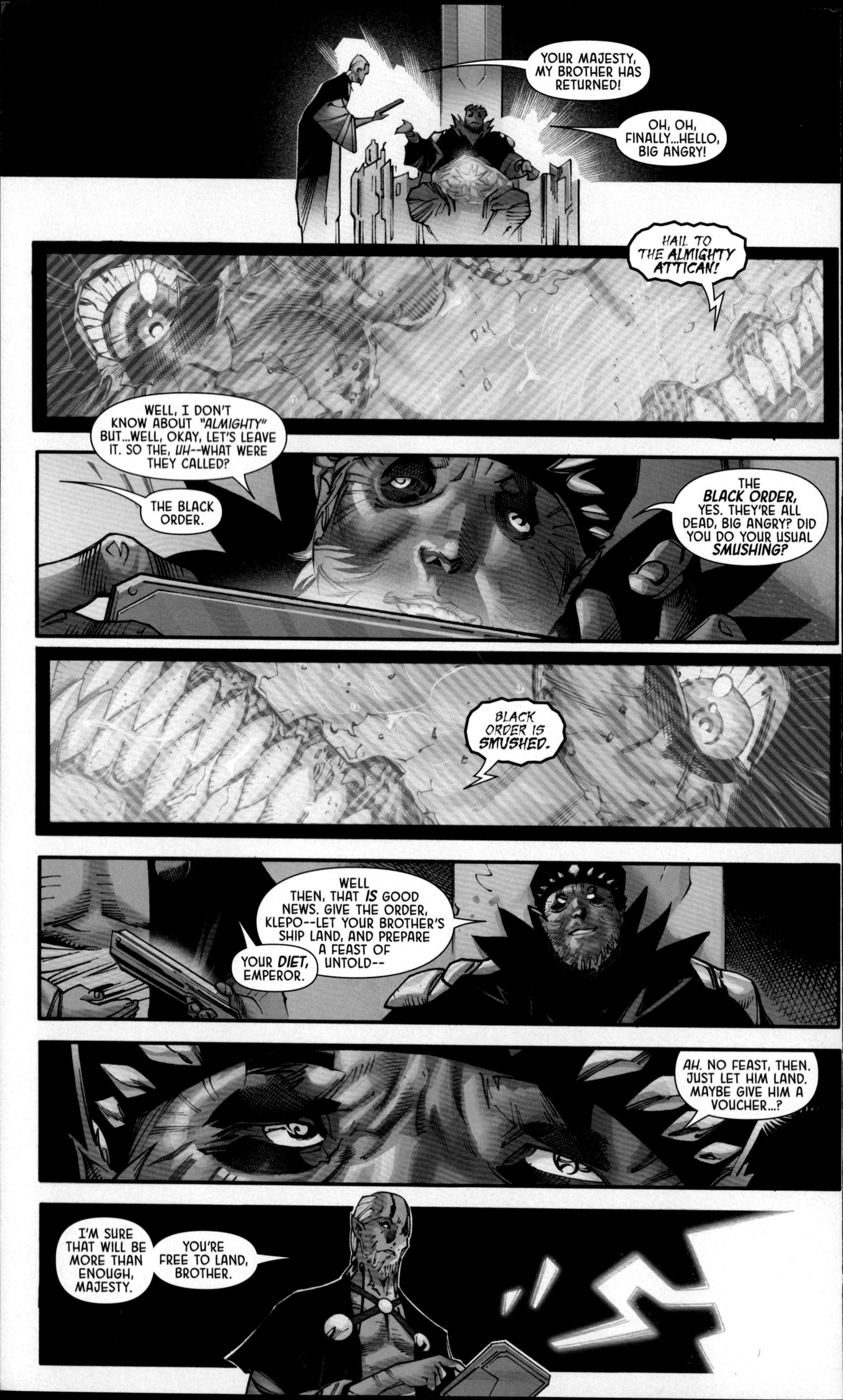
YOUR MAJESTY, MY BROTHER HAS RETURNED!
OH, OH, FINALLY...HELLO, BIG ANGRY!
HAIL TO THE ALMIGHTY ATTICAN!
WELL, I DON'T KNOW ABOUT "ALMIGHTY" BUT...WELL, OKAY, LET'S LEAVE IT. SO THE, UH--WHAT WERE THEY CALLED?
THE BLACK ORDER.
THE BLACK ORDER, YES. THEY'RE ALL DEAD, BIG ANGRY? DID YOU DO YOUR USUAL SMUSHING?
BLACK ORDER IS SMUSHED.
WELL THEN, THAT IS GOOD NEWS. GIVE THE ORDER, KLEPO--LET YOUR BROTHER'S SHIP LAND, AND PREPARE A FEAST OF UNTOLD--
YOUR DIET, EMPEROR.
AH. NO FEAST, THEN. JUST LET HIM LAND. MAYBE GIVE HIM A VOUCHER...?
I'M SURE THAT WILL BE MORE THAN ENOUGH, MAJESTY.
YOU'RE FREE TO LAND, BROTHER.

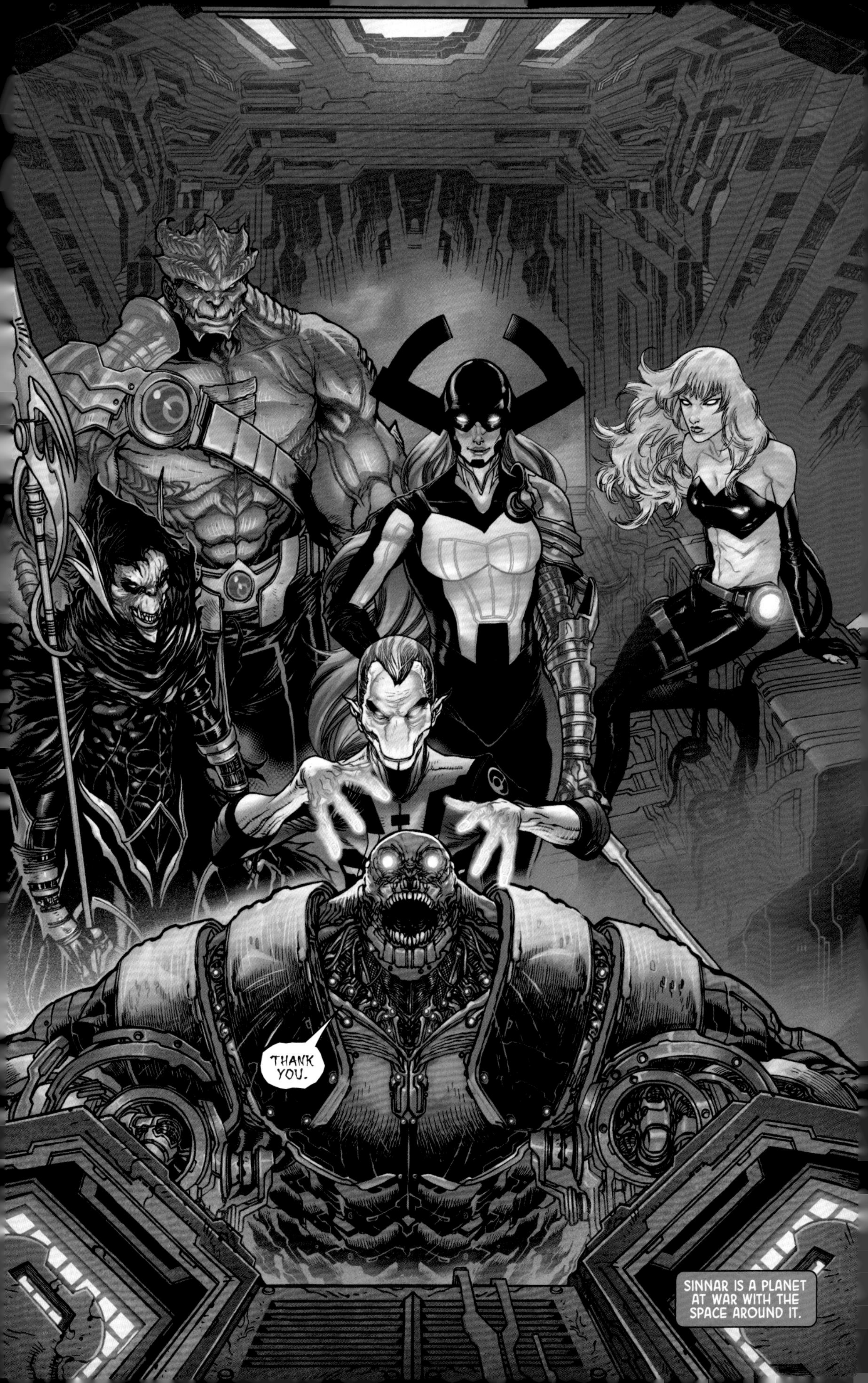
THANK YOU.
SINNAR IS A PLANET AT WAR WITH THE SPACE AROUND IT.

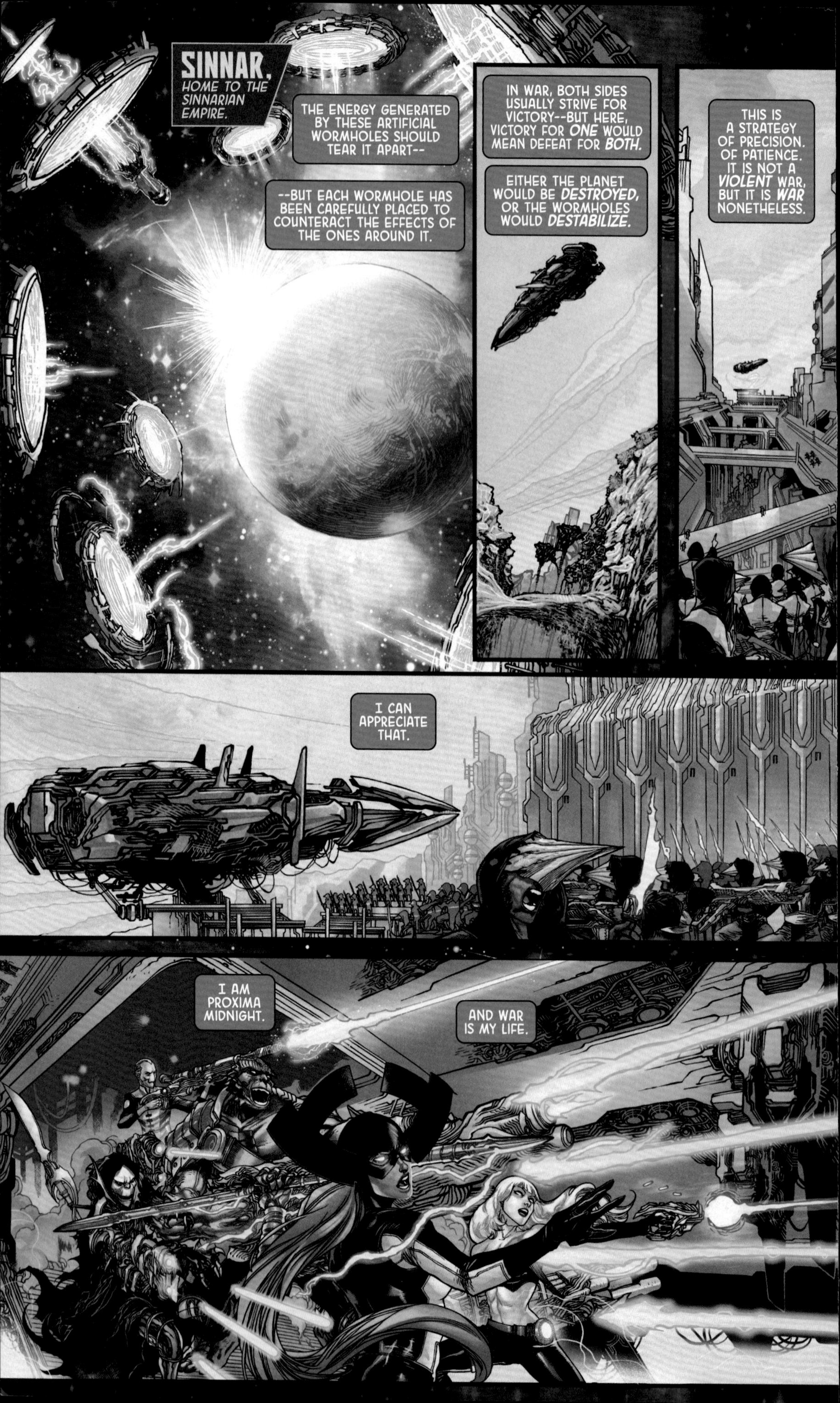
SINNAR, HOME TO THE SINNARIAN EMPIRE.
THE ENERGY GENERATED BY THESE ARTIFICIAL WORMHOLES SHOULD TEAR IT APART--
--BUT EACH WORMHOLE HAS BEEN CAREFULLY PLACED TO COUNTERACT THE EFFECTS OF THE ONES AROUND IT.
IN WAR, BOTH SIDES USUALLY STRIVE FOR VICTORY--BUT HERE, VICTORY FOR ONE WOULD MEAN DEFEAT FOR BOTH.
EITHER THE PLANET WOULD BE DESTROYED, OR THE WORMHOLES WOULD DESTABILIZE.
THIS IS A STRATEGY OF PRECISION. OF PATIENCE. IT IS NOT A VIOLENT WAR, BUT IT IS WAR NONETHELESS.
I CAN APPRECIATE THAT.
I AM PROXIMA MIDNIGHT.
AND WAR IS MY LIFE.

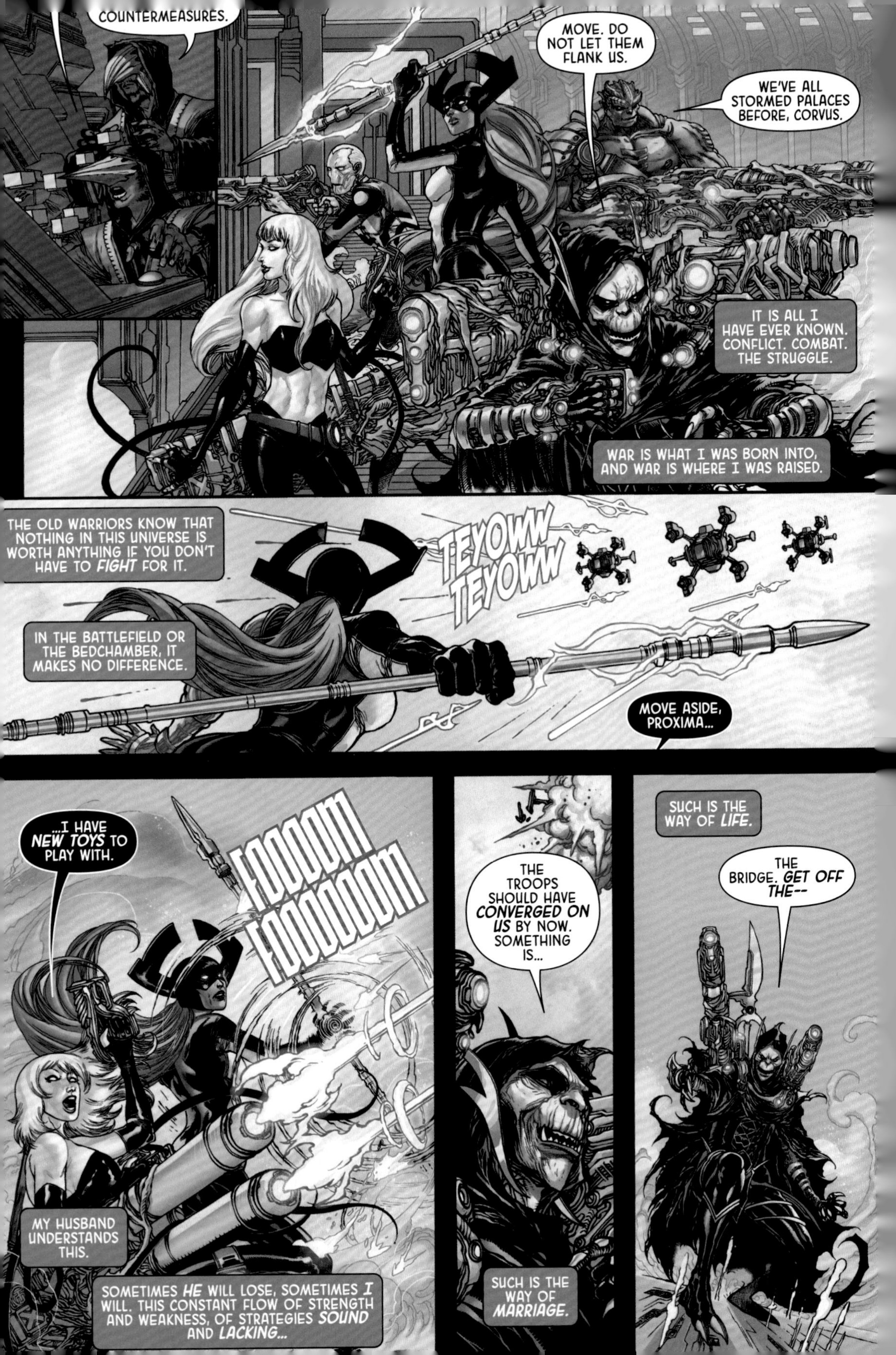

COUNTERMEASURES.
MOVE. DO NOT LET THEM FLANK US.
WE'VE ALL STORMED PALACES BEFORE, CORVUS.
IT IS ALL I HAVE EVER KNOWN. CONFLICT. COMBAT. THE STRUGGLE.
WAR IS WHAT I WAS BORN INTO, AND WAR IS WHERE I WAS RAISED.
THE OLD WARRIORS KNOW THAT NOTHING IN THIS UNIVERSE IS WORTH ANYTHING IF YOU DON'T HAVE TO FIGHT FOR IT.
TEYOWW TEYOWW
IN THE BATTLEFIELD OR THE BEDCHAMBER, IT MAKES NO DIFFERENCE.
MOVE ASIDE, PROXIMA...
...I HAVE NEW TOYS TO PLAY WITH.
FOOOOM FOOOOOOM
MY HUSBAND UNDERSTANDS THIS.
SOMETIMES HE WILL LOSE, SOMETIMES I WILL. THIS CONSTANT FLOW OF STRENGTH AND WEAKNESS, OF STRATEGIES SOUND AND LACKING...
THE TROOPS SHOULD HAVE CONVERGED ON US BY NOW. SOMETHING IS...
SUCH IS THE WAY OF MARRIAGE.
SUCH IS THE WAY OF LIFE.
THE BRIDGE. GET OFF THE--

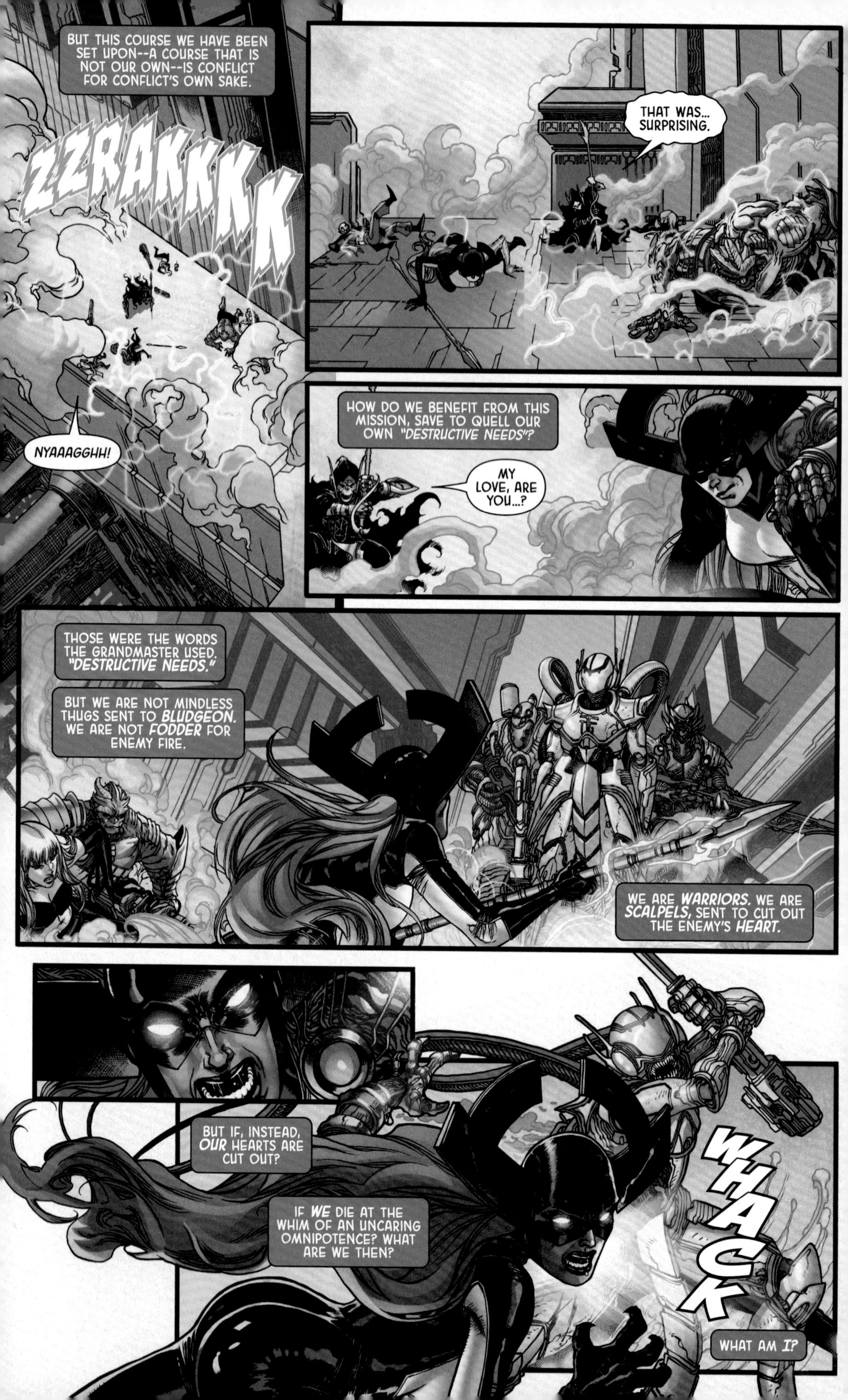
BUT THIS COURSE WE HAVE BEEN SET UPON--A COURSE THAT IS NOT OUR OWN--IS CONFLICT FOR CONFLICT'S OWN SAKE.
ZZRAKKKK
NYAAAGGHH!
THAT WAS... SURPRISING.
HOW DO WE BENEFIT FROM THIS MISSION, SAVE TO QUELL OUR OWN "DESTRUCTIVE NEEDS"?
MY LOVE, ARE YOU...?
THOSE WERE THE WORDS THE GRANDMASTER USED. "DESTRUCTIVE NEEDS."
BUT WE ARE NOT MINDLESS THUGS SENT TO BLUDGEON. WE ARE NOT FODDER FOR ENEMY FIRE.
WE ARE WARRIORS. WE ARE SCALPELS, SENT TO CUT OUT THE ENEMY'S HEART.
BUT IF, INSTEAD, OUR HEARTS ARE CUT OUT?
IF WE DIE AT THE WHIM OF AN UNCARING OMNIPOTENCE? WHAT ARE WE THEN?
WHACK
WHAT AM I?

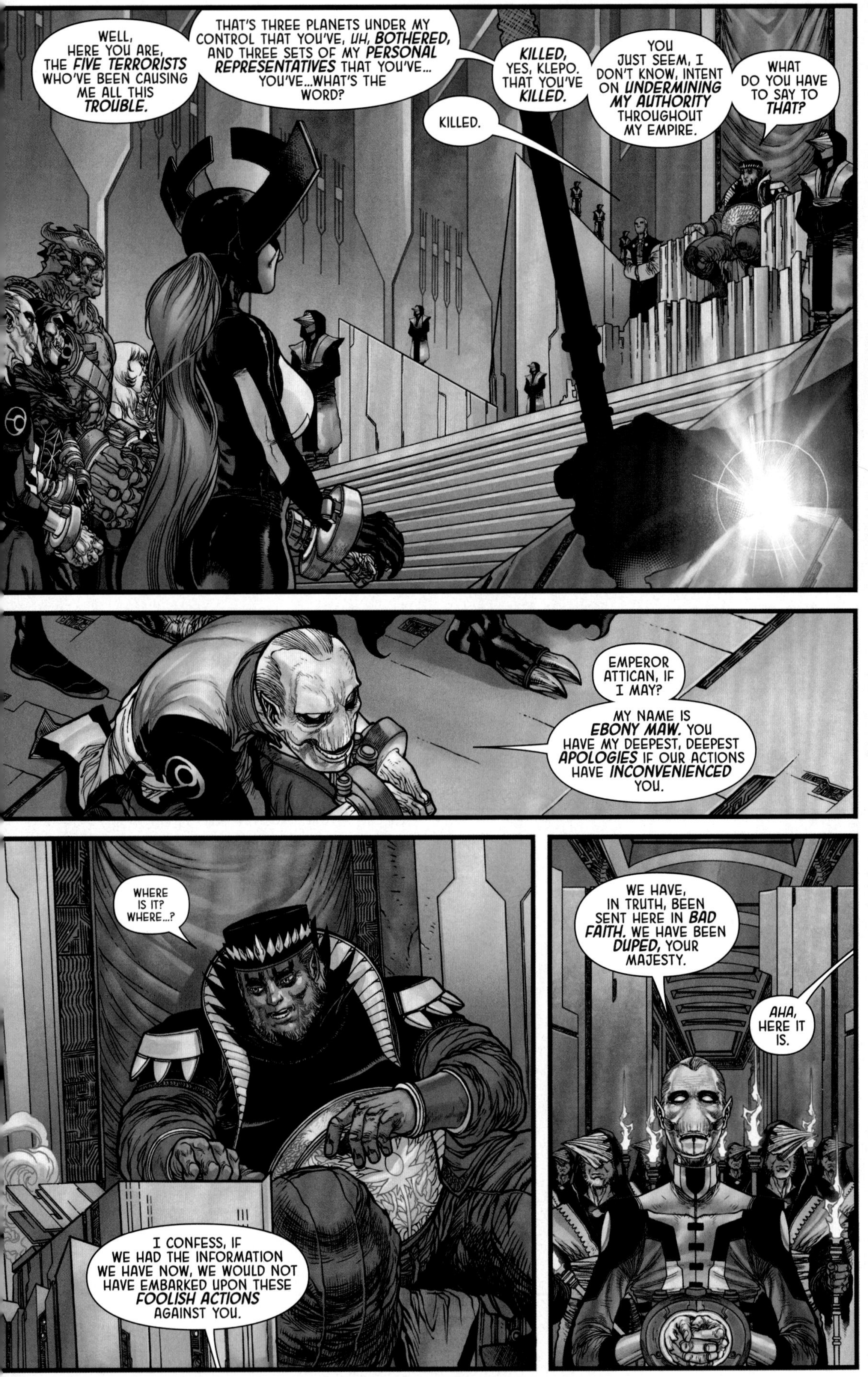
WELL, HERE YOU ARE, THE FIVE TERRORISTS WHO'VE BEEN CAUSING ME ALL THIS TROUBLE.
THAT'S THREE PLANETS UNDER MY CONTROL THAT YOU'VE, UH, BOTHERED, AND THREE SETS OF MY PERSONAL REPRESENTATIVES THAT YOU'VE... YOU'VE...WHAT'S THE WORD?
KILLED.
KILLED, YES, KLEPO. THAT YOU'VE KILLED.
YOU JUST SEEM, I DON'T KNOW, INTENT ON UNDERMINING MY AUTHORITY THROUGHOUT MY EMPIRE.
WHAT DO YOU HAVE TO SAY TO THAT?
EMPEROR ATTICAN, IF I MAY?
MY NAME IS EBONY MAW. YOU HAVE MY DEEPEST, DEEPEST APOLOGIES IF OUR ACTIONS HAVE INCONVENIENCED YOU.
WHERE IS IT? WHERE...?
I CONFESS, IF WE HAD THE INFORMATION WE HAVE NOW, WE WOULD NOT HAVE EMBARKED UPON THESE FOOLISH ACTIONS AGAINST YOU.
WE HAVE, IN TRUTH, BEEN SENT HERE IN BAD FAITH. WE HAVE BEEN DUPED, YOUR MAJESTY.
AHA, HERE IT IS.

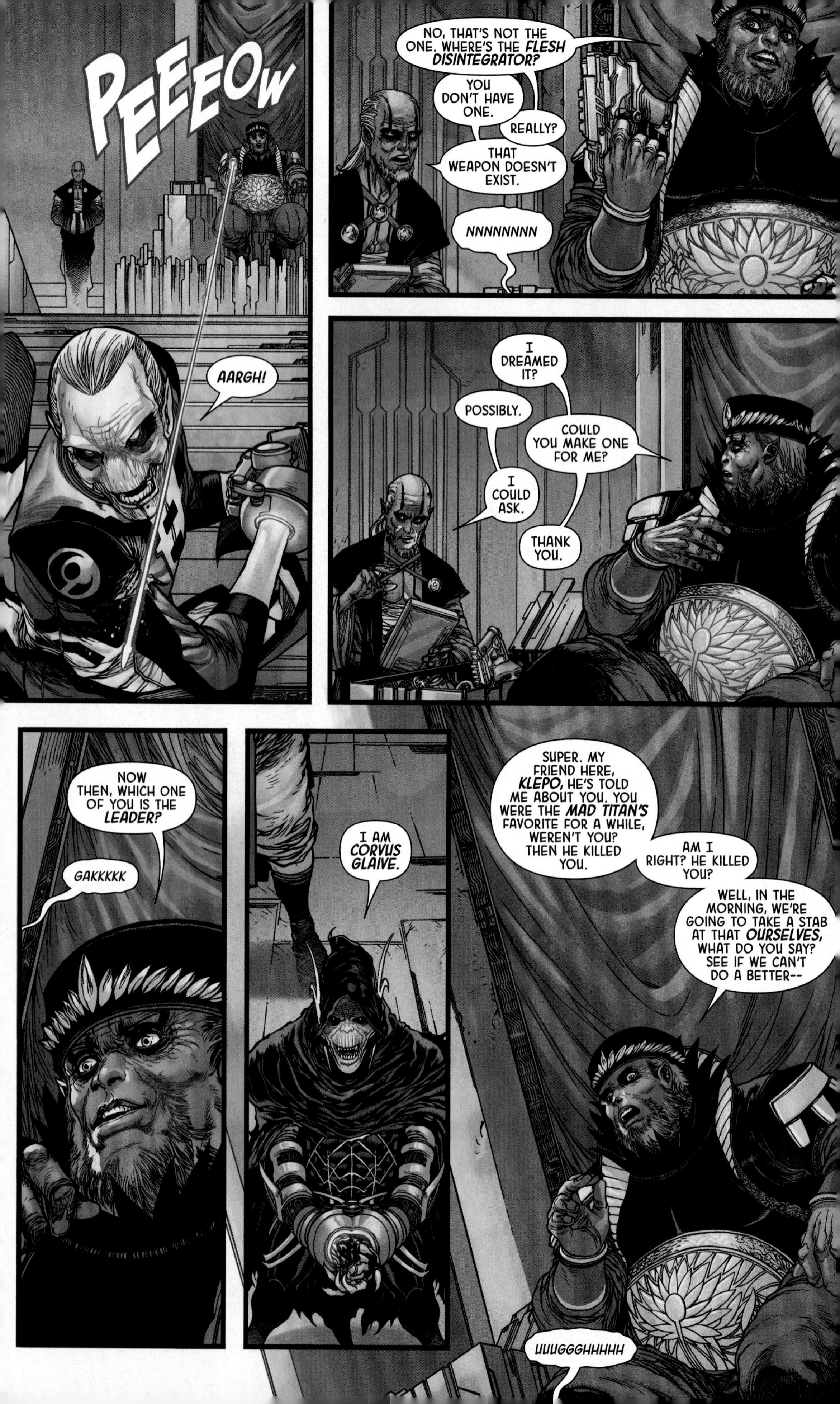
PEEEOW
NO, THAT'S NOT THE ONE. WHERE'S THE *FLESH DISINTEGRATOR?*
YOU DON'T HAVE ONE.
REALLY?
THAT WEAPON DOESN'T EXIST.
NNNNNNNN
AARGH!
I DREAMED IT?
POSSIBLY.
COULD YOU MAKE ONE FOR ME?
I COULD ASK.
THANK YOU.
NOW THEN, WHICH ONE OF YOU IS THE *LEADER?*
GAKKKKK
I AM *CORVUS GLAIVE.*
SUPER. MY FRIEND HERE, *KLEPO,* HE'S TOLD ME ABOUT YOU. YOU WERE THE *MAD TITAN'S* FAVORITE FOR A WHILE, WEREN'T YOU? THEN HE KILLED YOU.
AM I RIGHT? HE KILLED YOU?
WELL, IN THE MORNING, WE'RE GOING TO TAKE A STAB AT THAT *OURSELVES,* WHAT DO YOU SAY? SEE IF WE CAN'T DO A BETTER--
UUUGGGHHHHH

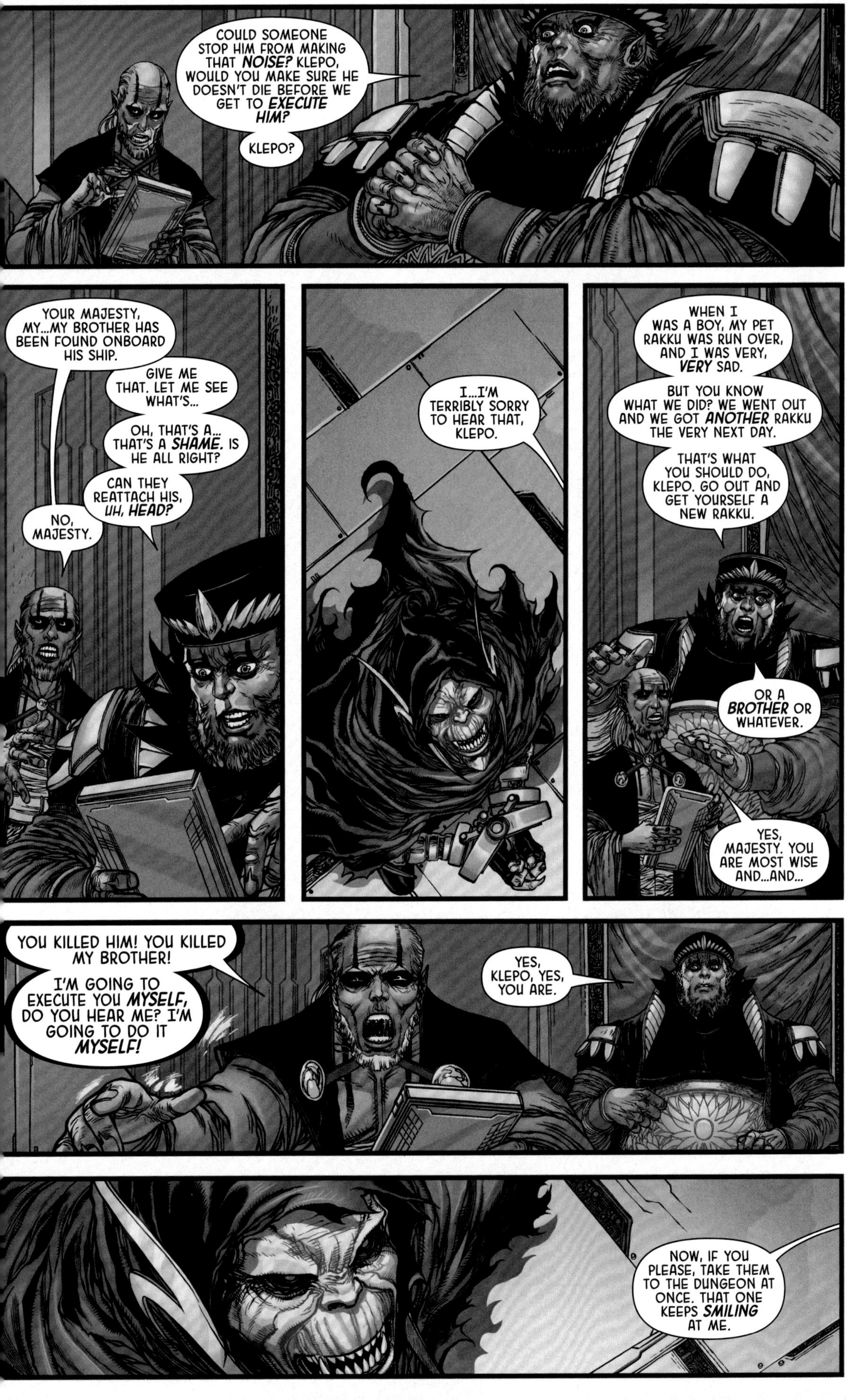
COULD SOMEONE STOP HIM FROM MAKING THAT NOISE? KLEPO, WOULD YOU MAKE SURE HE DOESN'T DIE BEFORE WE GET TO EXECUTE HIM?
KLEPO?
YOUR MAJESTY, MY...MY BROTHER HAS BEEN FOUND ONBOARD HIS SHIP.
GIVE ME THAT. LET ME SEE WHAT'S...
OH, THAT'S A... THAT'S A SHAME. IS HE ALL RIGHT?
CAN THEY REATTACH HIS, UH, HEAD?
NO, MAJESTY.
I...I'M TERRIBLY SORRY TO HEAR THAT, KLEPO.
WHEN I WAS A BOY, MY PET RAKKU WAS RUN OVER, AND I WAS VERY, VERY SAD.
BUT YOU KNOW WHAT WE DID? WE WENT OUT AND WE GOT ANOTHER RAKKU THE VERY NEXT DAY.
THAT'S WHAT YOU SHOULD DO, KLEPO. GO OUT AND GET YOURSELF A NEW RAKKU.
OR A BROTHER OR WHATEVER.
YES, MAJESTY. YOU ARE MOST WISE AND...AND...
YOU KILLED HIM! YOU KILLED MY BROTHER!
I'M GOING TO EXECUTE YOU MYSELF, DO YOU HEAR ME? I'M GOING TO DO IT MYSELF!
YES, KLEPO, YES, YOU ARE.
NOW, IF YOU PLEASE, TAKE THEM TO THE DUNGEON AT ONCE. THAT ONE KEEPS SMILING AT ME.

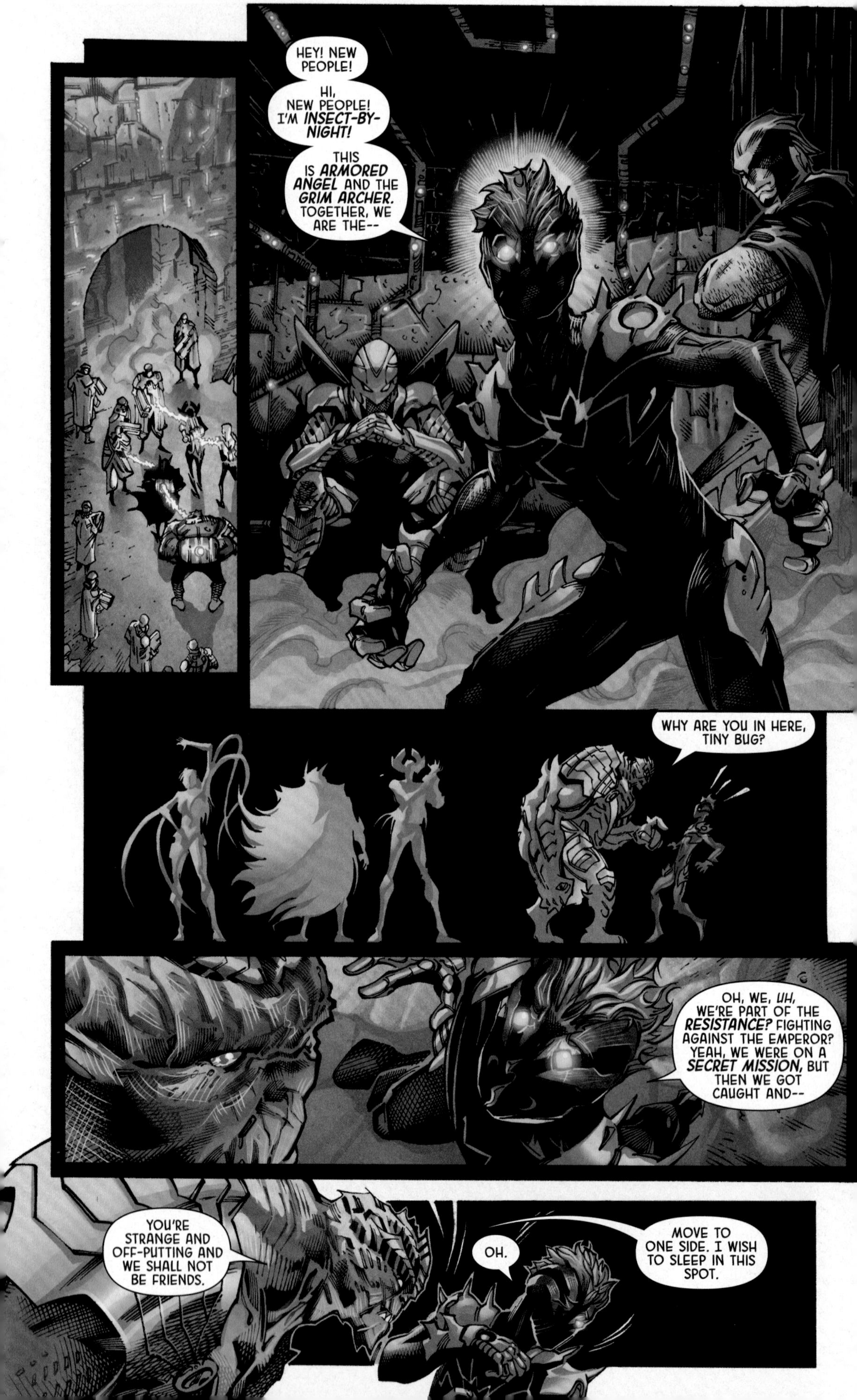
HEY! NEW PEOPLE!
HI, NEW PEOPLE! I'M INSECT-BY-NIGHT!
THIS IS ARMORED ANGEL AND THE GRIM ARCHER. TOGETHER, WE ARE THE--
WHY ARE YOU IN HERE, TINY BUG?
OH, WE, UH, WE'RE PART OF THE RESISTANCE? FIGHTING AGAINST THE EMPEROR? YEAH, WE WERE ON A SECRET MISSION, BUT THEN WE GOT CAUGHT AND--
YOU'RE STRANGE AND OFF-PUTTING AND WE SHALL NOT BE FRIENDS.
OH.
MOVE TO ONE SIDE. I WISH TO SLEEP IN THIS SPOT.

EVEN LOVE IS VIOLENCE.

THE CUT AND THRUST OF WORDS, SPOKEN IN WHISPERS.

WHAT TROUBLES YOU, MY LADY MIDNIGHT?

THIS IS NOT OUR WAR.

DID NOT YOU ONCE SAY TO ME THAT *EVERY* WAR IS OUR WAR?

THE PARRIES AND BLOCKS. THE REDIRECTS. THE EVASIONS.

I HAVE GROWN UP SINCE THEN. THIS MEANS *NOTHING* TO US. AN EMPIRE, A RESISTANCE... WE HAVE SEEN IT A THOUSAND TIMES.

THE REBELLION *SUCCEEDS* OR *FAILS.* THE PLANET KEEPS TURNING. EVERY REBEL IS AN *EMPEROR-IN-WAITING.*

YOU KNOW WHY WE'RE HERE.

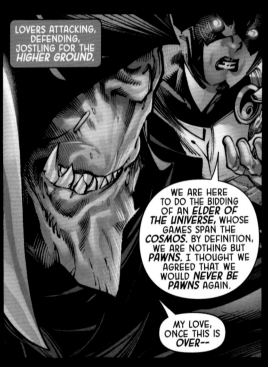

LOVERS ATTACKING, DEFENDING, JOSTLING FOR THE *HIGHER GROUND.*

WE ARE HERE TO DO THE BIDDING OF AN *ELDER OF THE UNIVERSE,* WHOSE GAMES SPAN THE *COSMOS.* BY DEFINITION, WE ARE NOTHING BUT *PAWNS.* I THOUGHT WE AGREED THAT WE WOULD *NEVER BE PAWNS* AGAIN.

MY LOVE, ONCE THIS IS *OVER--*

WHAT? WHAT THEN?

HE TASKS US WITH *ANOTHER* MISSION? HE HEALS OUR *WOUNDS* AND REVIVES OUR *DEAD* AND SENDS US OUT AGAIN? WE ARE MEANT FOR *MORE THAN THIS,* CORVUS.

HE CAN OFFER NO RIPOSTE.

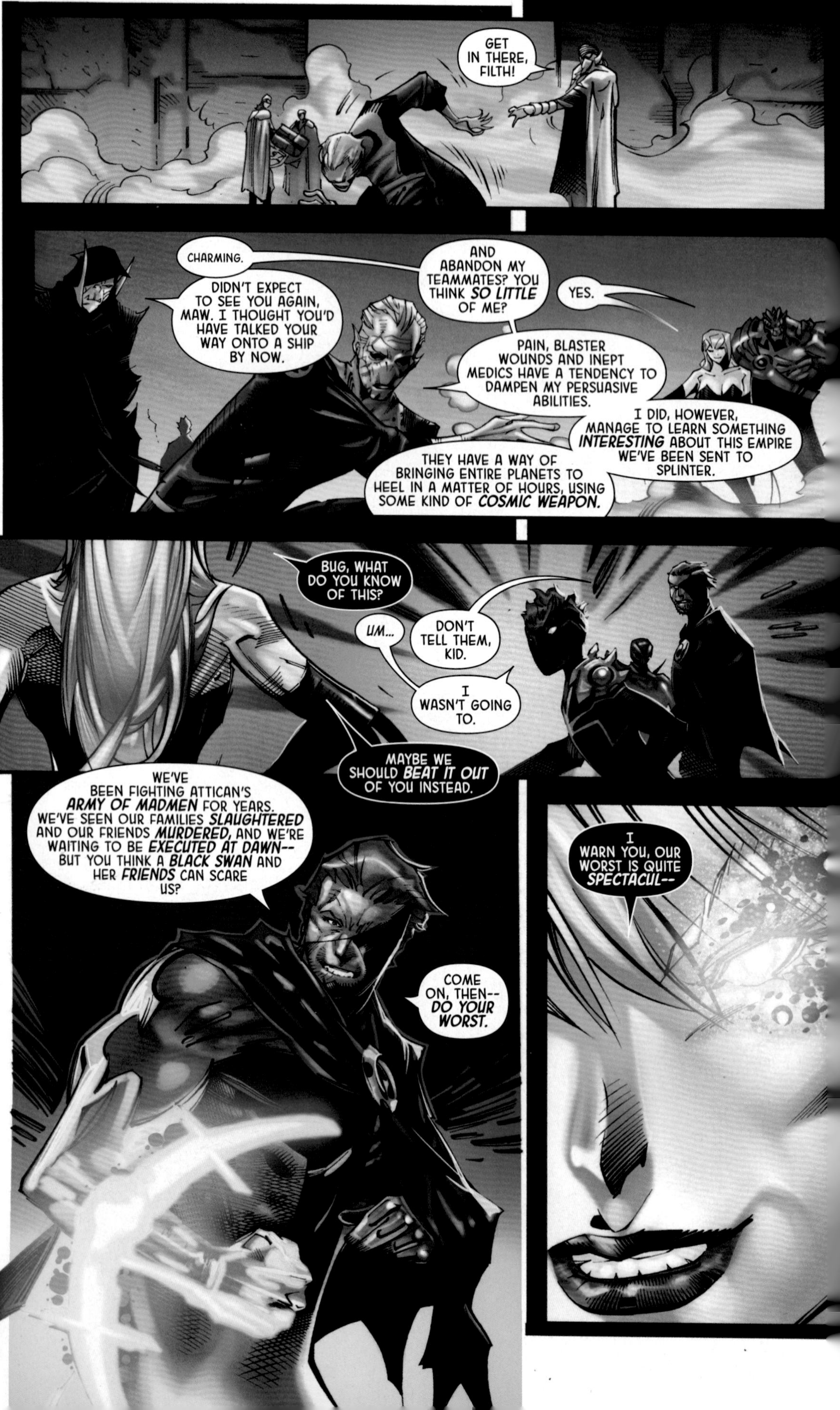
GET IN THERE, FILTH!
CHARMING.
DIDN'T EXPECT TO SEE YOU AGAIN, MAW. I THOUGHT YOU'D HAVE TALKED YOUR WAY ONTO A SHIP BY NOW.
AND ABANDON MY TEAMMATES? YOU THINK SO LITTLE OF ME?
YES.
PAIN, BLASTER WOUNDS AND INEPT MEDICS HAVE A TENDENCY TO DAMPEN MY PERSUASIVE ABILITIES.
I DID, HOWEVER, MANAGE TO LEARN SOMETHING INTERESTING ABOUT THIS EMPIRE WE'VE BEEN SENT TO SPLINTER.
THEY HAVE A WAY OF BRINGING ENTIRE PLANETS TO HEEL IN A MATTER OF HOURS, USING SOME KIND OF COSMIC WEAPON.
BUG, WHAT DO YOU KNOW OF THIS?
UM...
DON'T TELL THEM, KID.
I WASN'T GOING TO.
MAYBE WE SHOULD BEAT IT OUT OF YOU INSTEAD.
WE'VE BEEN FIGHTING ATTICAN'S ARMY OF MADMEN FOR YEARS. WE'VE SEEN OUR FAMILIES SLAUGHTERED AND OUR FRIENDS MURDERED, AND WE'RE WAITING TO BE EXECUTED AT DAWN-- BUT YOU THINK A BLACK SWAN AND HER FRIENDS CAN SCARE US?
COME ON, THEN-- DO YOUR WORST.
I WARN YOU, OUR WORST IS QUITE SPECTACUL--

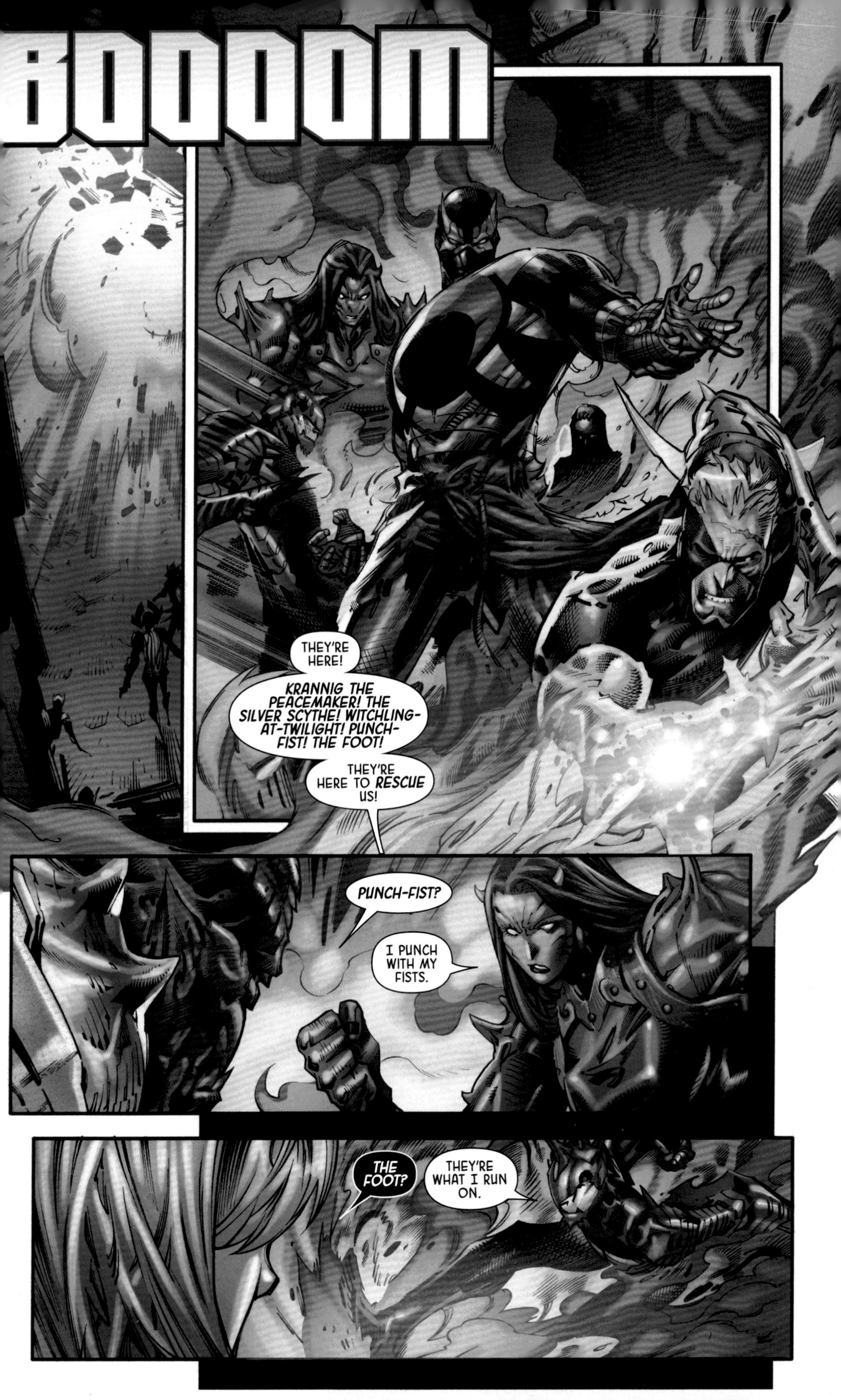
BOOOOM
THEY'RE HERE!
KRANNIG THE PEACEMAKER! THE SILVER SCYTHE! WITCHLING-AT-TWILIGHT! PUNCH-FIST! THE FOOT!
THEY'RE HERE TO RESCUE US!
PUNCH-FIST?
I PUNCH WITH MY FISTS.
THE FOOT?
THEY'RE WHAT I RUN ON.

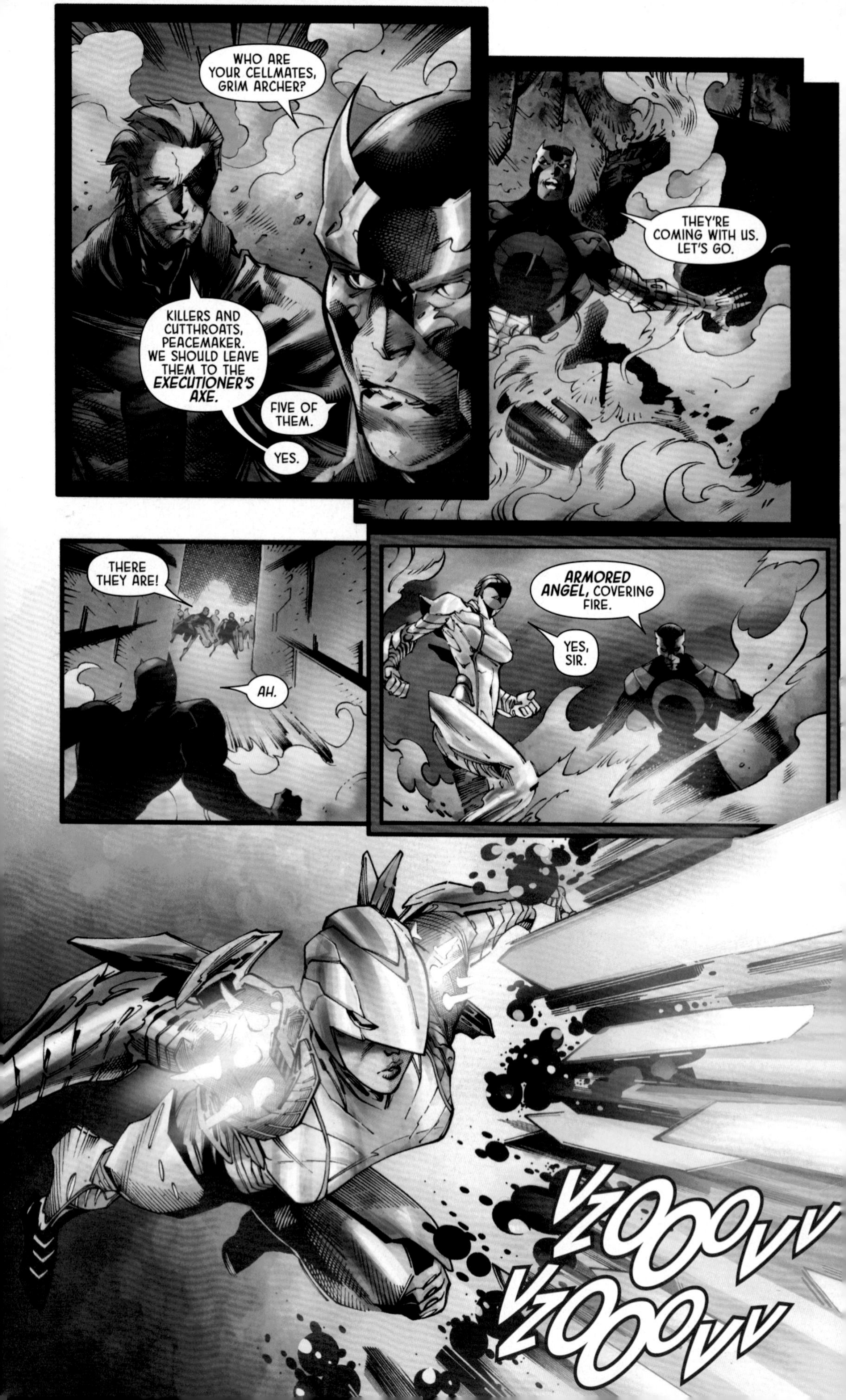
WHO ARE YOUR CELLMATES, GRIM ARCHER?
KILLERS AND CUTTHROATS, PEACEMAKER. WE SHOULD LEAVE THEM TO THE *EXECUTIONER'S AXE.*
FIVE OF THEM.
YES.
THEY'RE COMING WITH US. LET'S GO.
THERE THEY ARE!
AH.
ARMORED ANGEL, COVERING FIRE.
YES, SIR.
VZOOOVVV
VZOOOVVV

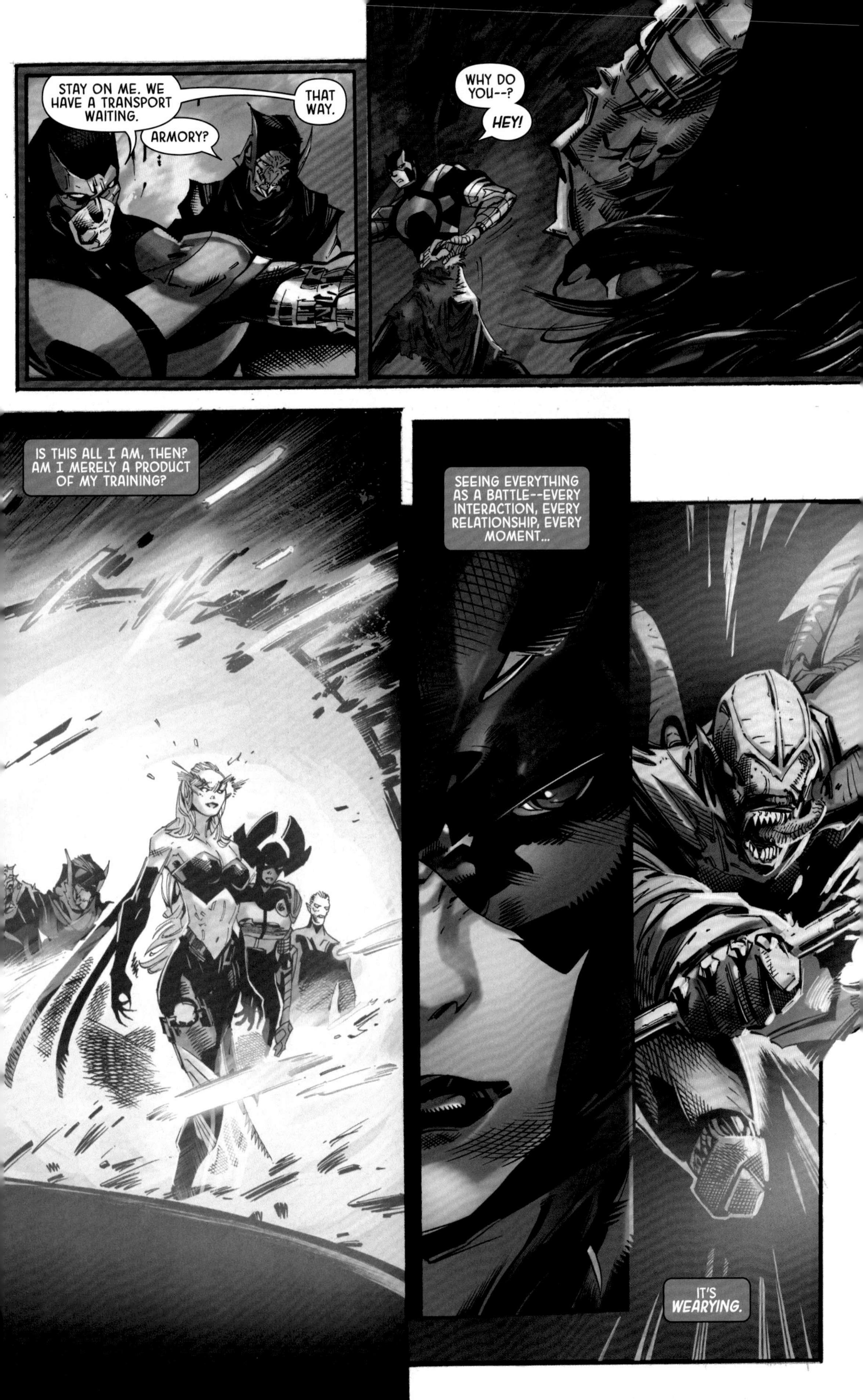

STAY ON ME. WE HAVE A TRANSPORT WAITING.
ARMORY?
THAT WAY.
WHY DO YOU--?
HEY!
IS THIS ALL I AM, THEN? AM I MERELY A PRODUCT OF MY TRAINING?
SEEING EVERYTHING AS A BATTLE--EVERY INTERACTION, EVERY RELATIONSHIP, EVERY MOMENT...
IT'S *WEARYING.*

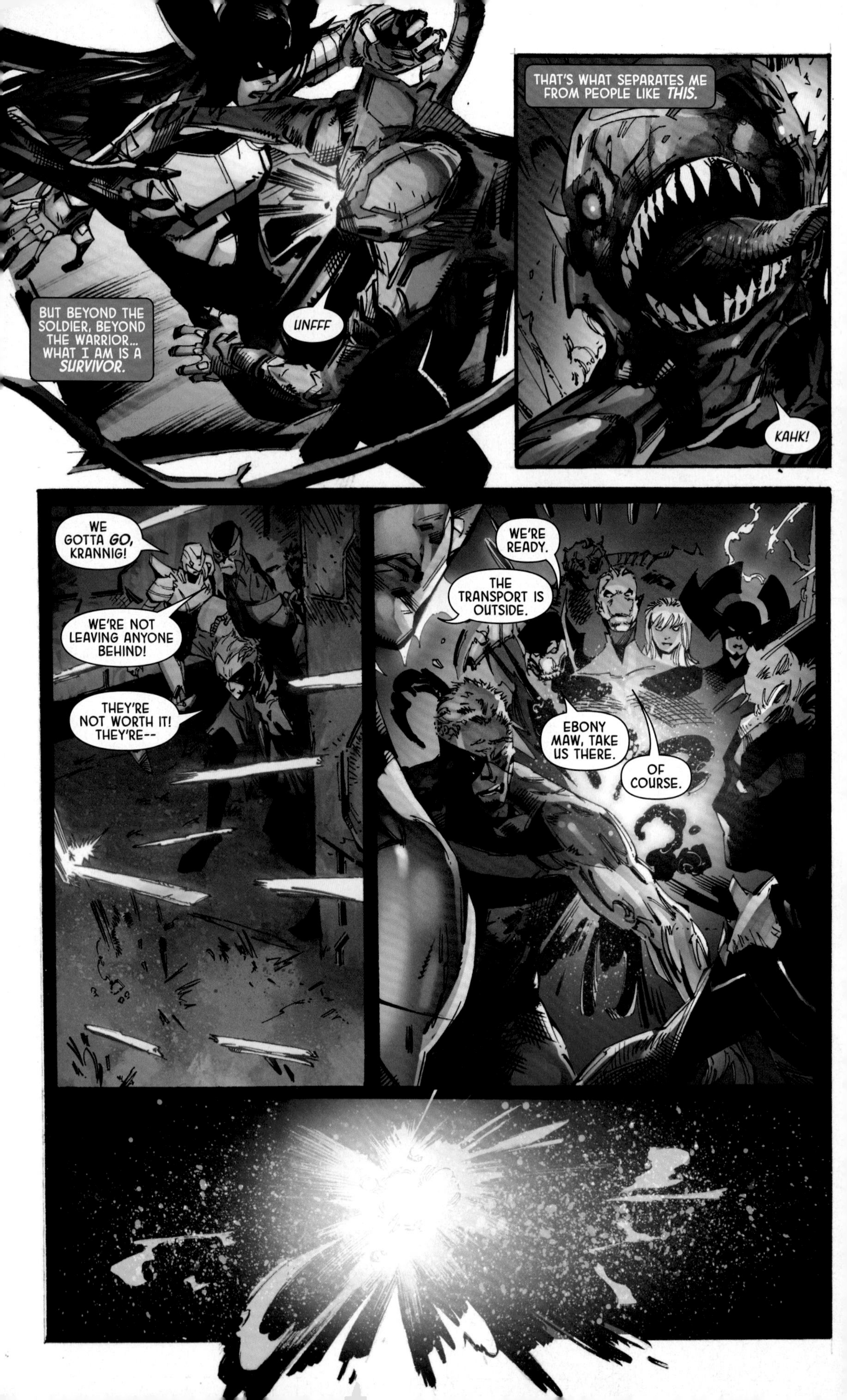
BUT BEYOND THE SOLDIER, BEYOND THE WARRIOR... WHAT I AM IS A SURVIVOR.
UNFFF
THAT'S WHAT SEPARATES ME FROM PEOPLE LIKE THIS.
KAHK!
WE GOTTA GO, KRANNIG!
WE'RE NOT LEAVING ANYONE BEHIND!
THEY'RE NOT WORTH IT! THEY'RE--
WE'RE READY.
THE TRANSPORT IS OUTSIDE.
EBONY MAW, TAKE US THERE.
OF COURSE.

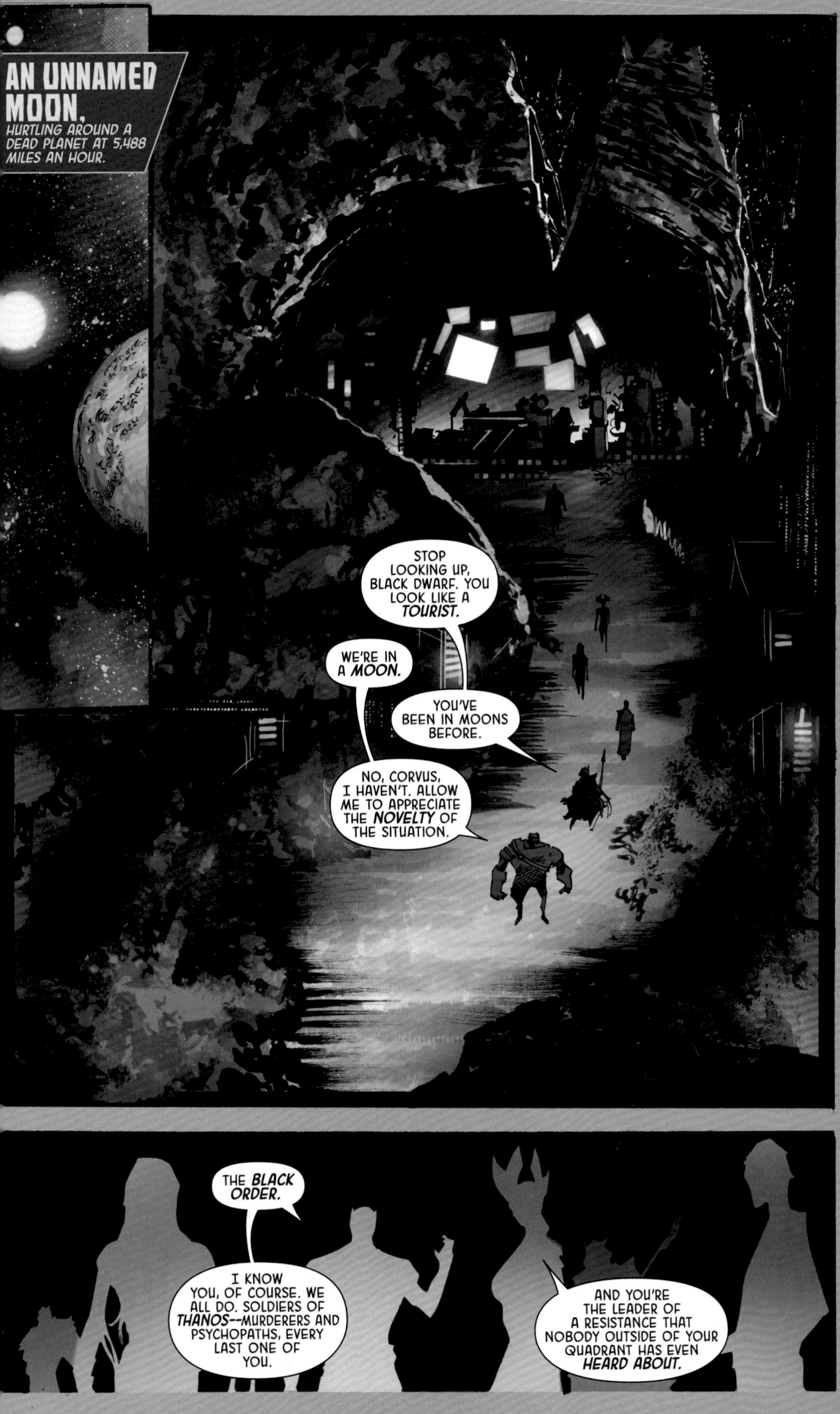
AN UNNAMED MOON,
HURTLING AROUND A DEAD PLANET AT 5,488 MILES AN HOUR.
STOP LOOKING UP, BLACK DWARF. YOU LOOK LIKE A TOURIST.
WE'RE IN A MOON.
YOU'VE BEEN IN MOONS BEFORE.
NO, CORVUS, I HAVEN'T. ALLOW ME TO APPRECIATE THE NOVELTY OF THE SITUATION.
THE BLACK ORDER.
I KNOW YOU, OF COURSE. WE ALL DO. SOLDIERS OF THANOS--MURDERERS AND PSYCHOPATHS, EVERY LAST ONE OF YOU.
AND YOU'RE THE LEADER OF A RESISTANCE THAT NOBODY OUTSIDE OF YOUR QUADRANT HAS EVEN HEARD ABOUT.

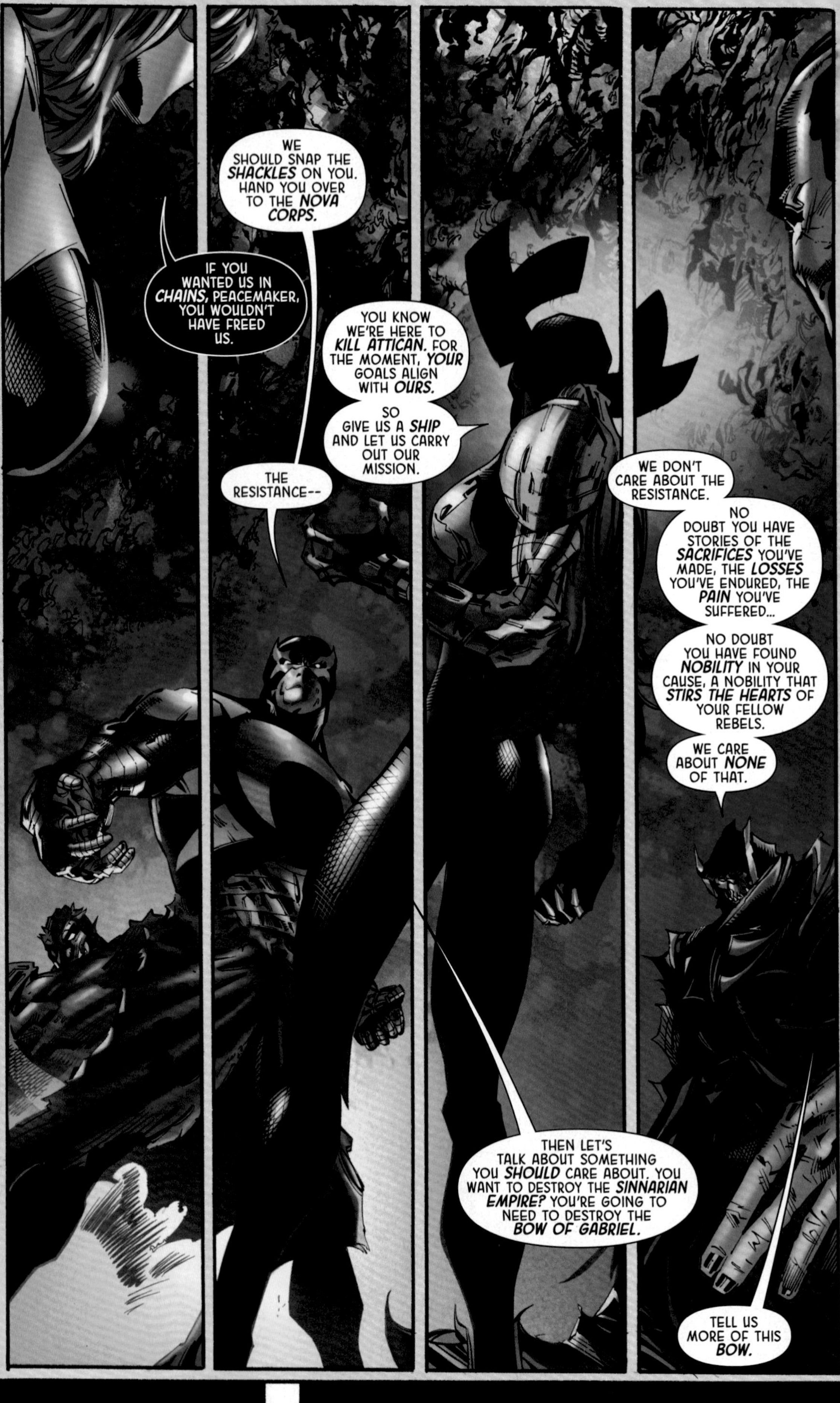
WE SHOULD SNAP THE SHACKLES ON YOU. HAND YOU OVER TO THE NOVA CORPS.
IF YOU WANTED US IN CHAINS, PEACEMAKER, YOU WOULDN'T HAVE FREED US.
YOU KNOW WE'RE HERE TO KILL ATTICAN. FOR THE MOMENT, YOUR GOALS ALIGN WITH OURS.
SO GIVE US A SHIP AND LET US CARRY OUT OUR MISSION.
THE RESISTANCE--
WE DON'T CARE ABOUT THE RESISTANCE.
NO DOUBT YOU HAVE STORIES OF THE SACRIFICES YOU'VE MADE, THE LOSSES YOU'VE ENDURED, THE PAIN YOU'VE SUFFERED...
NO DOUBT YOU HAVE FOUND NOBILITY IN YOUR CAUSE, A NOBILITY THAT STIRS THE HEARTS OF YOUR FELLOW REBELS.
WE CARE ABOUT NONE OF THAT.
THEN LET'S TALK ABOUT SOMETHING YOU SHOULD CARE ABOUT. YOU WANT TO DESTROY THE SINNARIAN EMPIRE? YOU'RE GOING TO NEED TO DESTROY THE BOW OF GABRIEL.
TELL US MORE OF THIS BOW.

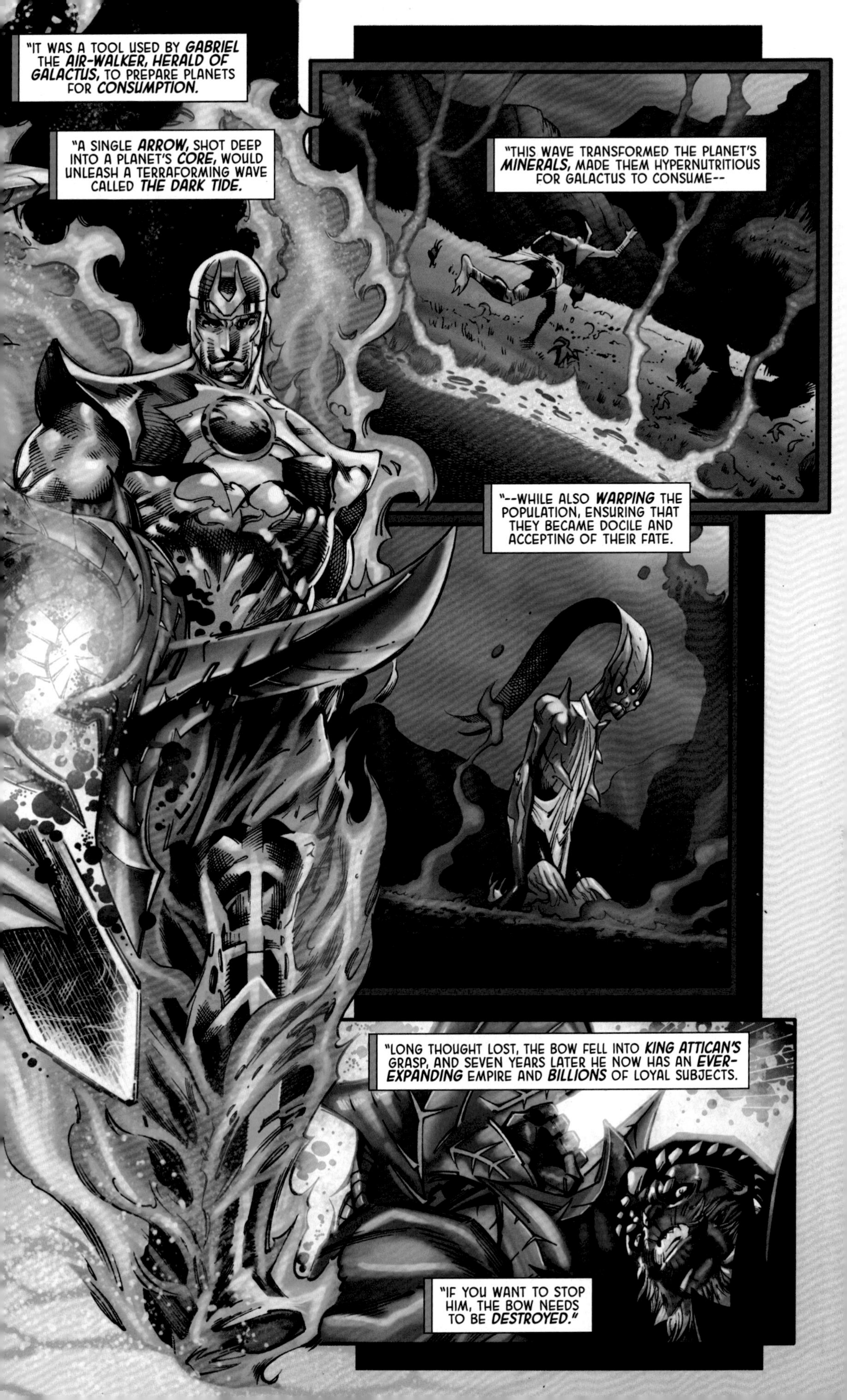
"IT WAS A TOOL USED BY GABRIEL THE AIR-WALKER, HERALD OF GALACTUS, TO PREPARE PLANETS FOR CONSUMPTION.
"A SINGLE ARROW, SHOT DEEP INTO A PLANET'S CORE, WOULD UNLEASH A TERRAFORMING WAVE CALLED THE DARK TIDE.
"THIS WAVE TRANSFORMED THE PLANET'S MINERALS, MADE THEM HYPERNUTRITIOUS FOR GALACTUS TO CONSUME--
"--WHILE ALSO WARPING THE POPULATION, ENSURING THAT THEY BECAME DOCILE AND ACCEPTING OF THEIR FATE.
"LONG THOUGHT LOST, THE BOW FELL INTO KING ATTICAN'S GRASP, AND SEVEN YEARS LATER HE NOW HAS AN EVER-EXPANDING EMPIRE AND BILLIONS OF LOYAL SUBJECTS.
"IF YOU WANT TO STOP HIM, THE BOW NEEDS TO BE DESTROYED."

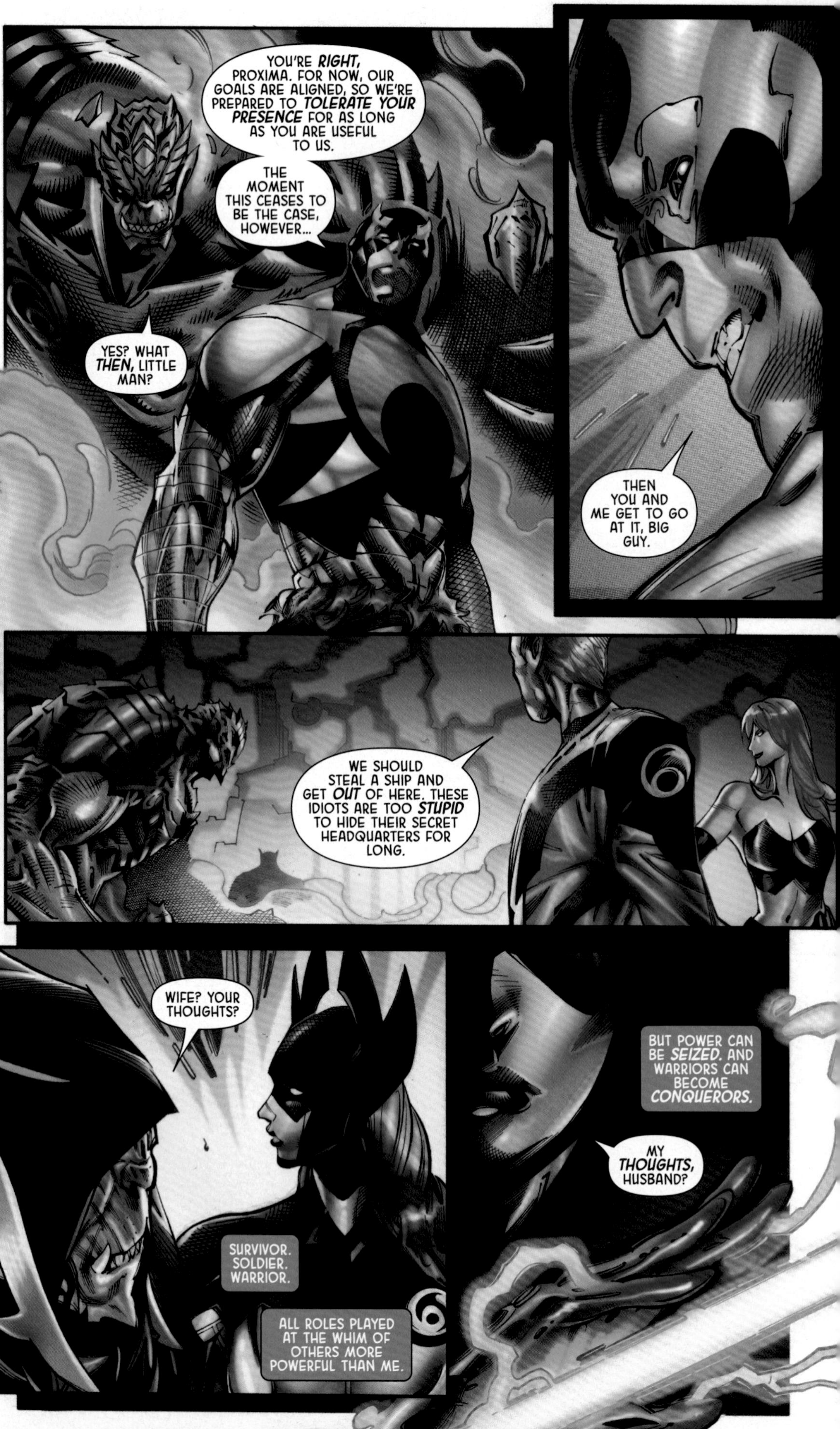
YOU'RE RIGHT, PROXIMA. FOR NOW, OUR GOALS ARE ALIGNED, SO WE'RE PREPARED TO TOLERATE YOUR PRESENCE FOR AS LONG AS YOU ARE USEFUL TO US.
THE MOMENT THIS CEASES TO BE THE CASE, HOWEVER...
YES? WHAT THEN, LITTLE MAN?
THEN YOU AND ME GET TO GO AT IT, BIG GUY.
WE SHOULD STEAL A SHIP AND GET OUT OF HERE. THESE IDIOTS ARE TOO STUPID TO HIDE THEIR SECRET HEADQUARTERS FOR LONG.
WIFE? YOUR THOUGHTS?
SURVIVOR. SOLDIER. WARRIOR.
ALL ROLES PLAYED AT THE WHIM OF OTHERS MORE POWERFUL THAN ME.
BUT POWER CAN BE SEIZED. AND WARRIORS CAN BECOME CONQUERORS.
MY THOUGHTS, HUSBAND?

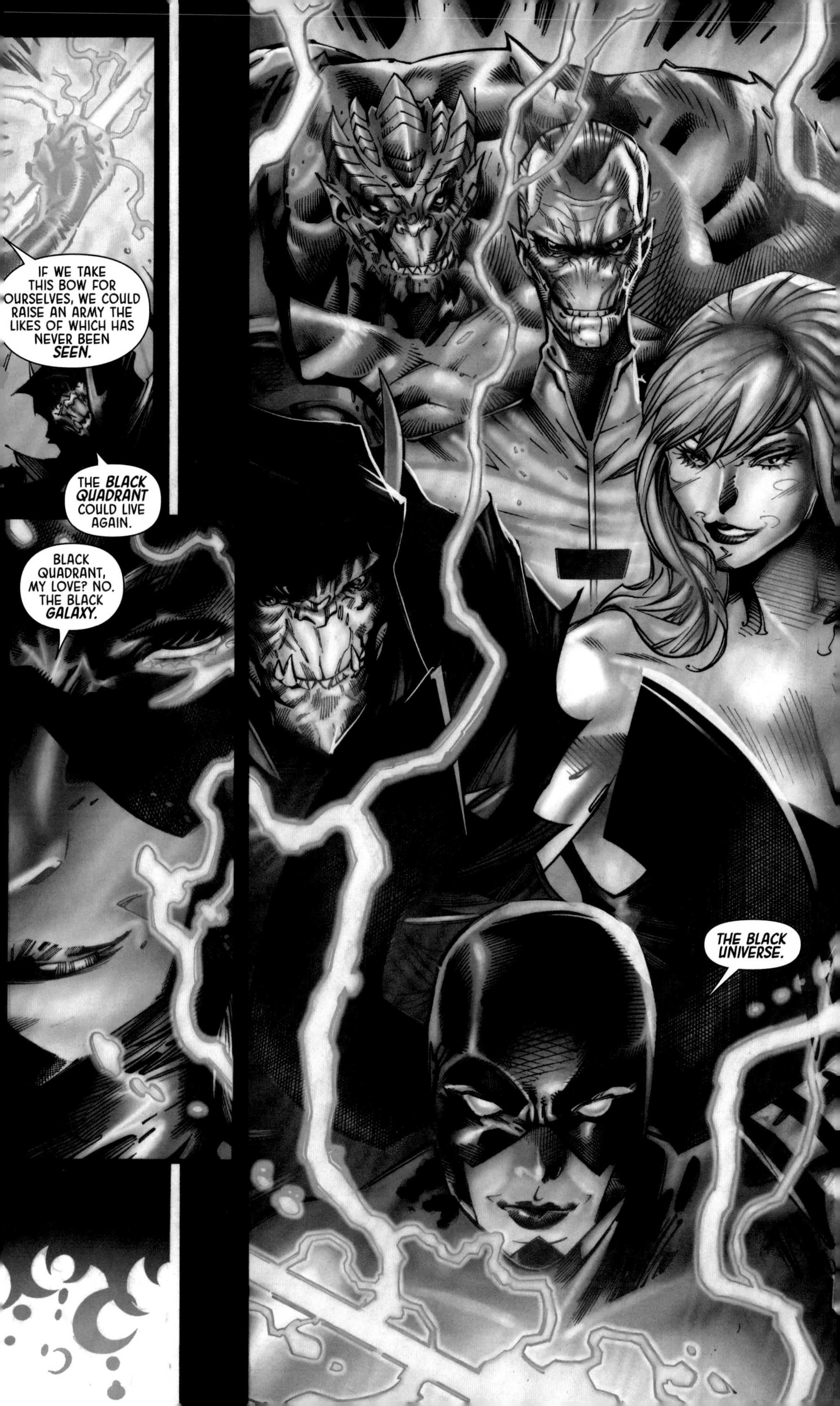

IF WE TAKE THIS BOW FOR OURSELVES, WE COULD RAISE AN ARMY THE LIKES OF WHICH HAS NEVER BEEN SEEN.
THE BLACK QUADRANT COULD LIVE AGAIN.
BLACK QUADRANT, MY LOVE? NO. THE BLACK GALAXY.
THE BLACK UNIVERSE.

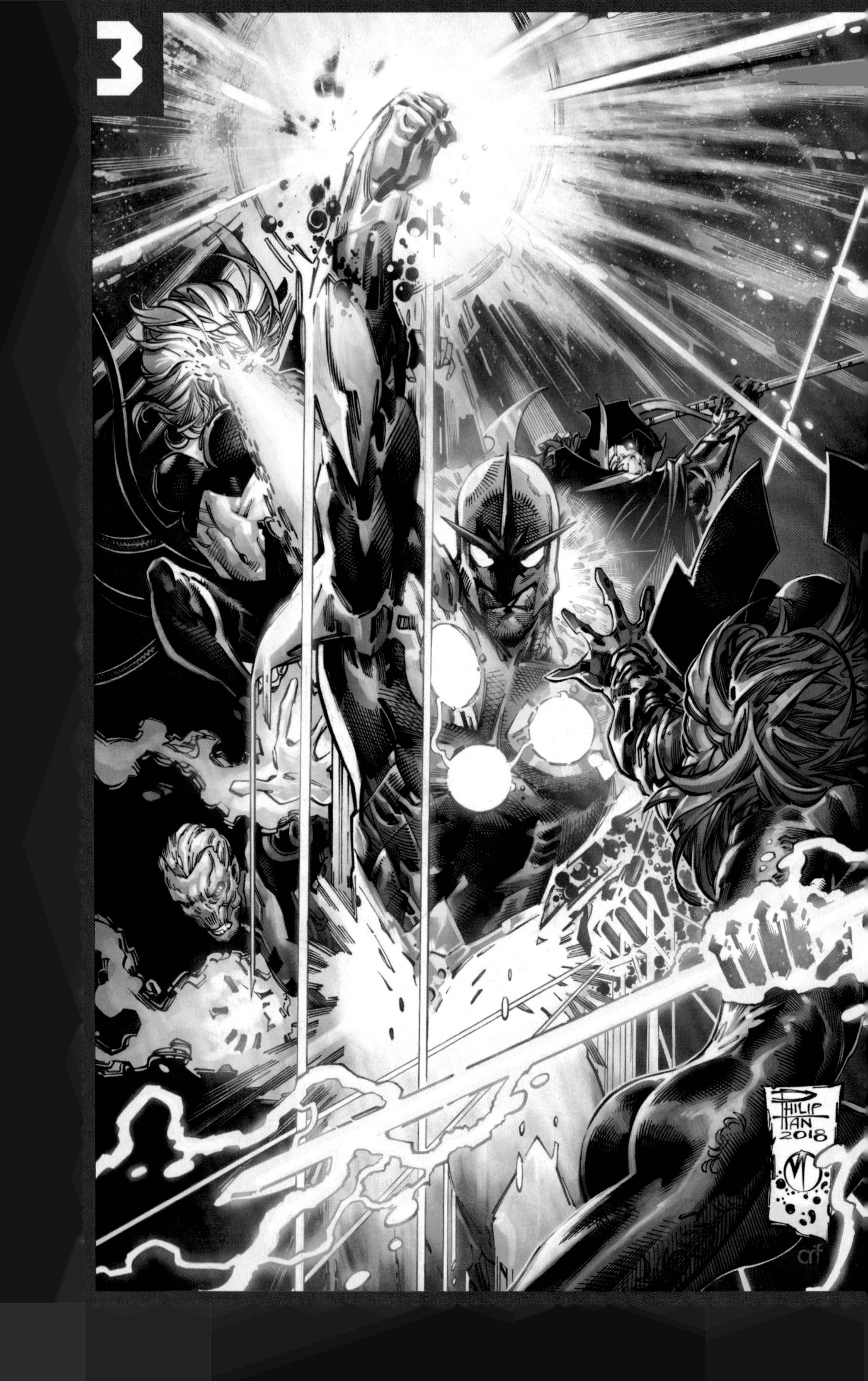
3
PHILIP TAN 2018

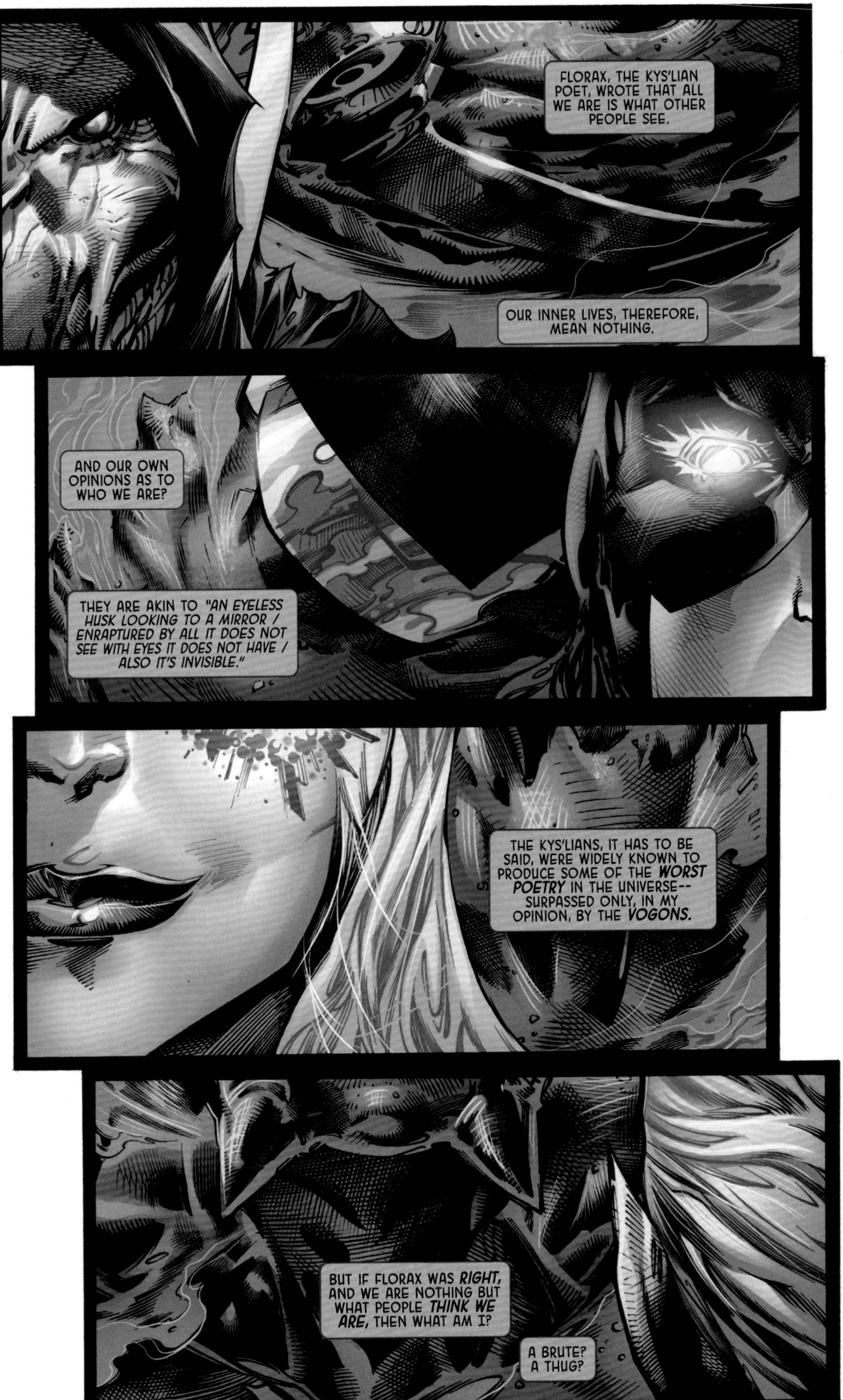

FLORAX, THE KYS'LIAN POET, WROTE THAT ALL WE ARE IS WHAT OTHER PEOPLE SEE.
OUR INNER LIVES, THEREFORE, MEAN NOTHING.
AND OUR OWN OPINIONS AS TO WHO WE ARE?
THEY ARE AKIN TO "AN EYELESS HUSK LOOKING TO A MIRROR / ENRAPTURED BY ALL IT DOES NOT SEE WITH EYES IT DOES NOT HAVE / ALSO IT'S INVISIBLE."
THE KYS'LIANS, IT HAS TO BE SAID, WERE WIDELY KNOWN TO PRODUCE SOME OF THE WORST POETRY IN THE UNIVERSE-- SURPASSED ONLY, IN MY OPINION, BY THE VOGONS.
BUT IF FLORAX WAS RIGHT, AND WE ARE NOTHING BUT WHAT PEOPLE THINK WE ARE, THEN WHAT AM I?
A BRUTE? A THUG?

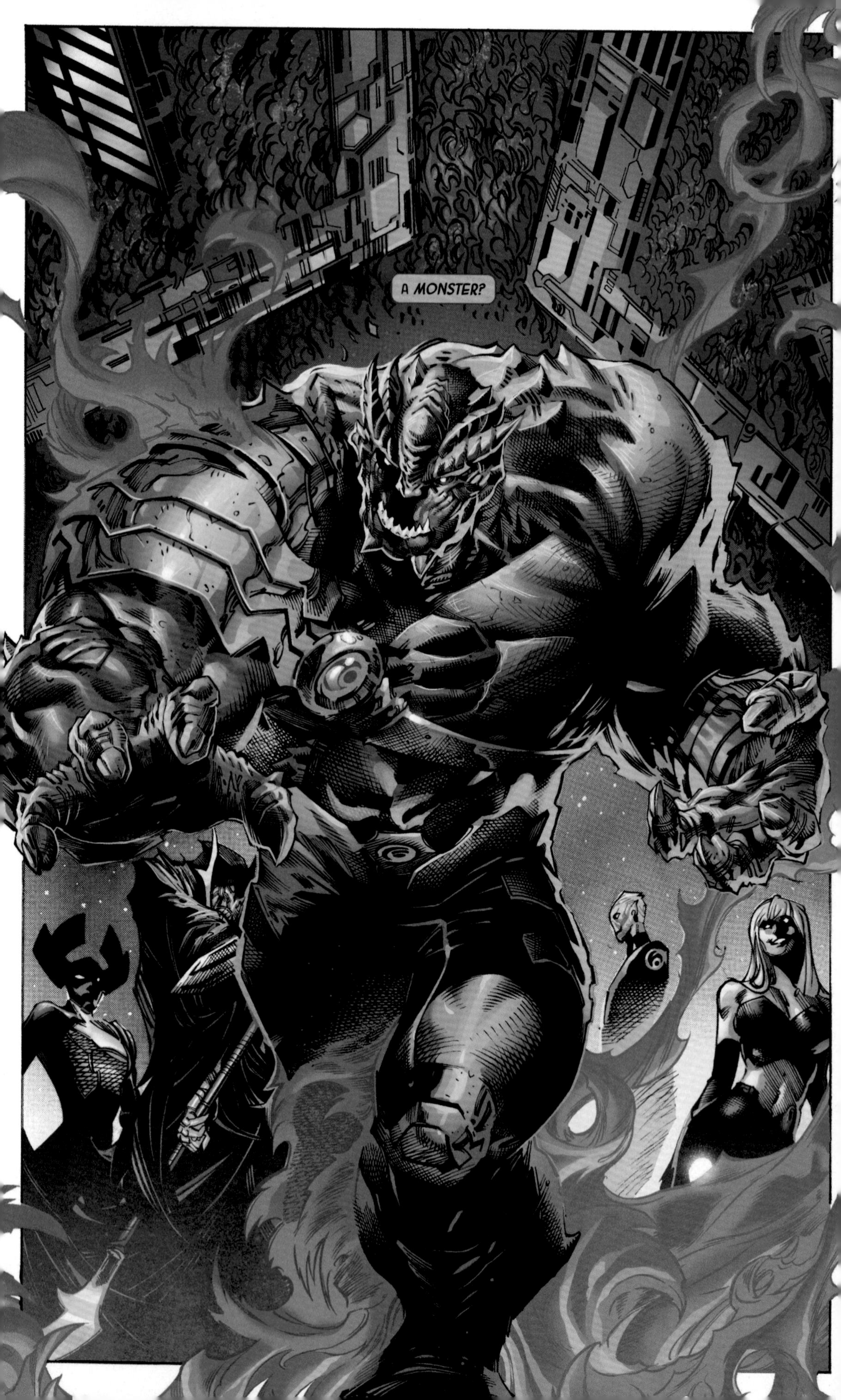
A MONSTER?

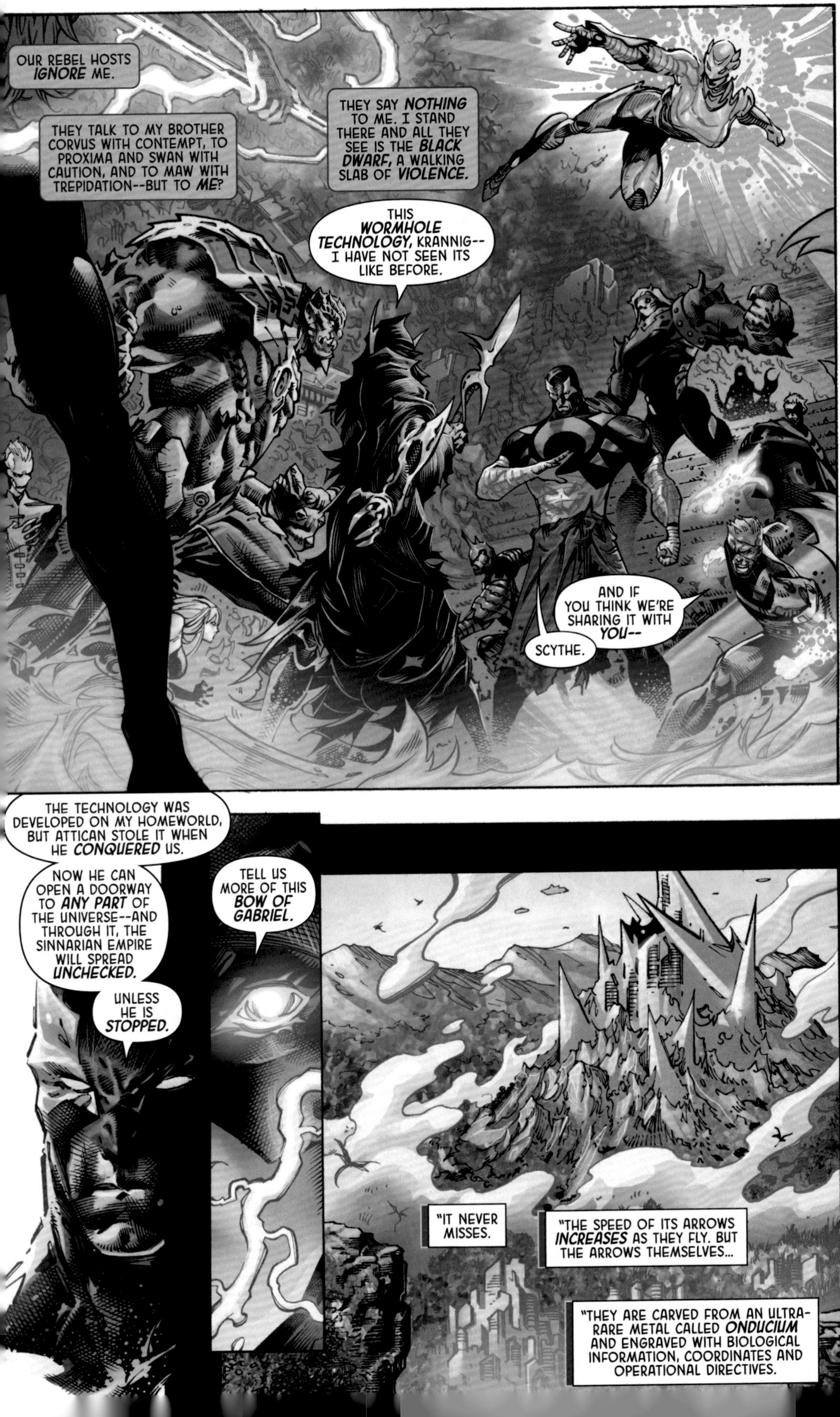
OUR REBEL HOSTS IGNORE ME.
THEY TALK TO MY BROTHER CORVUS WITH CONTEMPT, TO PROXIMA AND SWAN WITH CAUTION, AND TO MAW WITH TREPIDATION--BUT TO ME?
THEY SAY NOTHING TO ME. I STAND THERE AND ALL THEY SEE IS THE BLACK DWARF, A WALKING SLAB OF VIOLENCE.
THIS WORMHOLE TECHNOLOGY, KRANNIG--I HAVE NOT SEEN ITS LIKE BEFORE.
AND IF YOU THINK WE'RE SHARING IT WITH YOU--
SCYTHE.
THE TECHNOLOGY WAS DEVELOPED ON MY HOMEWORLD, BUT ATTICAN STOLE IT WHEN HE CONQUERED US.
NOW HE CAN OPEN A DOORWAY TO ANY PART OF THE UNIVERSE--AND THROUGH IT, THE SINNARIAN EMPIRE WILL SPREAD UNCHECKED.
UNLESS HE IS STOPPED.
TELL US MORE OF THIS BOW OF GABRIEL.
"IT NEVER MISSES.
"THE SPEED OF ITS ARROWS INCREASES AS THEY FLY. BUT THE ARROWS THEMSELVES...
"THEY ARE CARVED FROM AN ULTRA-RARE METAL CALLED ONDUCIUM AND ENGRAVED WITH BIOLOGICAL INFORMATION, COORDINATES AND OPERATIONAL DIRECTIVES.

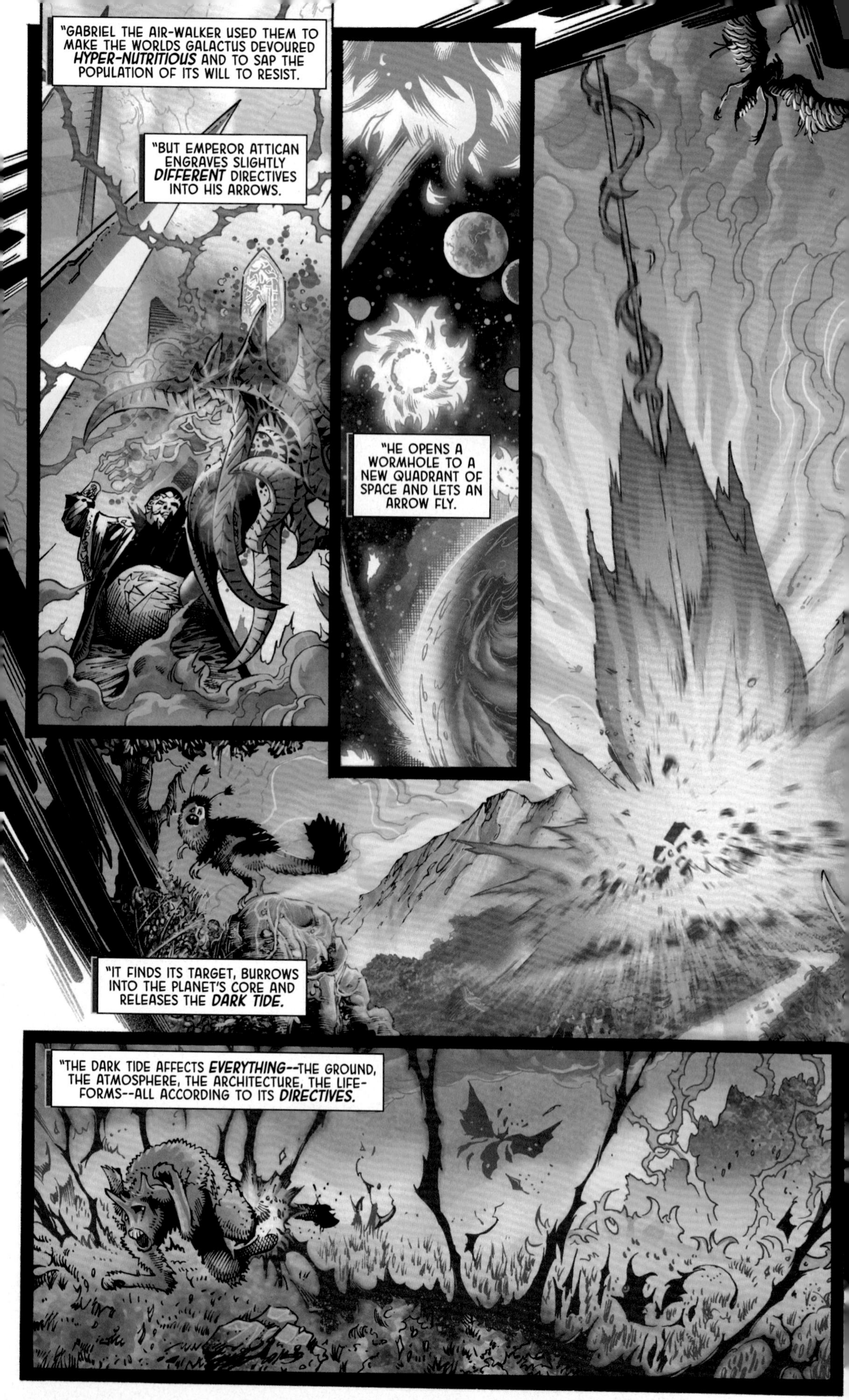
"GABRIEL THE AIR-WALKER USED THEM TO MAKE THE WORLDS GALACTUS DEVOURED *HYPER-NUTRITIOUS* AND TO SAP THE POPULATION OF ITS WILL TO RESIST.
"BUT EMPEROR ATTICAN ENGRAVES SLIGHTLY *DIFFERENT* DIRECTIVES INTO HIS ARROWS.
"HE OPENS A WORMHOLE TO A NEW QUADRANT OF SPACE AND LETS AN ARROW FLY.
"IT FINDS ITS TARGET, BURROWS INTO THE PLANET'S CORE AND RELEASES THE *DARK TIDE.*
"THE DARK TIDE AFFECTS *EVERYTHING*--THE GROUND, THE ATMOSPHERE, THE ARCHITECTURE, THE LIFE-FORMS--ALL ACCORDING TO ITS *DIRECTIVES.*

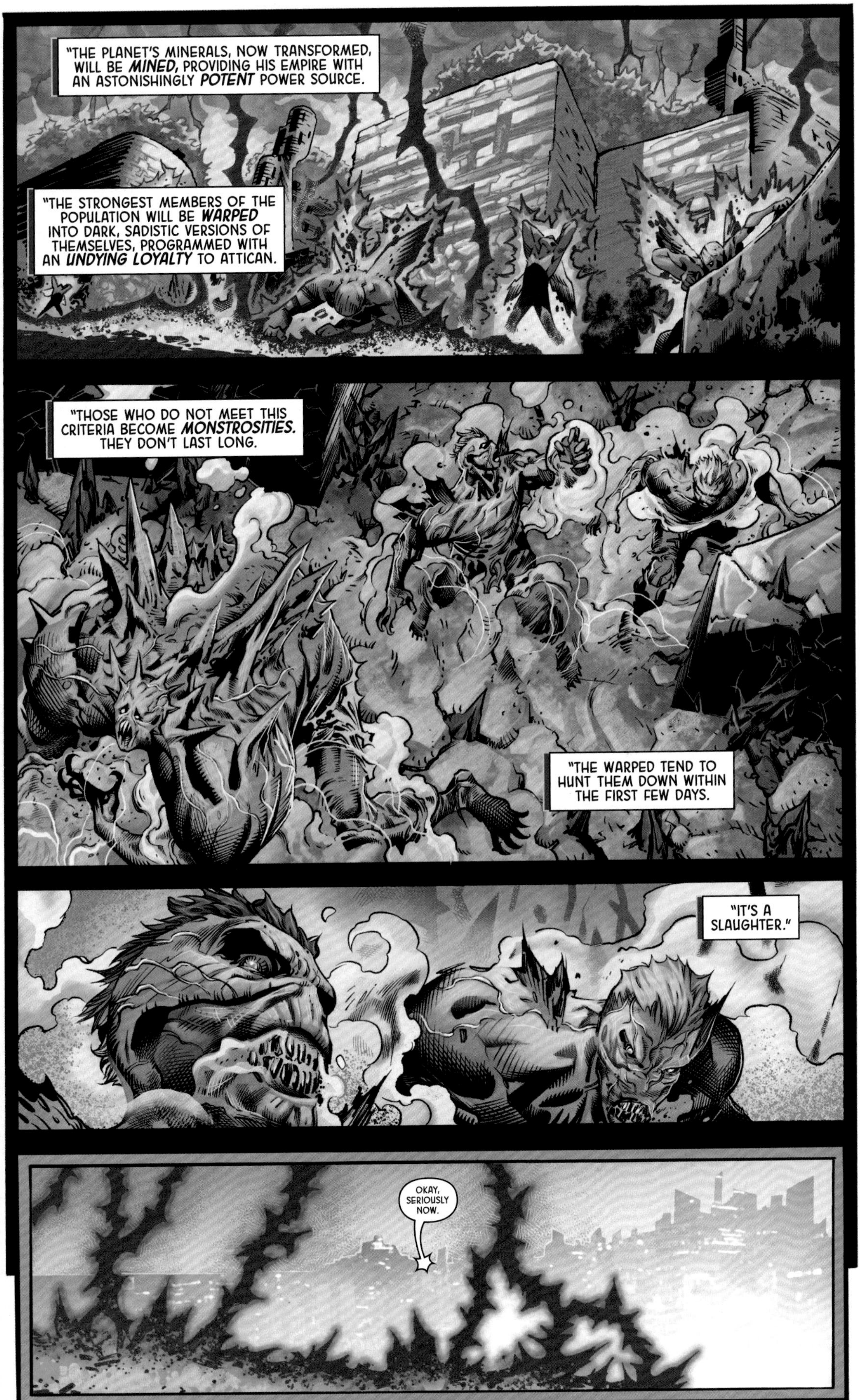
"THE PLANET'S MINERALS, NOW TRANSFORMED, WILL BE MINED, PROVIDING HIS EMPIRE WITH AN ASTONISHINGLY POTENT POWER SOURCE.
"THE STRONGEST MEMBERS OF THE POPULATION WILL BE WARPED INTO DARK, SADISTIC VERSIONS OF THEMSELVES, PROGRAMMED WITH AN UNDYING LOYALTY TO ATTICAN.
"THOSE WHO DO NOT MEET THIS CRITERIA BECOME MONSTROSITIES. THEY DON'T LAST LONG.
"THE WARPED TEND TO HUNT THEM DOWN WITHIN THE FIRST FEW DAYS.
"IT'S A SLAUGHTER."
OKAY, SERIOUSLY NOW.

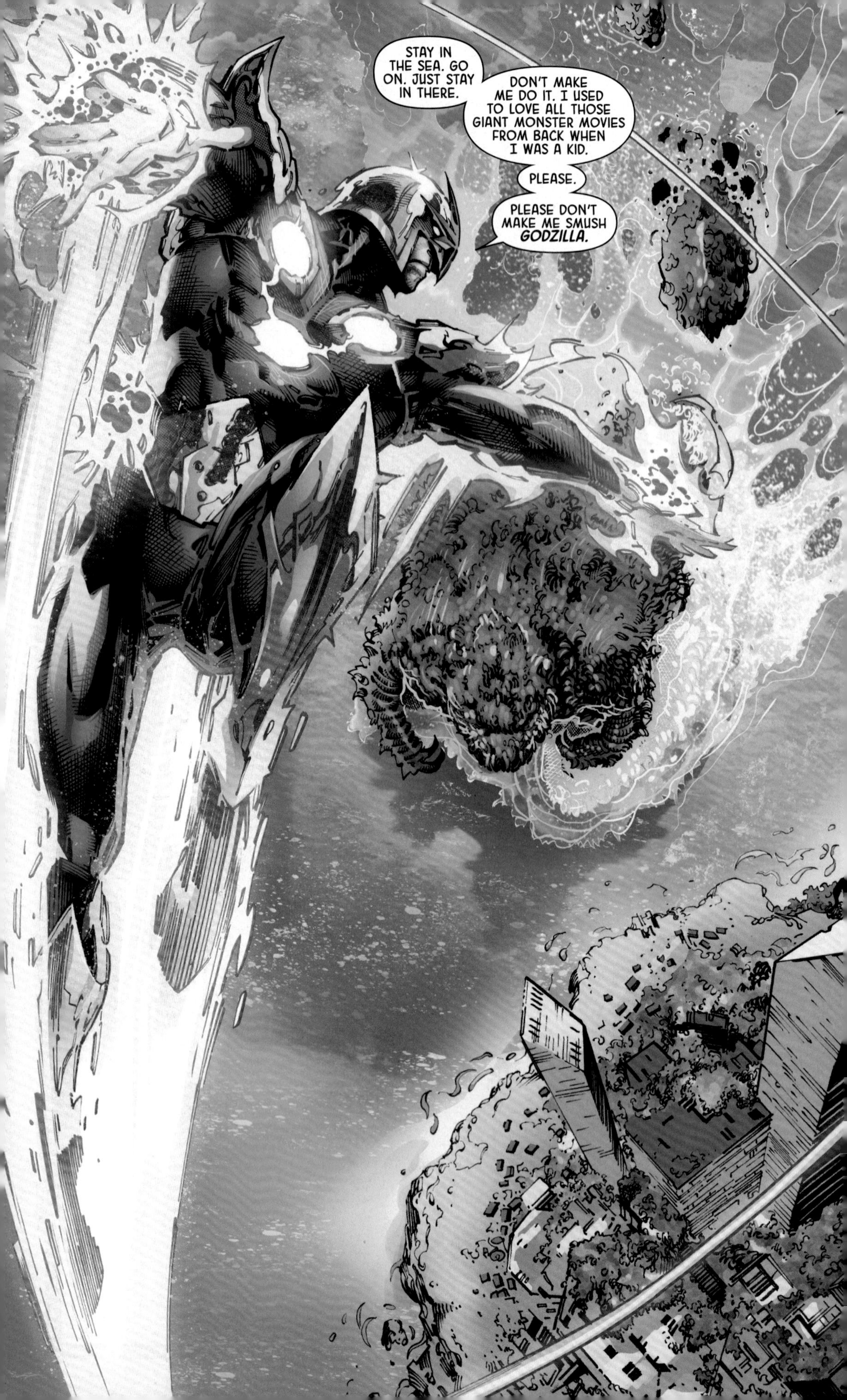
STAY IN THE SEA. GO ON. JUST STAY IN THERE.
DON'T MAKE ME DO IT. I USED TO LOVE ALL THOSE GIANT MONSTER MOVIES FROM BACK WHEN I WAS A KID.
PLEASE.
PLEASE DON'T MAKE ME SMUSH GODZILLA.

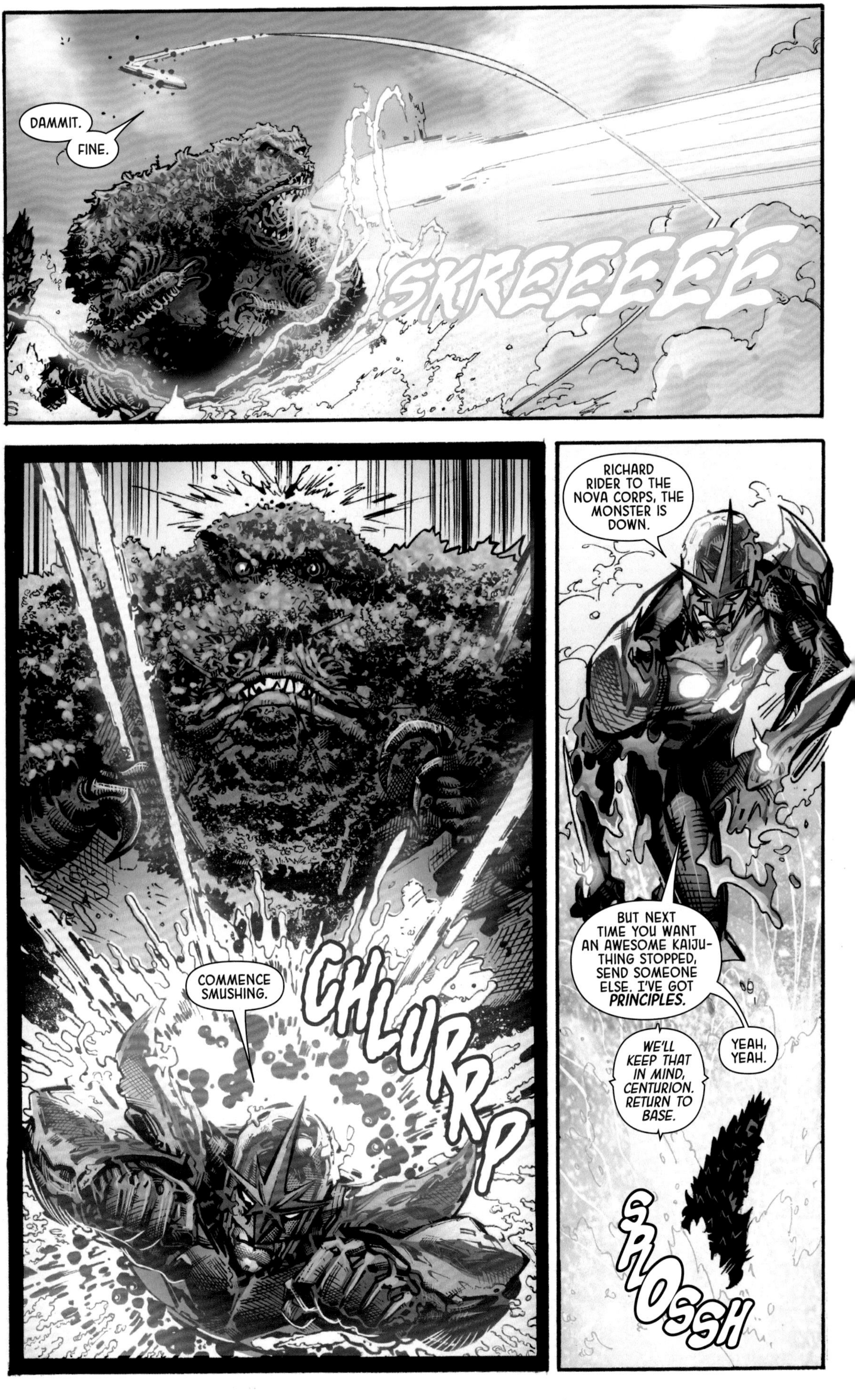
DAMMIT.
FINE.
SKREEEEEE
COMMENCE SMUSHING.
CHLURRP
RICHARD RIDER TO THE NOVA CORPS, THE MONSTER IS DOWN.
BUT NEXT TIME YOU WANT AN AWESOME KAIJU-THING STOPPED, SEND SOMEONE ELSE. I'VE GOT PRINCIPLES.
WE'LL KEEP THAT IN MIND, CENTURION. RETURN TO BASE.
YEAH, YEAH.
SPLOSSH

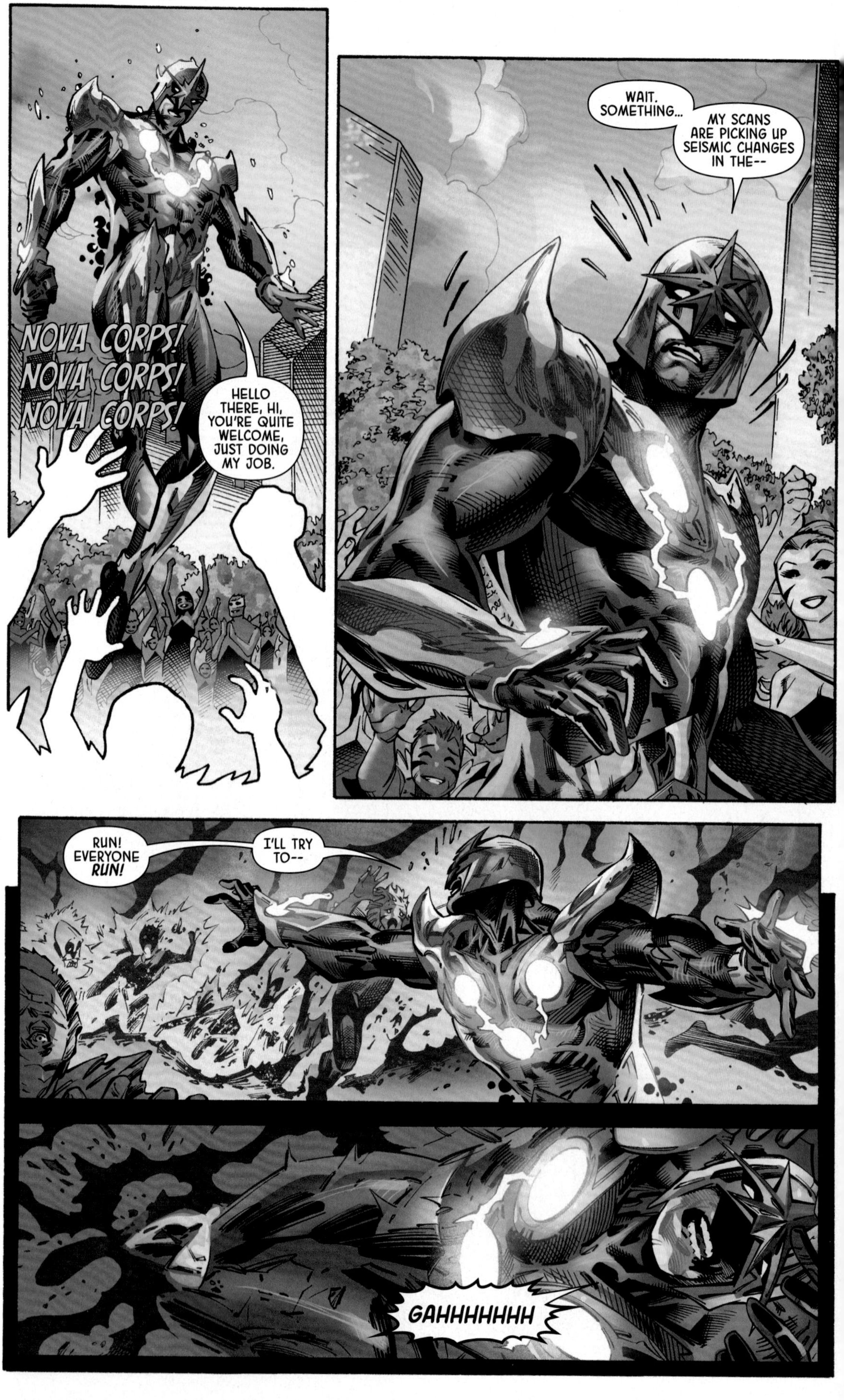
NOVA CORPS! NOVA CORPS! NOVA CORPS!
HELLO THERE, HI, YOU'RE QUITE WELCOME, JUST DOING MY JOB.
WAIT. SOMETHING...
MY SCANS ARE PICKING UP SEISMIC CHANGES IN THE--
RUN! EVERYONE RUN!
I'LL TRY TO--
GAHHHHHHH

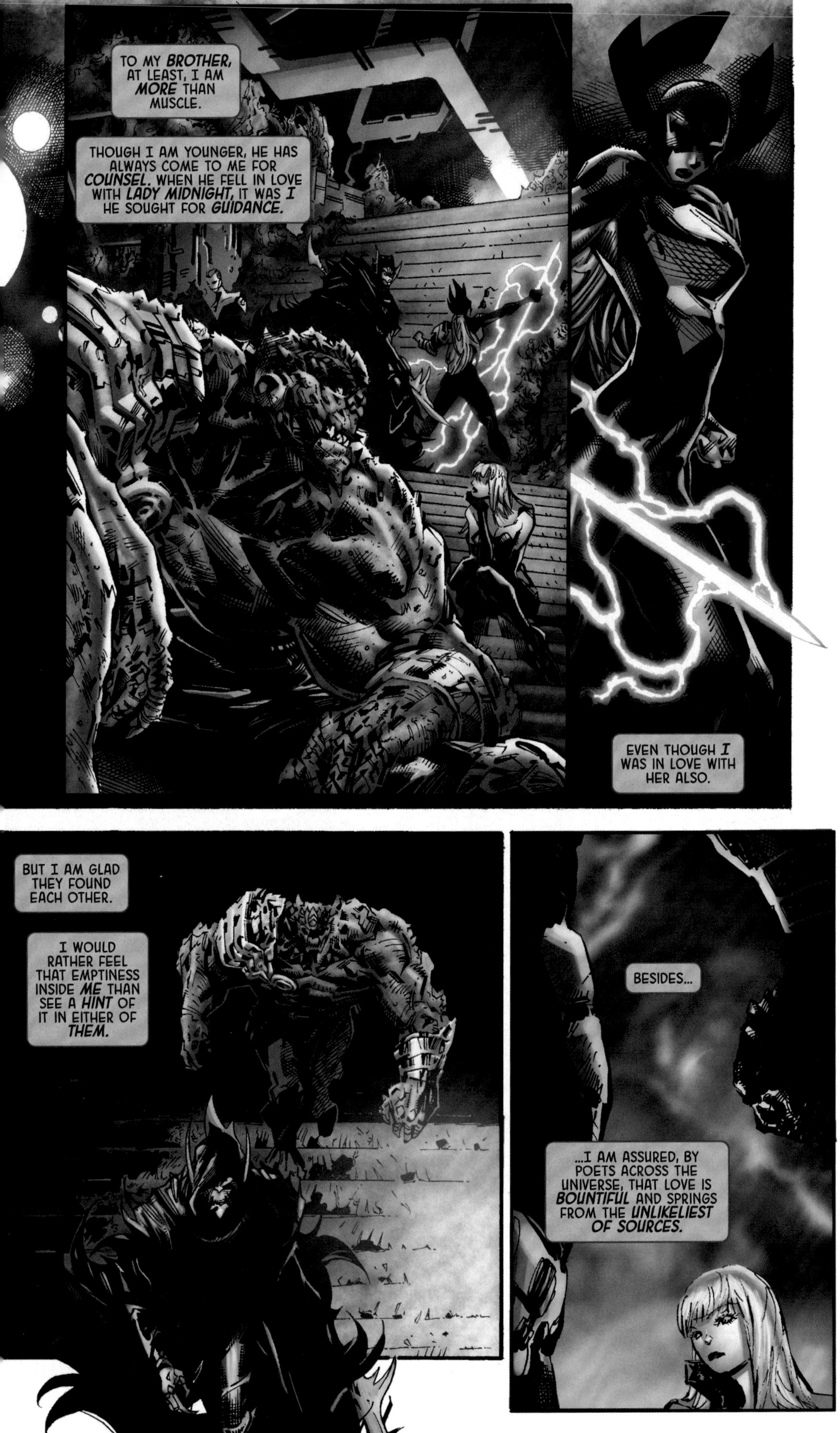
TO MY BROTHER, AT LEAST, I AM MORE THAN MUSCLE.
THOUGH I AM YOUNGER, HE HAS ALWAYS COME TO ME FOR COUNSEL. WHEN HE FELL IN LOVE WITH LADY MIDNIGHT, IT WAS I HE SOUGHT FOR GUIDANCE.
EVEN THOUGH I WAS IN LOVE WITH HER ALSO.
BUT I AM GLAD THEY FOUND EACH OTHER.
I WOULD RATHER FEEL THAT EMPTINESS INSIDE ME THAN SEE A HINT OF IT IN EITHER OF THEM.
BESIDES...
...I AM ASSURED, BY POETS ACROSS THE UNIVERSE, THAT LOVE IS BOUNTIFUL AND SPRINGS FROM THE UNLIKELIEST OF SOURCES.

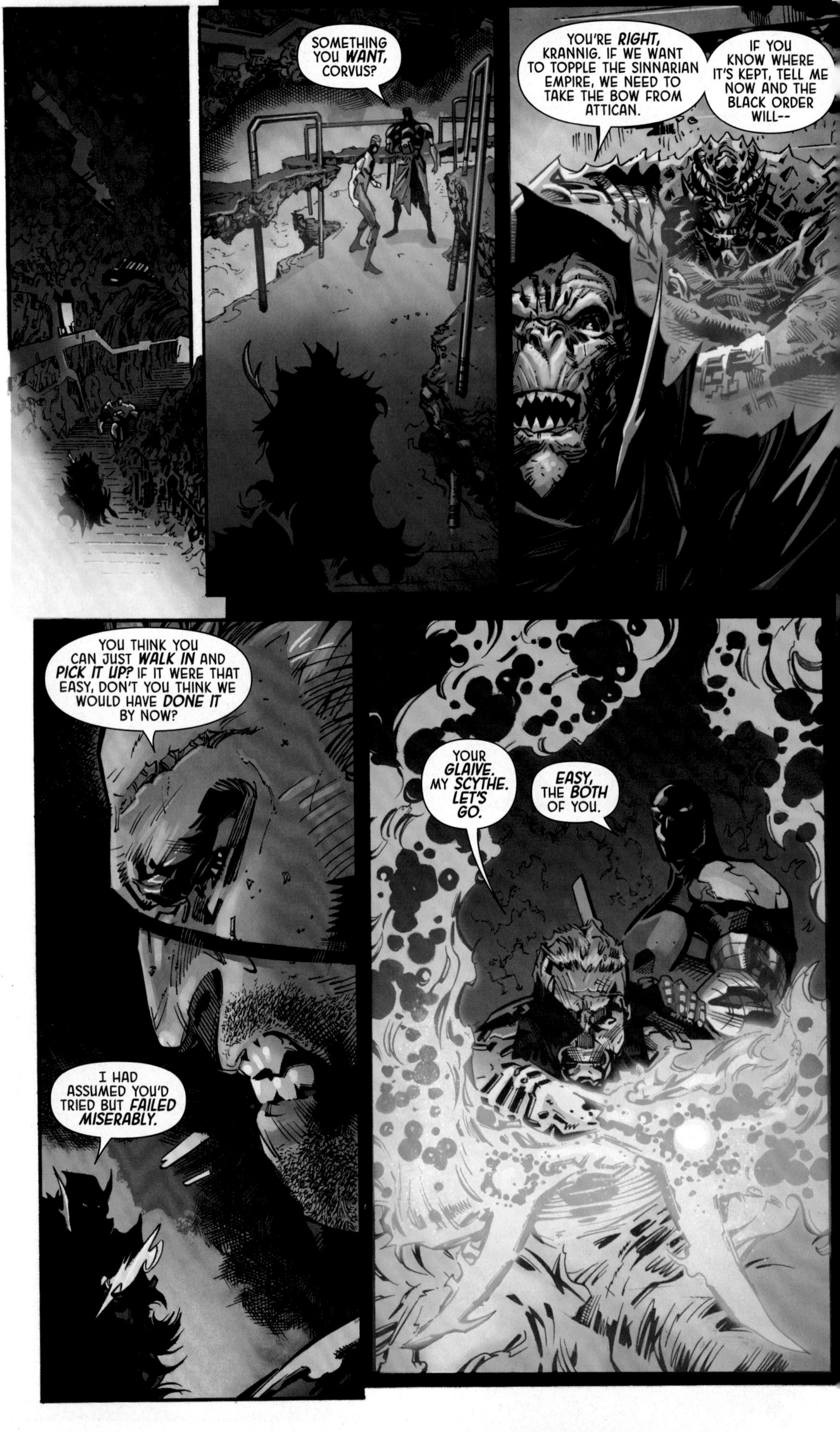

SOMETHING YOU WANT, CORVUS?
YOU'RE RIGHT, KRANNIG. IF WE WANT TO TOPPLE THE SINNARIAN EMPIRE, WE NEED TO TAKE THE BOW FROM ATTICAN.
IF YOU KNOW WHERE IT'S KEPT, TELL ME NOW AND THE BLACK ORDER WILL--
YOU THINK YOU CAN JUST WALK IN AND PICK IT UP? IF IT WERE THAT EASY, DON'T YOU THINK WE WOULD HAVE DONE IT BY NOW?
I HAD ASSUMED YOU'D TRIED BUT FAILED MISERABLY.
YOUR GLAIVE. MY SCYTHE. LET'S GO.
EASY, THE BOTH OF YOU.

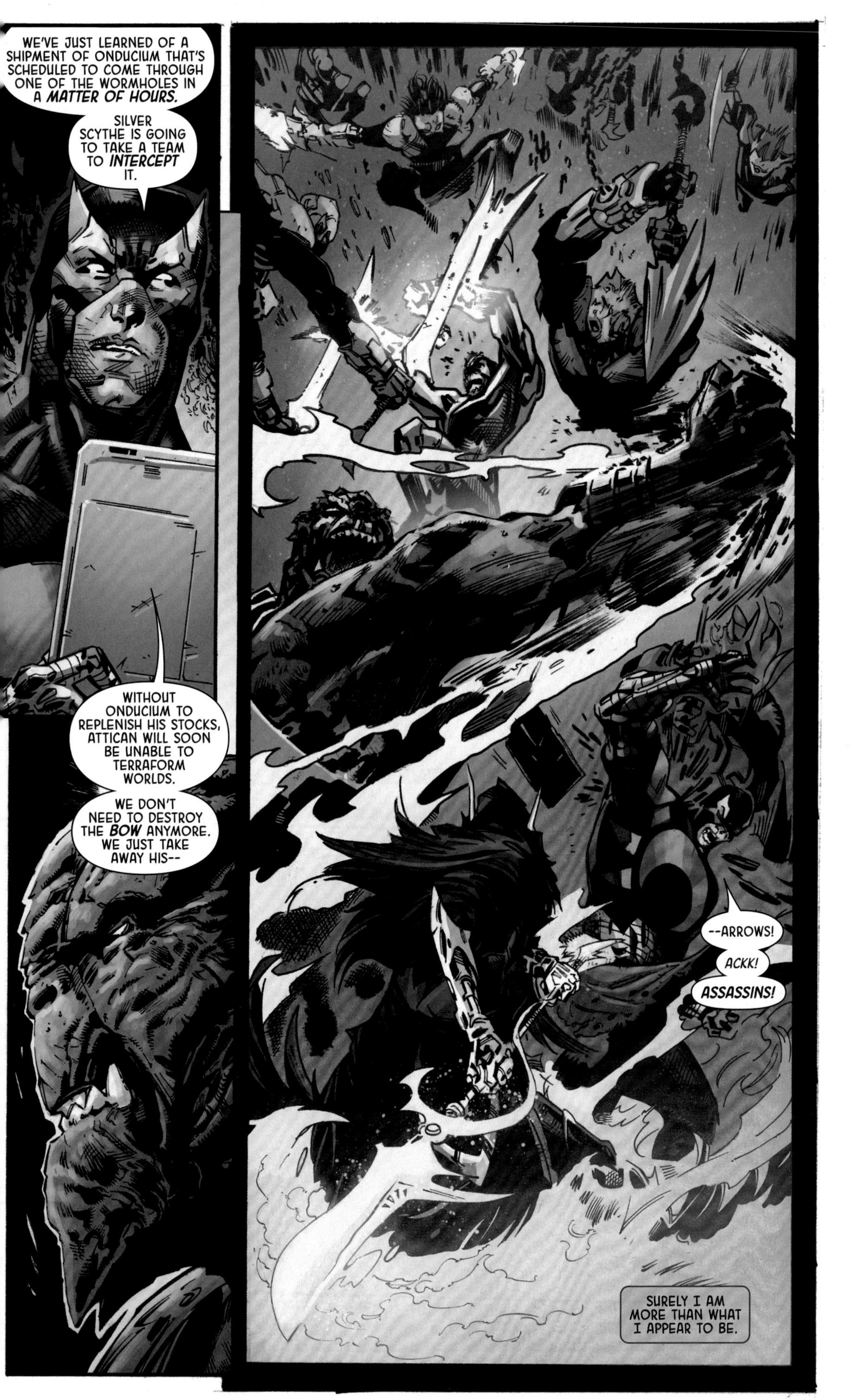
WE'VE JUST LEARNED OF A SHIPMENT OF ONDUCIUM THAT'S SCHEDULED TO COME THROUGH ONE OF THE WORMHOLES IN A MATTER OF HOURS.
SILVER SCYTHE IS GOING TO TAKE A TEAM TO INTERCEPT IT.
WITHOUT ONDUCIUM TO REPLENISH HIS STOCKS, ATTICAN WILL SOON BE UNABLE TO TERRAFORM WORLDS.
WE DON'T NEED TO DESTROY THE BOW ANYMORE. WE JUST TAKE AWAY HIS--
--ARROWS!
ACKK!
ASSASSINS!
SURELY I AM MORE THAN WHAT I APPEAR TO BE.

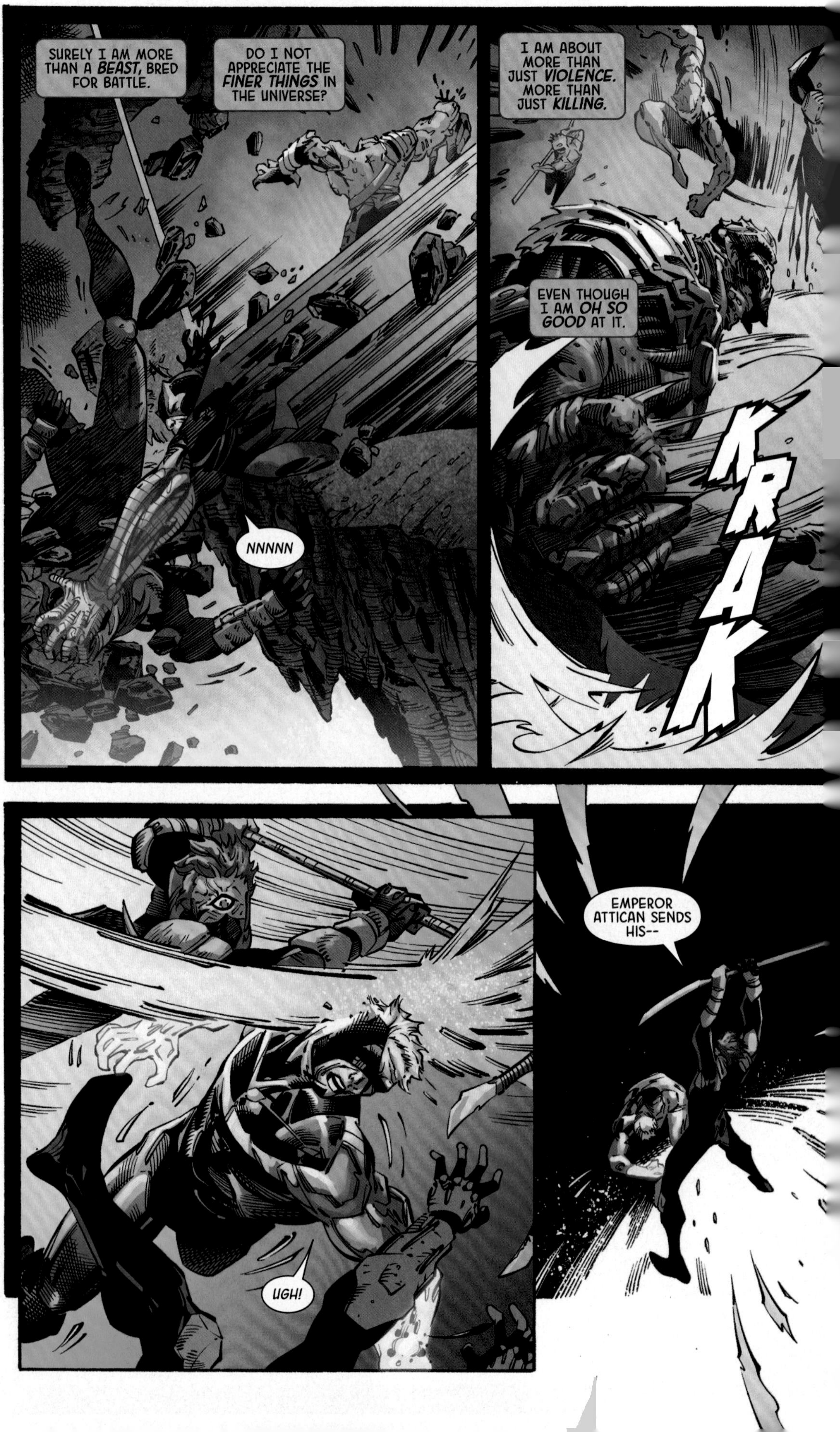
SURELY I AM MORE THAN A BEAST, BRED FOR BATTLE.
DO I NOT APPRECIATE THE FINER THINGS IN THE UNIVERSE?
NNNNN
I AM ABOUT MORE THAN JUST VIOLENCE. MORE THAN JUST KILLING.
EVEN THOUGH I AM OH SO GOOD AT IT.
KRAK
UGH!
EMPEROR ATTICAN SENDS HIS--

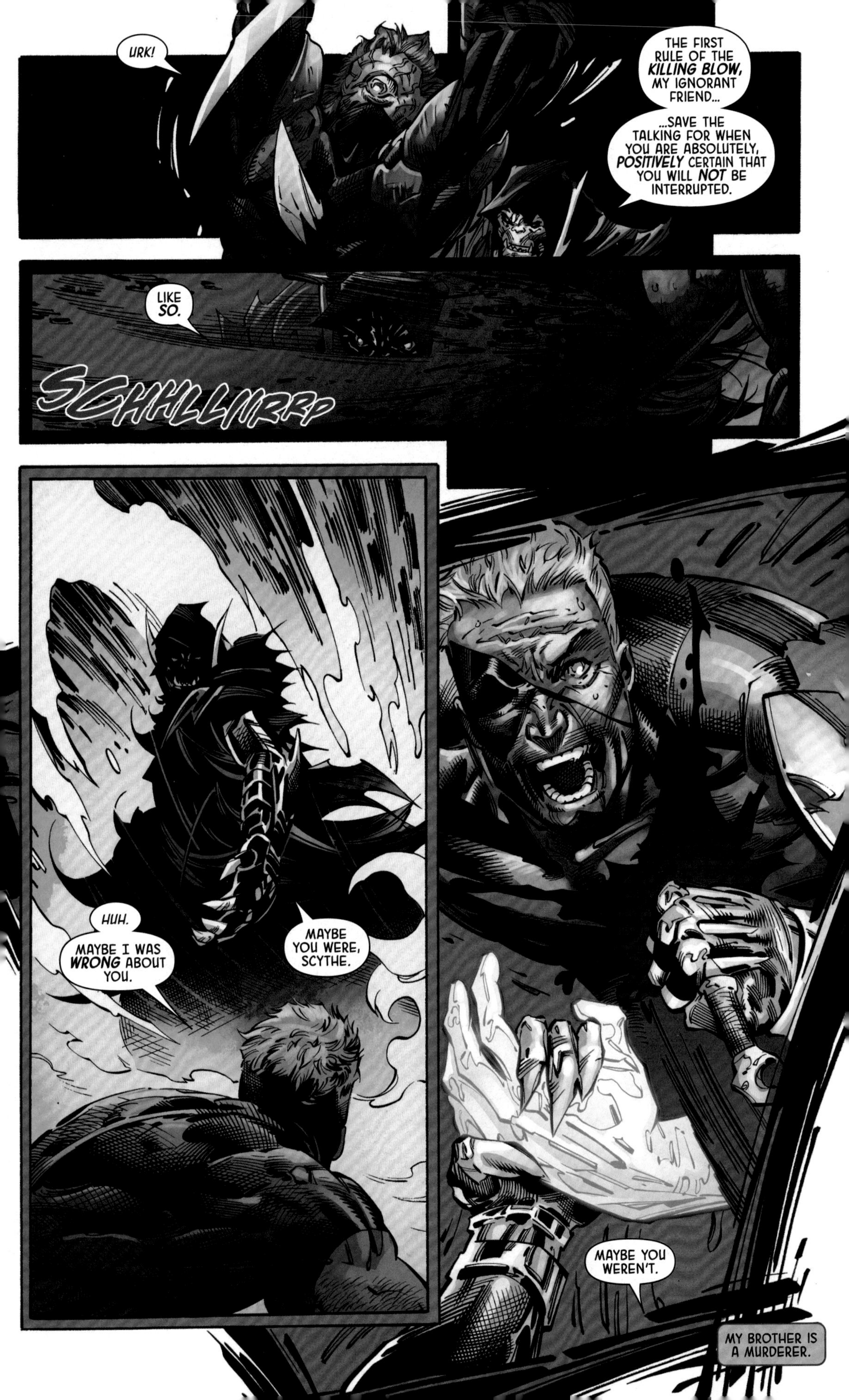
URK!
THE FIRST RULE OF THE KILLING BLOW, MY IGNORANT FRIEND...
...SAVE THE TALKING FOR WHEN YOU ARE ABSOLUTELY, POSITIVELY CERTAIN THAT YOU WILL NOT BE INTERRUPTED.
LIKE SO.
SCHHLLIIRRP
HUH.
MAYBE I WAS WRONG ABOUT YOU.
MAYBE YOU WERE, SCYTHE.
MAYBE YOU WEREN'T.
MY BROTHER IS A MURDERER.

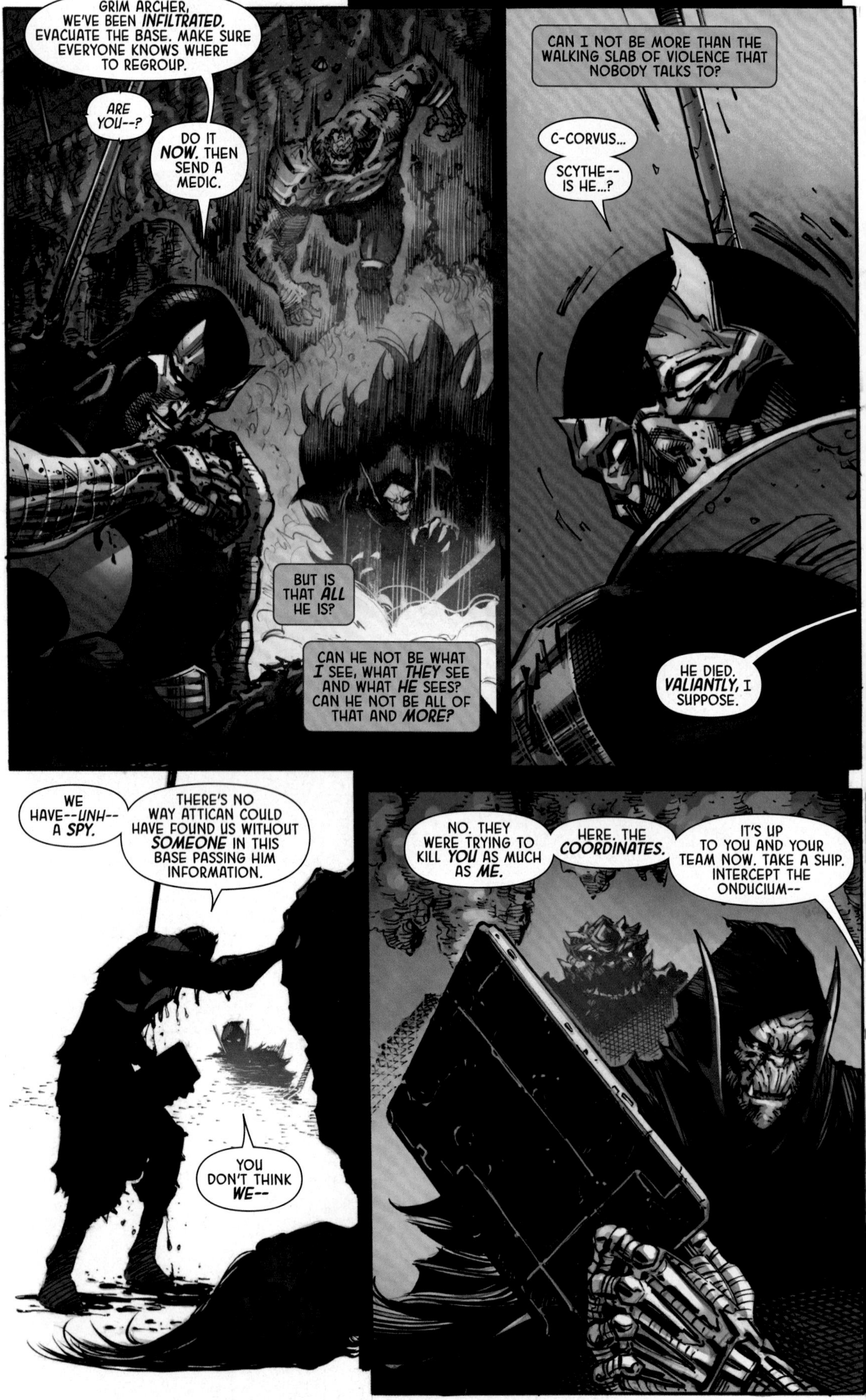
GRIM ARCHER, WE'VE BEEN INFILTRATED. EVACUATE THE BASE. MAKE SURE EVERYONE KNOWS WHERE TO REGROUP.
ARE YOU--?
DO IT NOW. THEN SEND A MEDIC.
BUT IS THAT ALL HE IS?
CAN HE NOT BE WHAT I SEE, WHAT THEY SEE AND WHAT HE SEES? CAN HE NOT BE ALL OF THAT AND MORE?
CAN I NOT BE MORE THAN THE WALKING SLAB OF VIOLENCE THAT NOBODY TALKS TO?
C-CORVUS...
SCYTHE--IS HE...?
HE DIED. VALIANTLY, I SUPPOSE.
WE HAVE--UNH--A SPY.
THERE'S NO WAY ATTICAN COULD HAVE FOUND US WITHOUT SOMEONE IN THIS BASE PASSING HIM INFORMATION.
YOU DON'T THINK WE--
NO. THEY WERE TRYING TO KILL YOU AS MUCH AS ME.
HERE. THE COORDINATES.
IT'S UP TO YOU AND YOUR TEAM NOW. TAKE A SHIP. INTERCEPT THE ONDUCIUM--

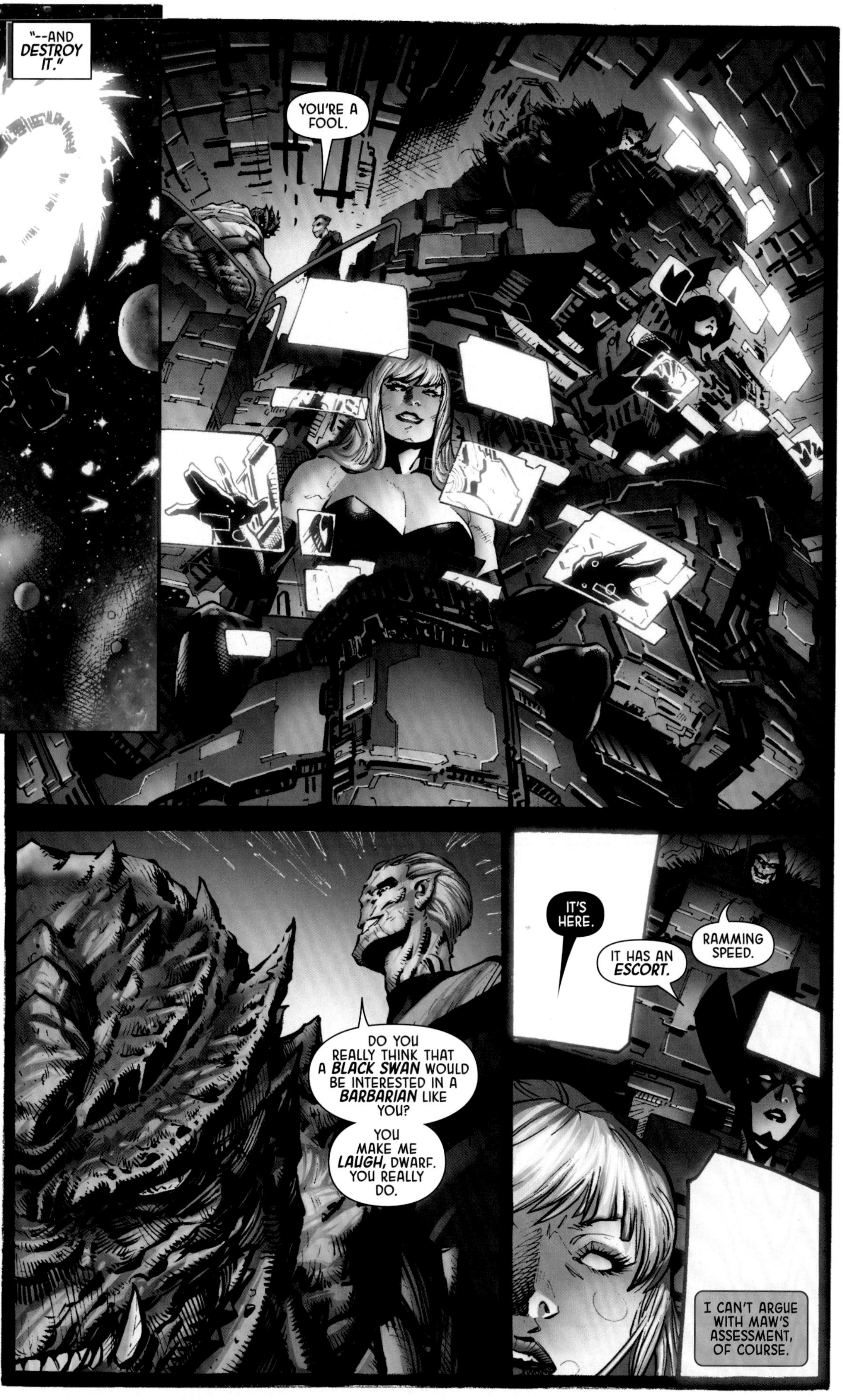
"--AND DESTROY IT."
YOU'RE A FOOL.
DO YOU REALLY THINK THAT A BLACK SWAN WOULD BE INTERESTED IN A BARBARIAN LIKE YOU?
YOU MAKE ME LAUGH, DWARF. YOU REALLY DO.
IT'S HERE.
IT HAS AN ESCORT.
RAMMING SPEED.
I CAN'T ARGUE WITH MAW'S ASSESSMENT, OF COURSE.

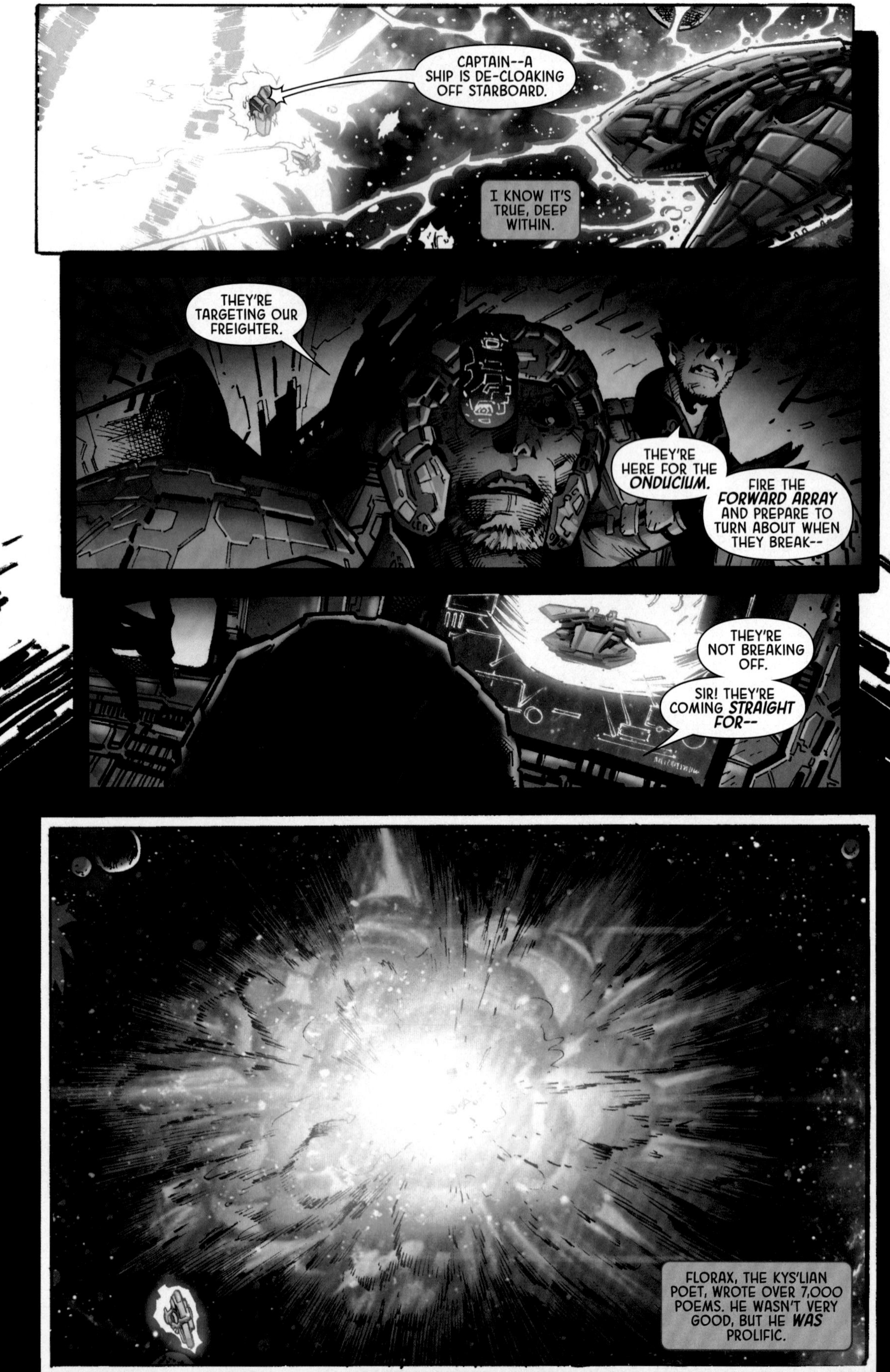
CAPTAIN--A SHIP IS DE-CLOAKING OFF STARBOARD.
I KNOW IT'S TRUE, DEEP WITHIN.
THEY'RE TARGETING OUR FREIGHTER.
THEY'RE HERE FOR THE ONDUCIUM.
FIRE THE FORWARD ARRAY AND PREPARE TO TURN ABOUT WHEN THEY BREAK--
THEY'RE NOT BREAKING OFF.
SIR! THEY'RE COMING STRAIGHT FOR--
FLORAX, THE KYS'LIAN POET, WROTE OVER 7,000 POEMS. HE WASN'T VERY GOOD, BUT HE WAS PROLIFIC.

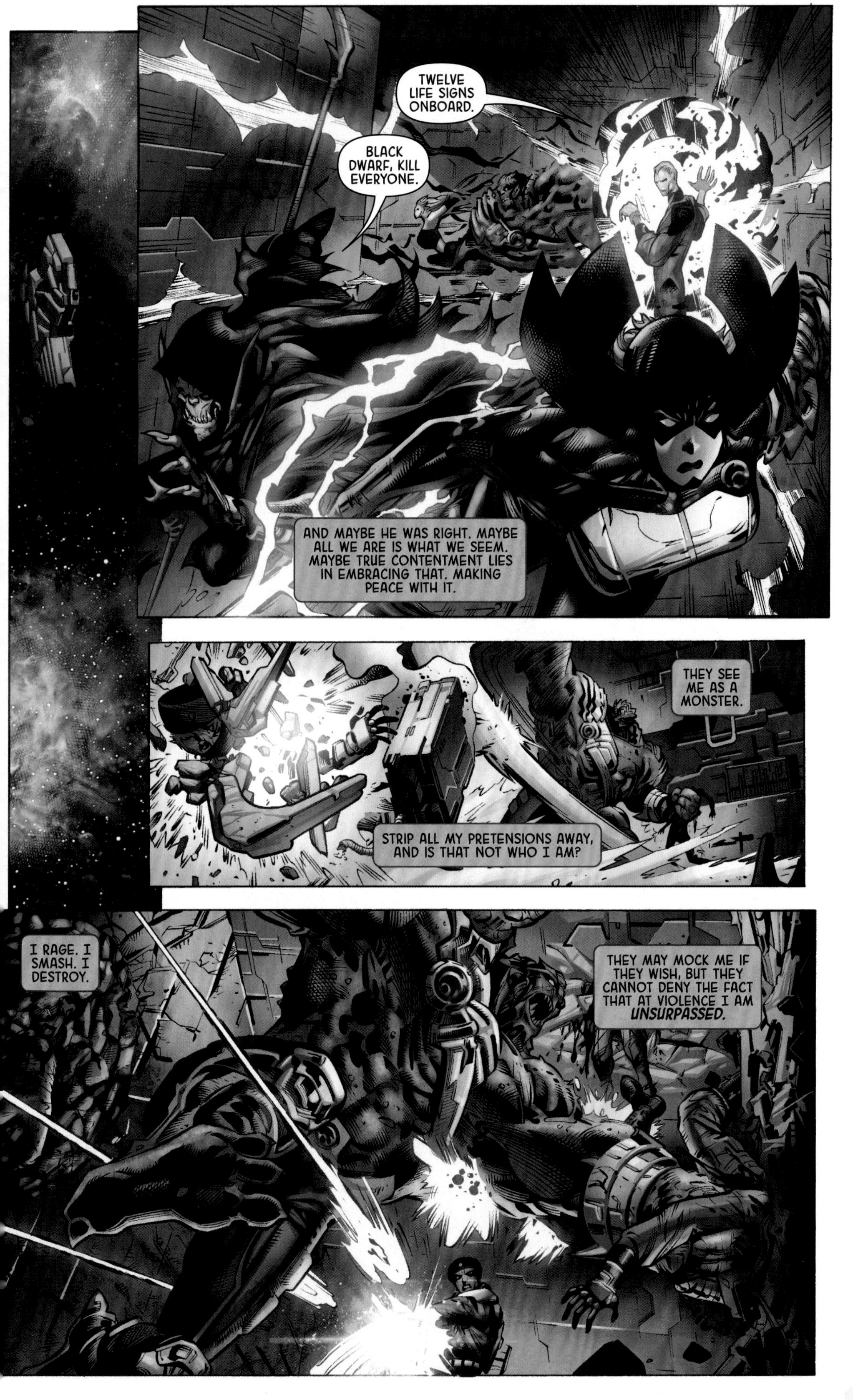
TWELVE LIFE SIGNS ONBOARD.
BLACK DWARF, KILL EVERYONE.
AND MAYBE HE WAS RIGHT. MAYBE ALL WE ARE IS WHAT WE SEEM. MAYBE TRUE CONTENTMENT LIES IN EMBRACING THAT. MAKING PEACE WITH IT.
THEY SEE ME AS A MONSTER.
STRIP ALL MY PRETENSIONS AWAY, AND IS THAT NOT WHO I AM?
I RAGE. I SMASH. I DESTROY.
THEY MAY MOCK ME IF THEY WISH, BUT THEY CANNOT DENY THE FACT THAT AT VIOLENCE I AM *UNSURPASSED.*

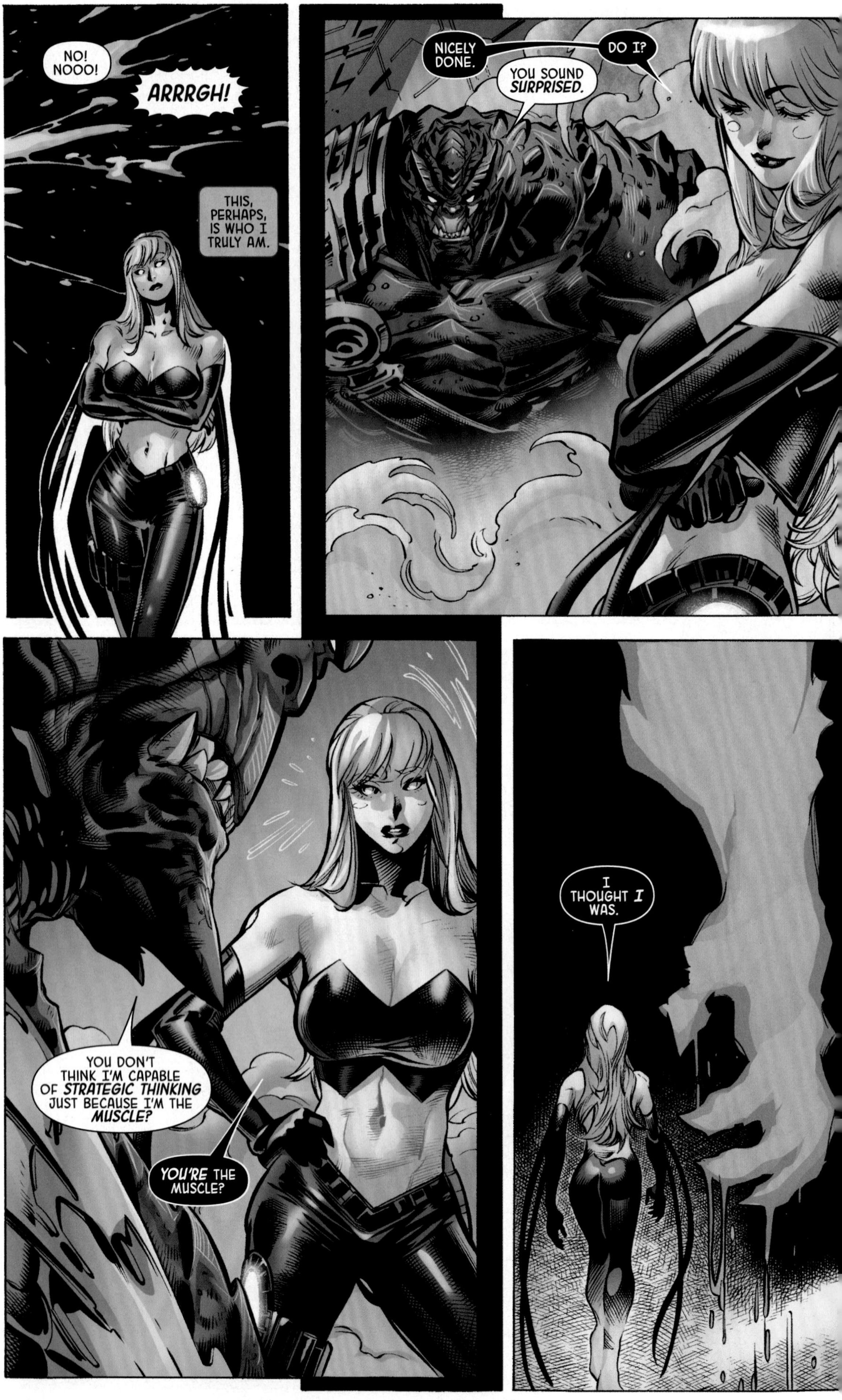
NO! NOOO!
ARRRGH!
THIS, PERHAPS, IS WHO I TRULY AM.
NICELY DONE.
DO I?
YOU SOUND *SURPRISED.*
YOU DON'T THINK I'M CAPABLE OF *STRATEGIC THINKING* JUST BECAUSE I'M THE *MUSCLE?*
YOU'RE THE MUSCLE?
I THOUGHT *I* WAS.

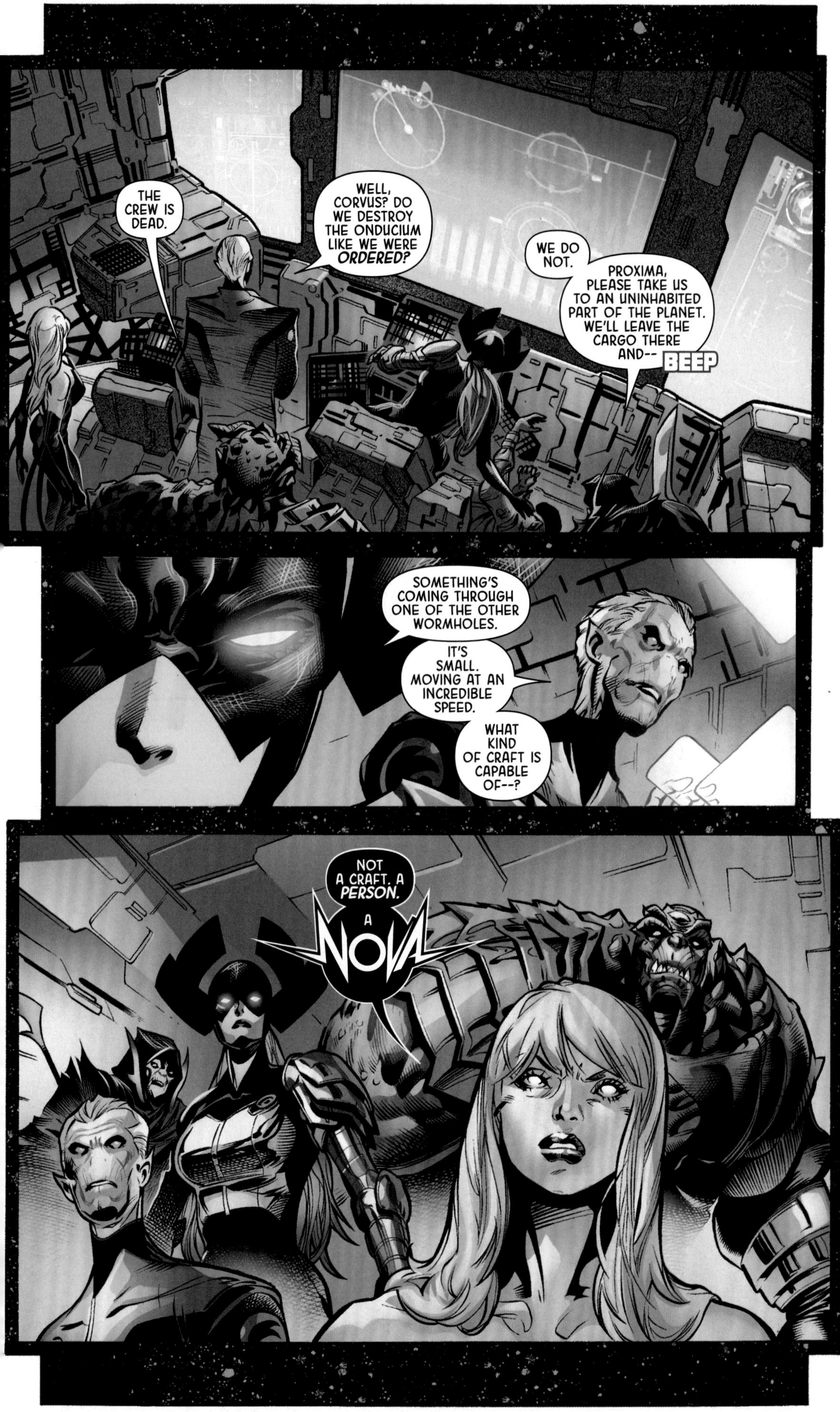
THE CREW IS DEAD.
WELL, CORVUS? DO WE DESTROY THE ONDUCIUM LIKE WE WERE *ORDERED?*
WE DO NOT.
PROXIMA, PLEASE TAKE US TO AN UNINHABITED PART OF THE PLANET. WE'LL LEAVE THE CARGO THERE AND--
BEEP
SOMETHING'S COMING THROUGH ONE OF THE OTHER WORMHOLES.
IT'S SMALL. MOVING AT AN INCREDIBLE SPEED.
WHAT KIND OF CRAFT IS CAPABLE OF--?
NOT A CRAFT. A *PERSON.*
A NOVA

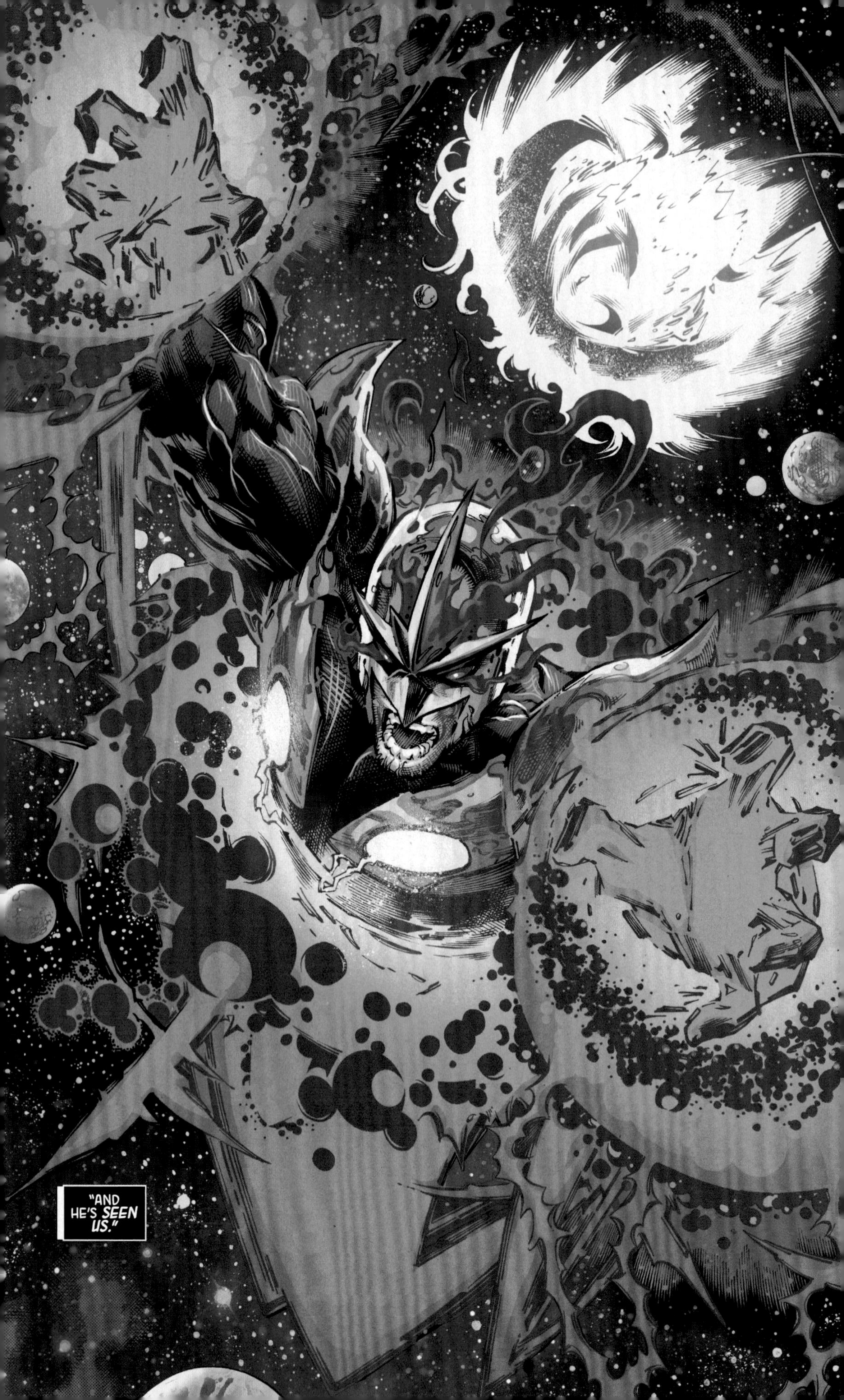
"AND HE'S SEEN US."

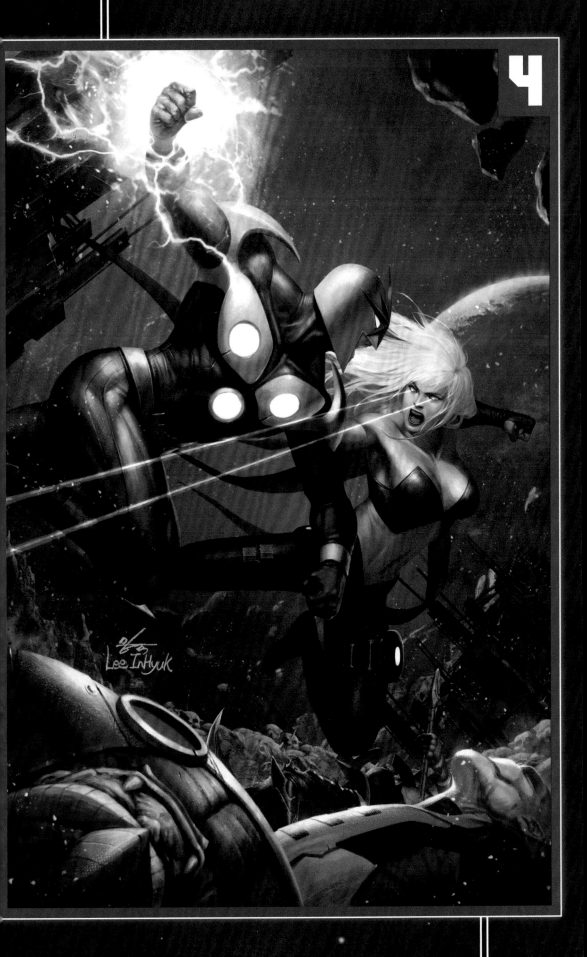

4

Lee InHyuk

THERE ONCE WAS A PRINCESS WHO LIVED IN A PALACE.

SINNARIAN EMPIRE FREIGHTER. *TRANSPORTING RARE ONDUCIUM ORE TO THE EMPIRE.*

SURROUNDED BY HER MOTHER, HER SISTERS AND HER BROTHERS, SHE KNEW ONLY LOVE.

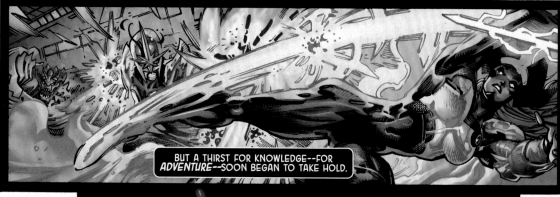

BUT A THIRST FOR KNOWLEDGE--FOR *ADVENTURE*--SOON BEGAN TO TAKE HOLD.

SO ONE DAY SHE SLIPPED BY THE PALACE GUARDS AND SNEAKED OUT THROUGH A GAP IN THE WALLS OF THE HIDDEN CITY--

--INTO THE WILDERNESS.

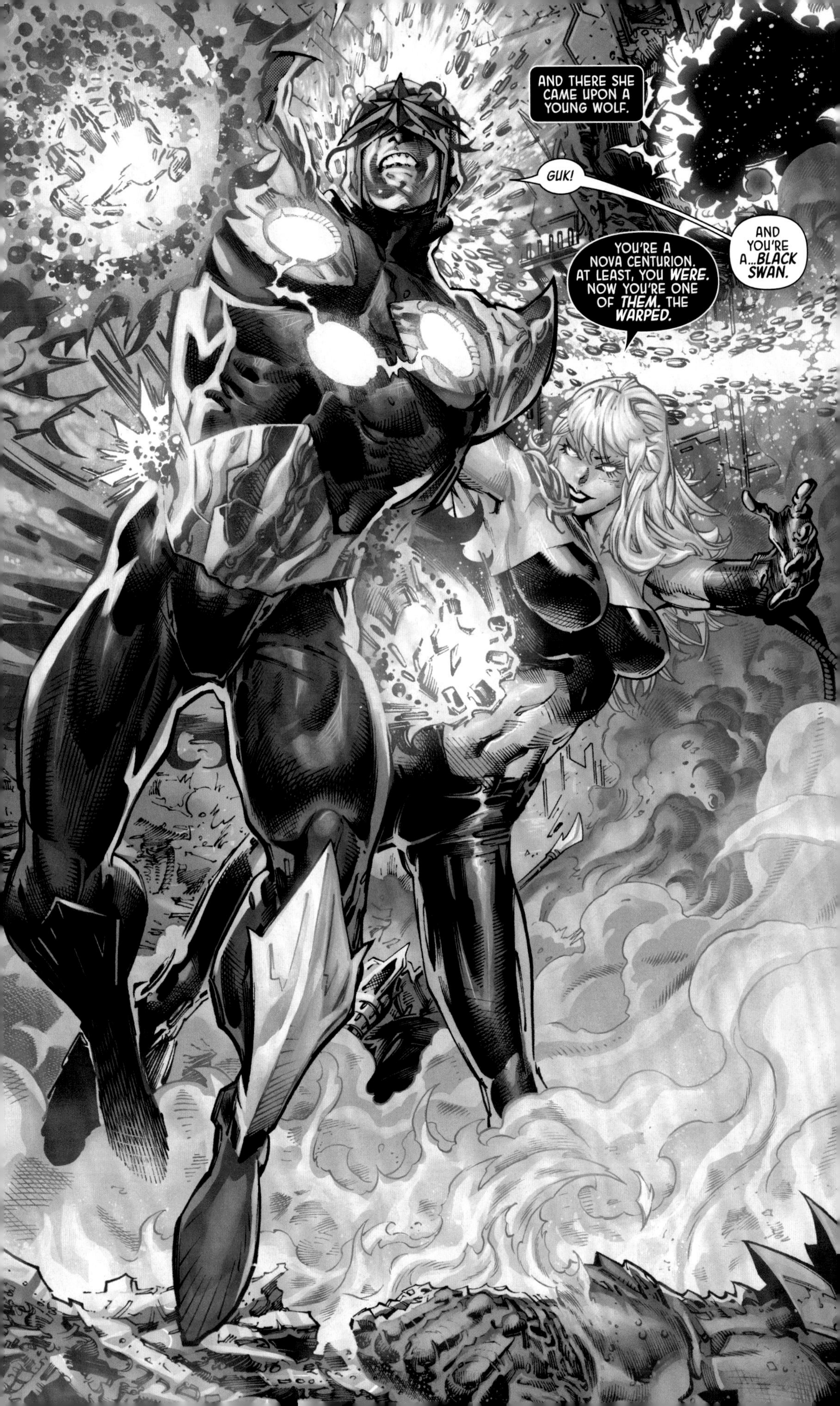
AND THERE SHE CAME UPON A YOUNG WOLF.
GUK!
AND YOU'RE A...BLACK SWAN.
YOU'RE A NOVA CENTURION. AT LEAST, YOU WERE. NOW YOU'RE ONE OF THEM. THE WARPED.

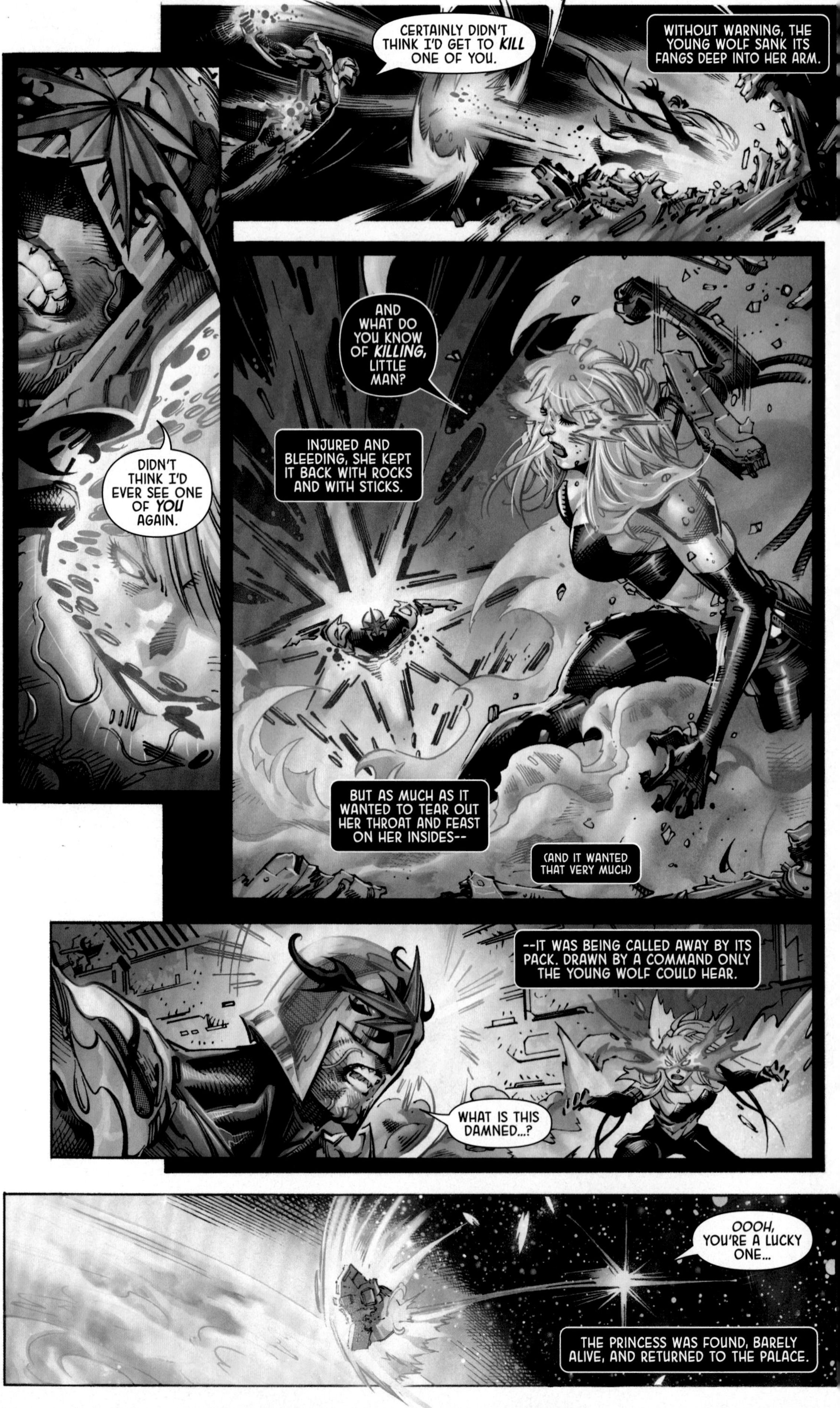
CERTAINLY DIDN'T THINK I'D GET TO KILL ONE OF YOU.
WITHOUT WARNING, THE YOUNG WOLF SANK ITS FANGS DEEP INTO HER ARM.
DIDN'T THINK I'D EVER SEE ONE OF YOU AGAIN.
AND WHAT DO YOU KNOW OF KILLING, LITTLE MAN?
INJURED AND BLEEDING, SHE KEPT IT BACK WITH ROCKS AND WITH STICKS.
BUT AS MUCH AS IT WANTED TO TEAR OUT HER THROAT AND FEAST ON HER INSIDES--
(AND IT WANTED THAT VERY MUCH)
--IT WAS BEING CALLED AWAY BY ITS PACK. DRAWN BY A COMMAND ONLY THE YOUNG WOLF COULD HEAR.
WHAT IS THIS DAMNED...?
OOOH, YOU'RE A LUCKY ONE...
THE PRINCESS WAS FOUND, BARELY ALIVE, AND RETURNED TO THE PALACE.

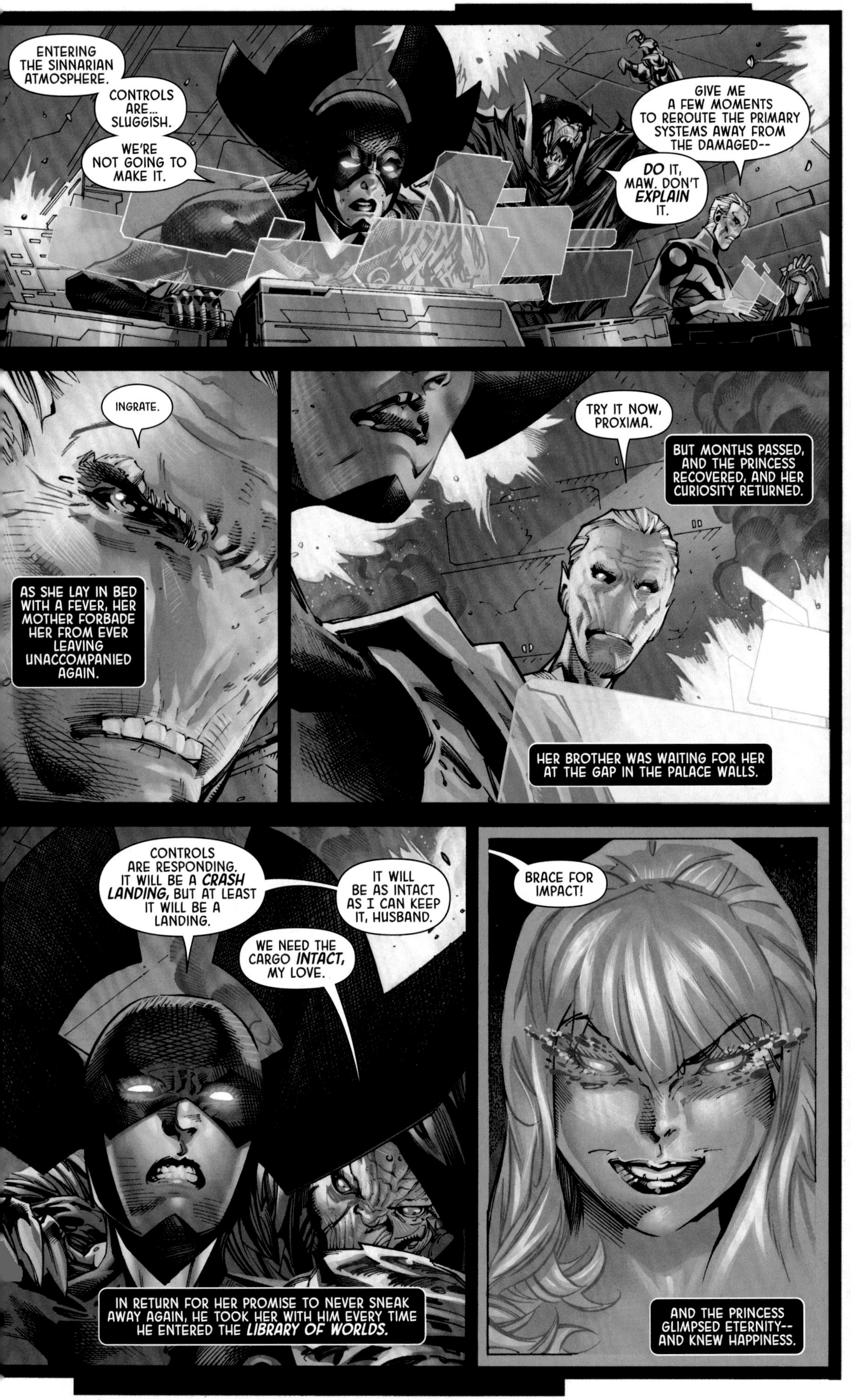

ENTERING THE SINNARIAN ATMOSPHERE.
CONTROLS ARE... SLUGGISH.
WE'RE NOT GOING TO MAKE IT.
GIVE ME A FEW MOMENTS TO REROUTE THE PRIMARY SYSTEMS AWAY FROM THE DAMAGED--
DO IT, MAW. DON'T EXPLAIN IT.
INGRATE.
AS SHE LAY IN BED WITH A FEVER, HER MOTHER FORBADE HER FROM EVER LEAVING UNACCOMPANIED AGAIN.
TRY IT NOW, PROXIMA.
BUT MONTHS PASSED, AND THE PRINCESS RECOVERED, AND HER CURIOSITY RETURNED.
HER BROTHER WAS WAITING FOR HER AT THE GAP IN THE PALACE WALLS.
CONTROLS ARE RESPONDING. IT WILL BE A CRASH LANDING, BUT AT LEAST IT WILL BE A LANDING.
WE NEED THE CARGO INTACT, MY LOVE.
IT WILL BE AS INTACT AS I CAN KEEP IT, HUSBAND.
IN RETURN FOR HER PROMISE TO NEVER SNEAK AWAY AGAIN, HE TOOK HER WITH HIM EVERY TIME HE ENTERED THE LIBRARY OF WORLDS.
BRACE FOR IMPACT!
AND THE PRINCESS GLIMPSED ETERNITY-- AND KNEW HAPPINESS.

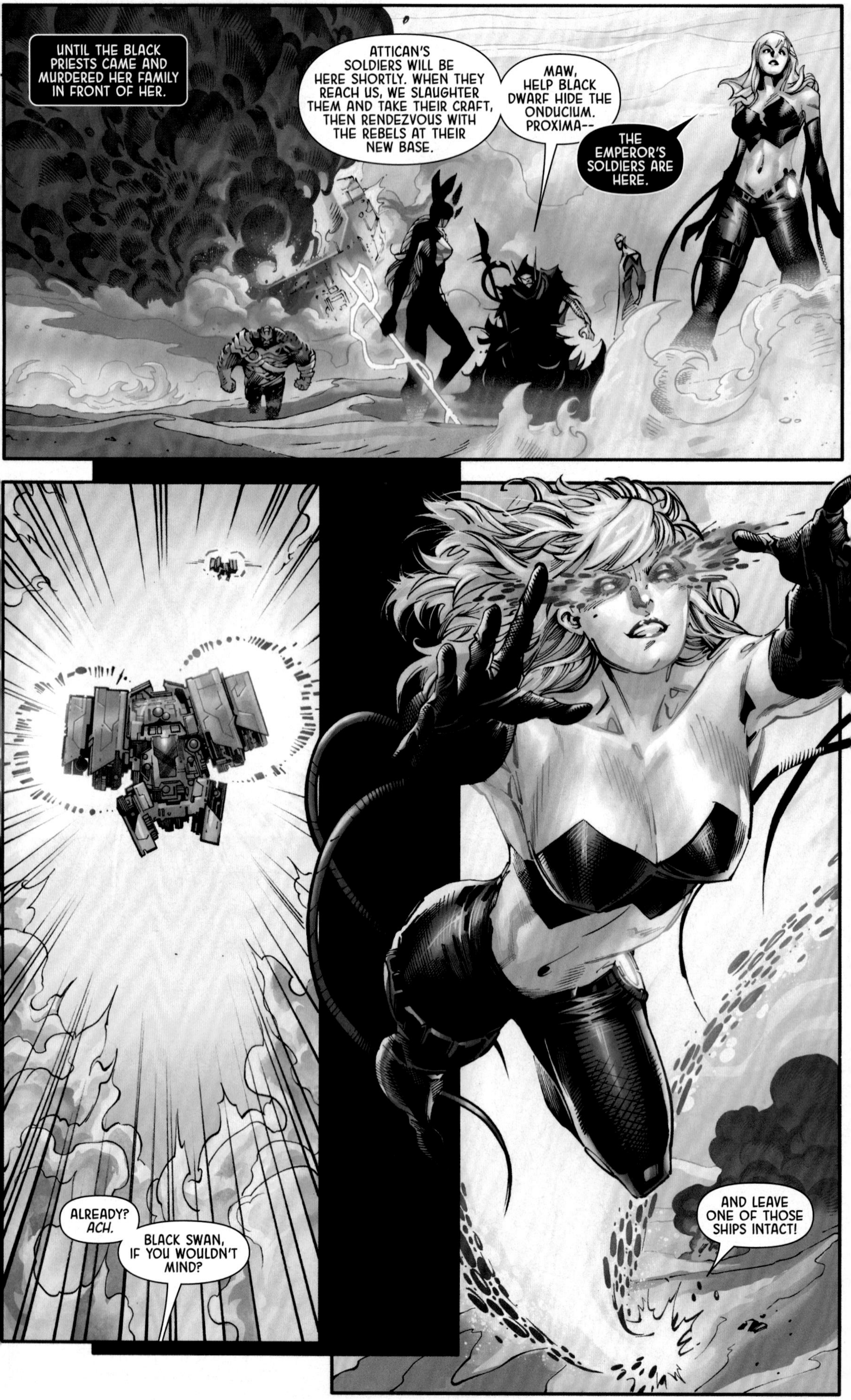
UNTIL THE BLACK PRIESTS CAME AND MURDERED HER FAMILY IN FRONT OF HER.
ATTICAN'S SOLDIERS WILL BE HERE SHORTLY. WHEN THEY REACH US, WE SLAUGHTER THEM AND TAKE THEIR CRAFT, THEN RENDEZVOUS WITH THE REBELS AT THEIR NEW BASE.
MAW, HELP BLACK DWARF HIDE THE ONDUCIUM. PROXIMA--
THE EMPEROR'S SOLDIERS ARE HERE.
ALREADY? ACH.
BLACK SWAN, IF YOU WOULDN'T MIND?
AND LEAVE ONE OF THOSE SHIPS INTACT!

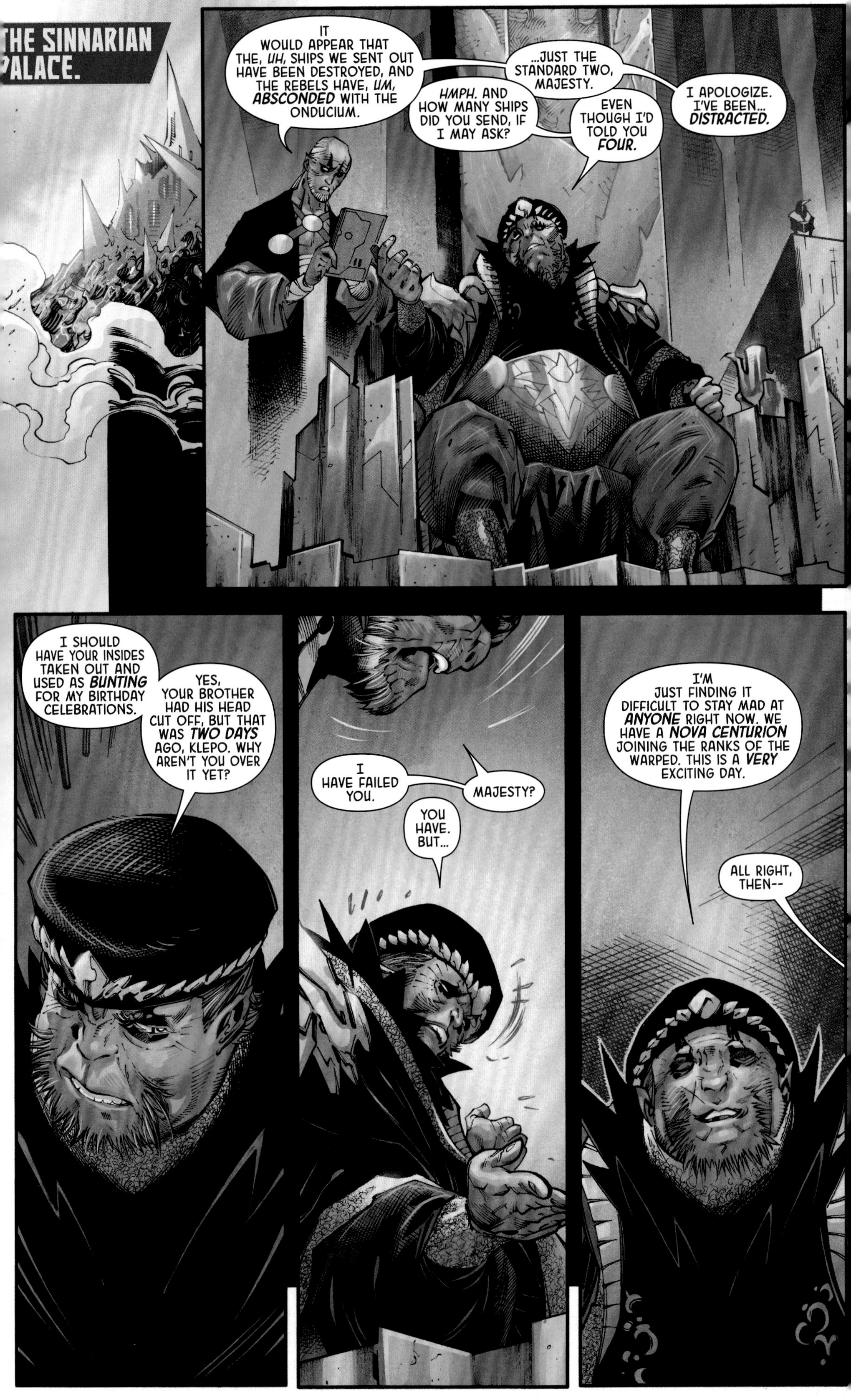
THE SINNARIAN PALACE.
IT WOULD APPEAR THAT THE, UH, SHIPS WE SENT OUT HAVE BEEN DESTROYED, AND THE REBELS HAVE, UM, ABSCONDED WITH THE ONDUCIUM.
HMPH. AND HOW MANY SHIPS DID YOU SEND, IF I MAY ASK?
...JUST THE STANDARD TWO, MAJESTY.
EVEN THOUGH I'D TOLD YOU FOUR.
I APOLOGIZE. I'VE BEEN... DISTRACTED.
I SHOULD HAVE YOUR INSIDES TAKEN OUT AND USED AS BUNTING FOR MY BIRTHDAY CELEBRATIONS.
YES, YOUR BROTHER HAD HIS HEAD CUT OFF, BUT THAT WAS TWO DAYS AGO, KLEPO. WHY AREN'T YOU OVER IT YET?
I HAVE FAILED YOU.
MAJESTY?
YOU HAVE. BUT...
I'M JUST FINDING IT DIFFICULT TO STAY MAD AT ANYONE RIGHT NOW. WE HAVE A NOVA CENTURION JOINING THE RANKS OF THE WARPED. THIS IS A VERY EXCITING DAY.
ALL RIGHT, THEN--

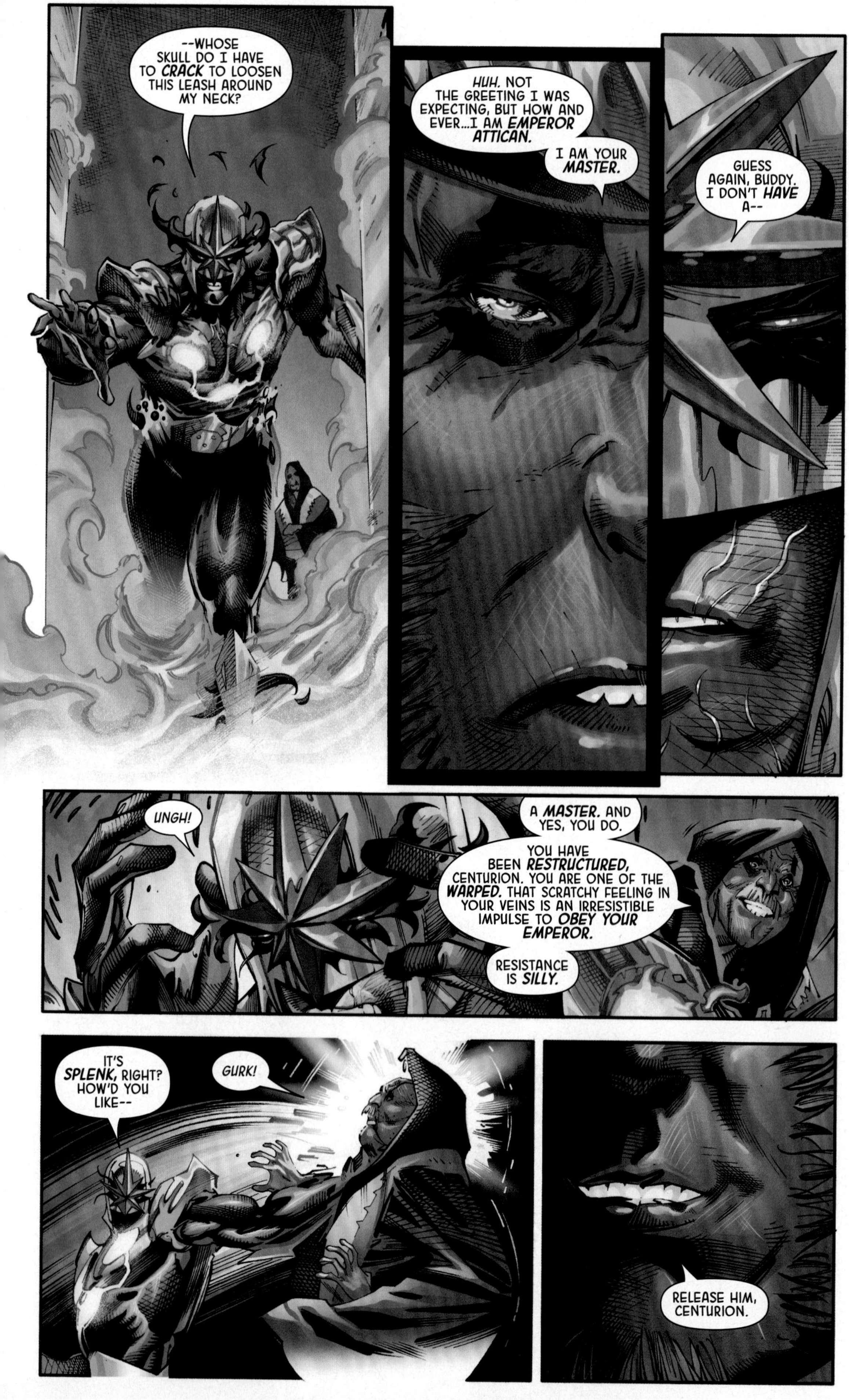
--WHOSE SKULL DO I HAVE TO CRACK TO LOOSEN THIS LEASH AROUND MY NECK?
HUH. NOT THE GREETING I WAS EXPECTING, BUT HOW AND EVER...I AM EMPEROR ATTICAN.
I AM YOUR MASTER.
GUESS AGAIN, BUDDY. I DON'T HAVE A--
UNGH!
A MASTER. AND YES, YOU DO.
YOU HAVE BEEN RESTRUCTURED, CENTURION. YOU ARE ONE OF THE WARPED. THAT SCRATCHY FEELING IN YOUR VEINS IS AN IRRESISTIBLE IMPULSE TO OBEY YOUR EMPEROR.
RESISTANCE IS SILLY.
IT'S SPLENK, RIGHT? HOW'D YOU LIKE--
GURK!
RELEASE HIM, CENTURION.

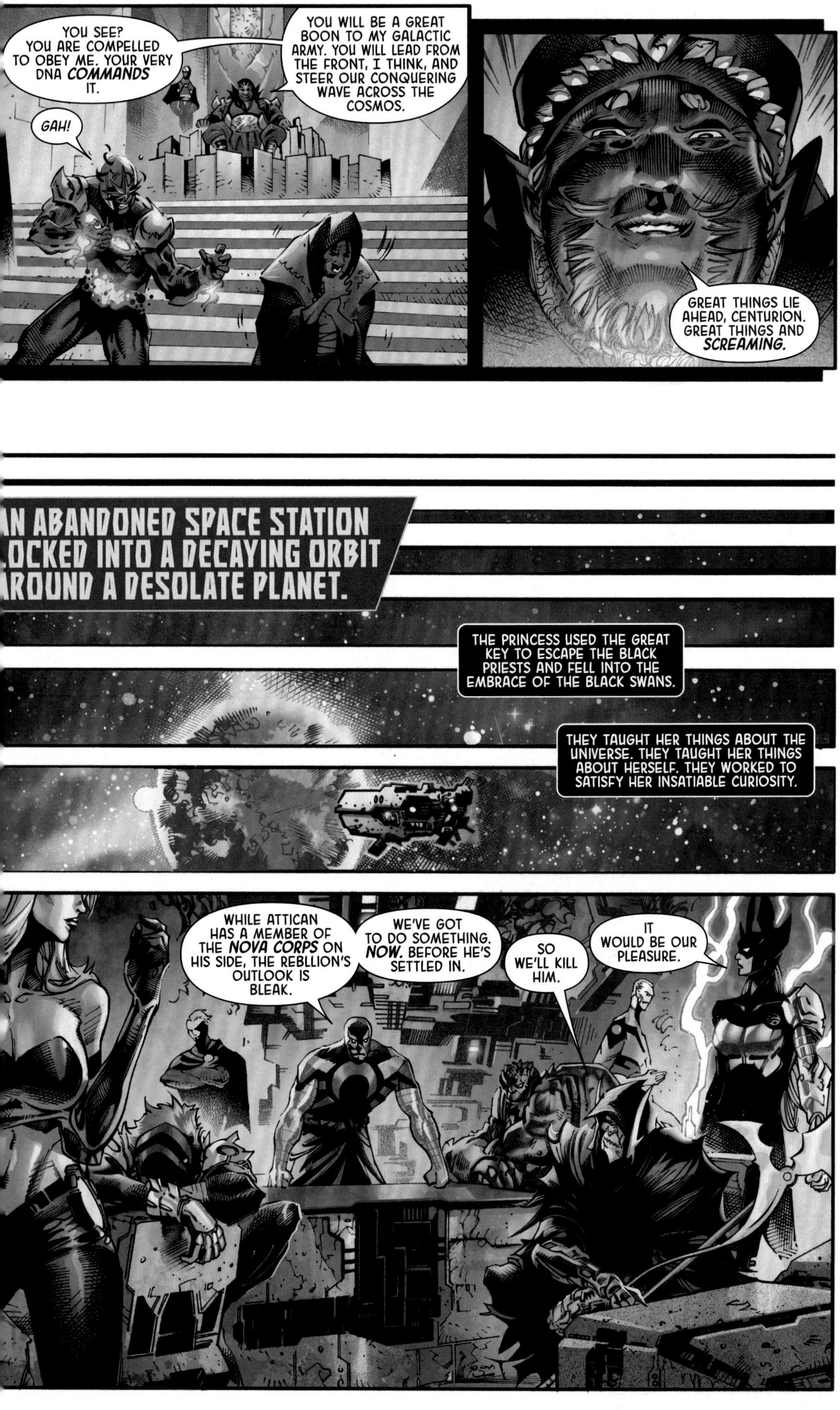

YOU SEE? YOU ARE COMPELLED TO OBEY ME. YOUR VERY DNA **COMMANDS** IT.
YOU WILL BE A GREAT BOON TO MY GALACTIC ARMY. YOU WILL LEAD FROM THE FRONT, I THINK, AND STEER OUR CONQUERING WAVE ACROSS THE COSMOS.
GAH!
GREAT THINGS LIE AHEAD, CENTURION. GREAT THINGS AND ***SCREAMING.***
N ABANDONED SPACE STATION
OCKED INTO A DECAYING ORBIT
ROUND A DESOLATE PLANET.
THE PRINCESS USED THE GREAT KEY TO ESCAPE THE BLACK PRIESTS AND FELL INTO THE EMBRACE OF THE BLACK SWANS.
THEY TAUGHT HER THINGS ABOUT THE UNIVERSE. THEY TAUGHT HER THINGS ABOUT HERSELF. THEY WORKED TO SATISFY HER INSATIABLE CURIOSITY.
WHILE ATTICAN HAS A MEMBER OF THE ***NOVA CORPS*** ON HIS SIDE, THE REBLLION'S OUTLOOK IS BLEAK.
WE'VE GOT TO DO SOMETHING. ***NOW.*** BEFORE HE'S SETTLED IN.
SO WE'LL KILL HIM.
IT WOULD BE OUR PLEASURE.

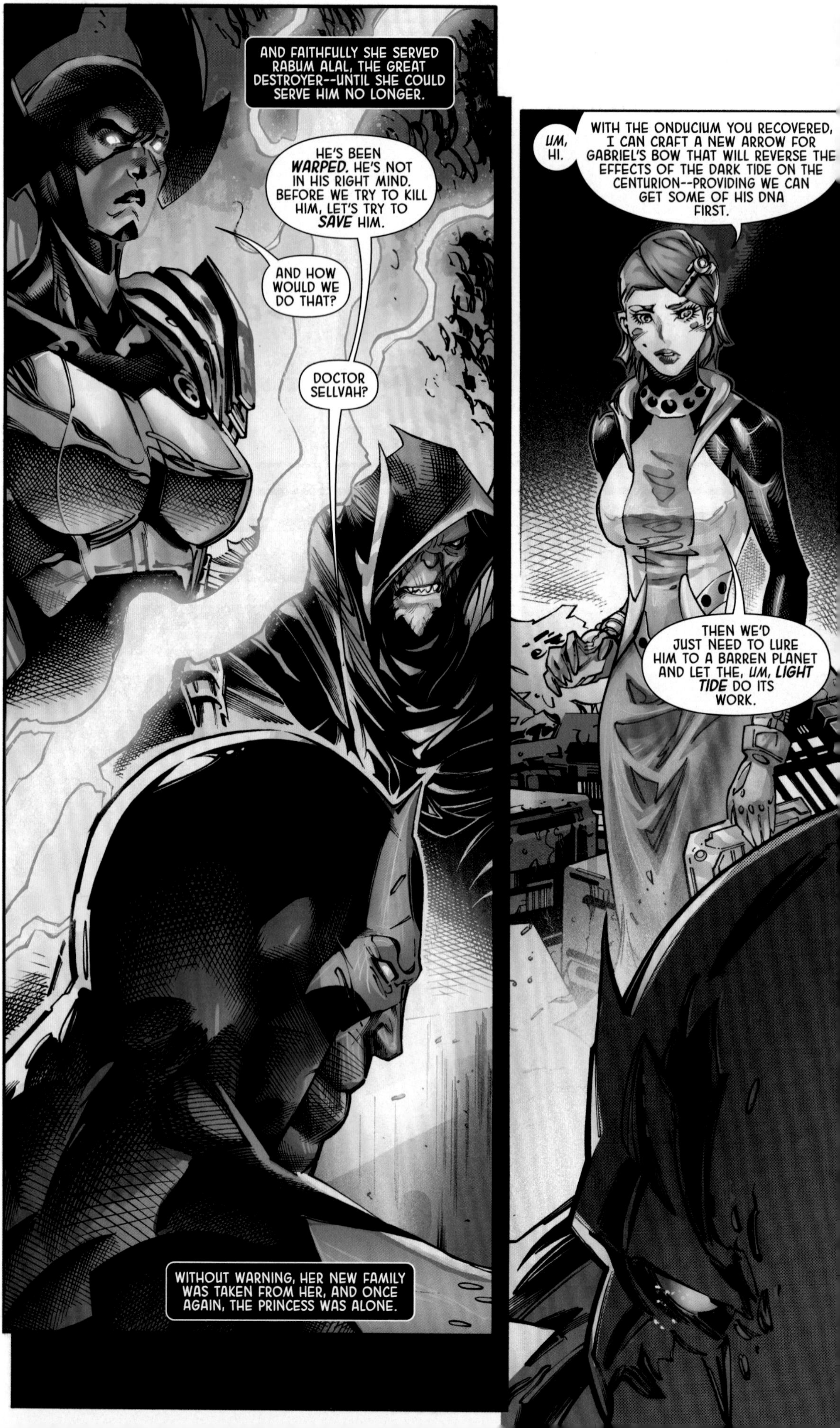
AND FAITHFULLY SHE SERVED RABUM ALAL, THE GREAT DESTROYER--UNTIL SHE COULD SERVE HIM NO LONGER.
HE'S BEEN WARPED. HE'S NOT IN HIS RIGHT MIND. BEFORE WE TRY TO KILL HIM, LET'S TRY TO SAVE HIM.
AND HOW WOULD WE DO THAT?
DOCTOR SELLVAH?
WITHOUT WARNING, HER NEW FAMILY WAS TAKEN FROM HER, AND ONCE AGAIN, THE PRINCESS WAS ALONE.
UM, HI.
WITH THE ONDUCIUM YOU RECOVERED, I CAN CRAFT A NEW ARROW FOR GABRIEL'S BOW THAT WILL REVERSE THE EFFECTS OF THE DARK TIDE ON THE CENTURION--PROVIDING WE CAN GET SOME OF HIS DNA FIRST.
THEN WE'D JUST NEED TO LURE HIM TO A BARREN PLANET AND LET THE, UM, LIGHT TIDE DO ITS WORK.

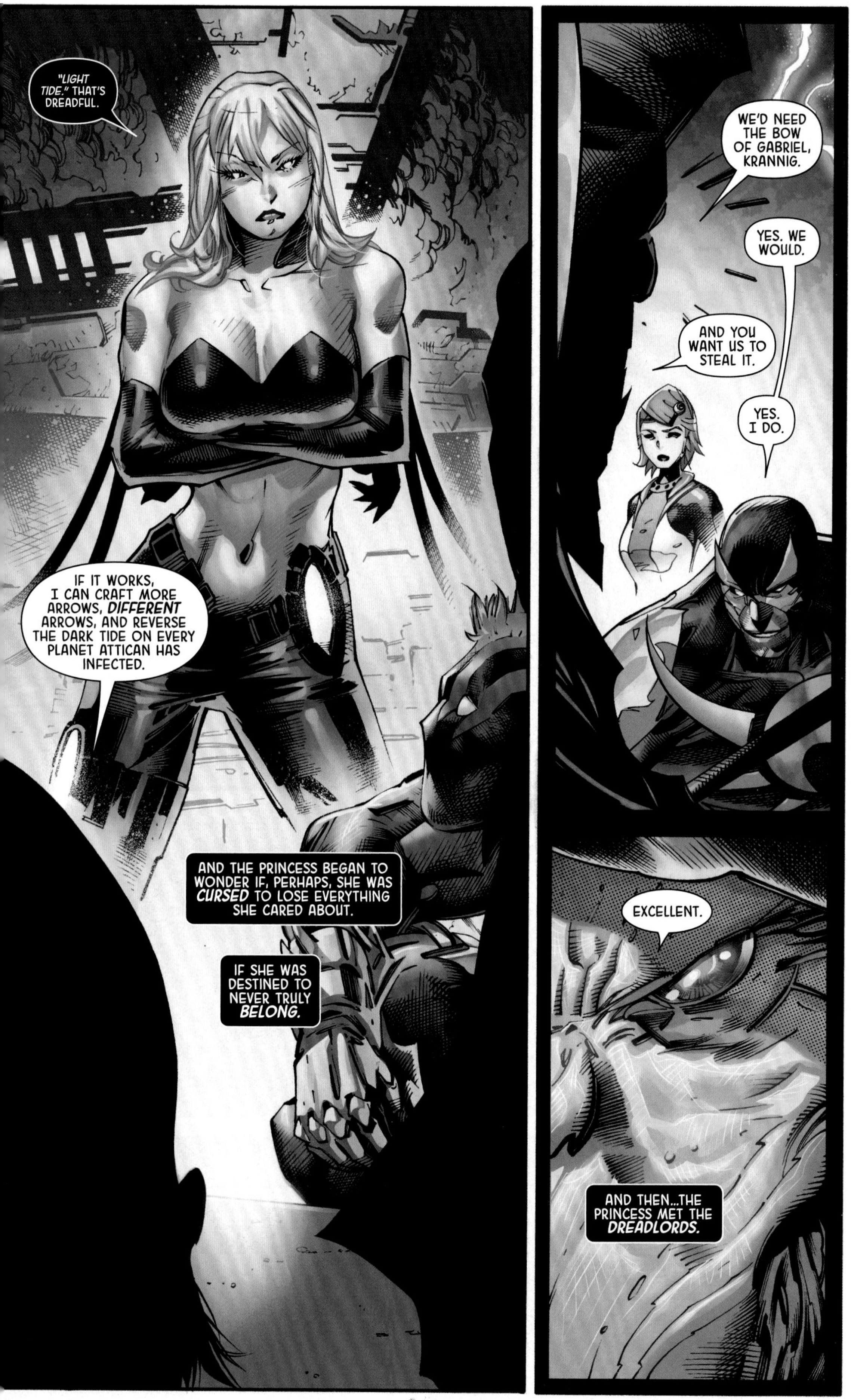
"LIGHT TIDE." THAT'S DREADFUL.
IF IT WORKS, I CAN CRAFT MORE ARROWS, DIFFERENT ARROWS, AND REVERSE THE DARK TIDE ON EVERY PLANET ATTICAN HAS INFECTED.
AND THE PRINCESS BEGAN TO WONDER IF, PERHAPS, SHE WAS CURSED TO LOSE EVERYTHING SHE CARED ABOUT.
IF SHE WAS DESTINED TO NEVER TRULY BELONG.
WE'D NEED THE BOW OF GABRIEL, KRANNIG.
YES. WE WOULD.
AND YOU WANT US TO STEAL IT.
YES. I DO.
EXCELLENT.
AND THEN...THE PRINCESS MET THE DREADLORDS.

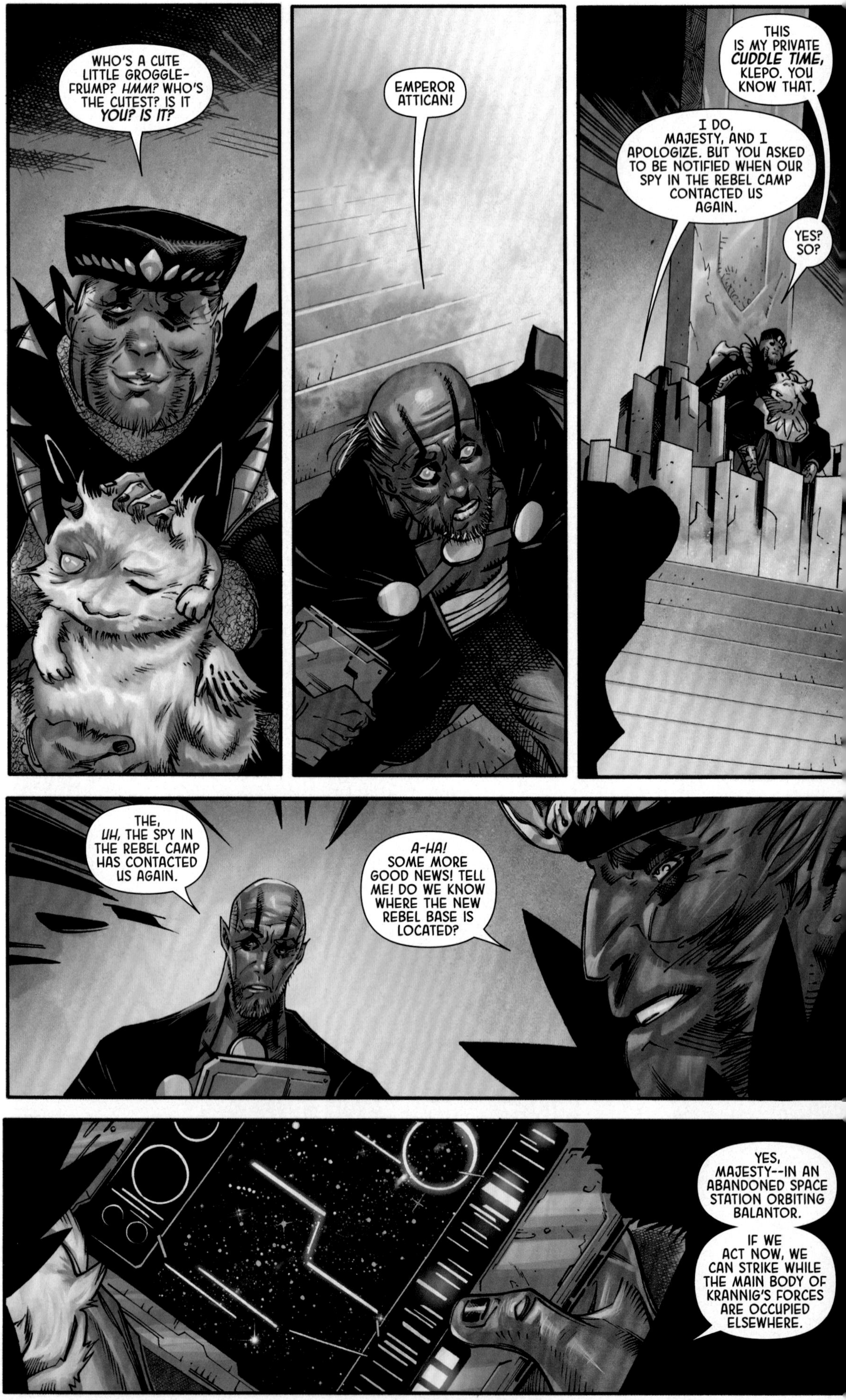
WHO'S A CUTE LITTLE GROGGLE-FRUMP? HMM? WHO'S THE CUTEST? IS IT YOU? IS IT?
EMPEROR ATTICAN!
THIS IS MY PRIVATE CUDDLE TIME, KLEPO. YOU KNOW THAT.
I DO, MAJESTY, AND I APOLOGIZE. BUT YOU ASKED TO BE NOTIFIED WHEN OUR SPY IN THE REBEL CAMP CONTACTED US AGAIN.
YES? SO?
THE, UH, THE SPY IN THE REBEL CAMP HAS CONTACTED US AGAIN.
A-HA! SOME MORE GOOD NEWS! TELL ME! DO WE KNOW WHERE THE NEW REBEL BASE IS LOCATED?
YES, MAJESTY--IN AN ABANDONED SPACE STATION ORBITING BALANTOR.
IF WE ACT NOW, WE CAN STRIKE WHILE THE MAIN BODY OF KRANNIG'S FORCES ARE OCCUPIED ELSEWHERE.

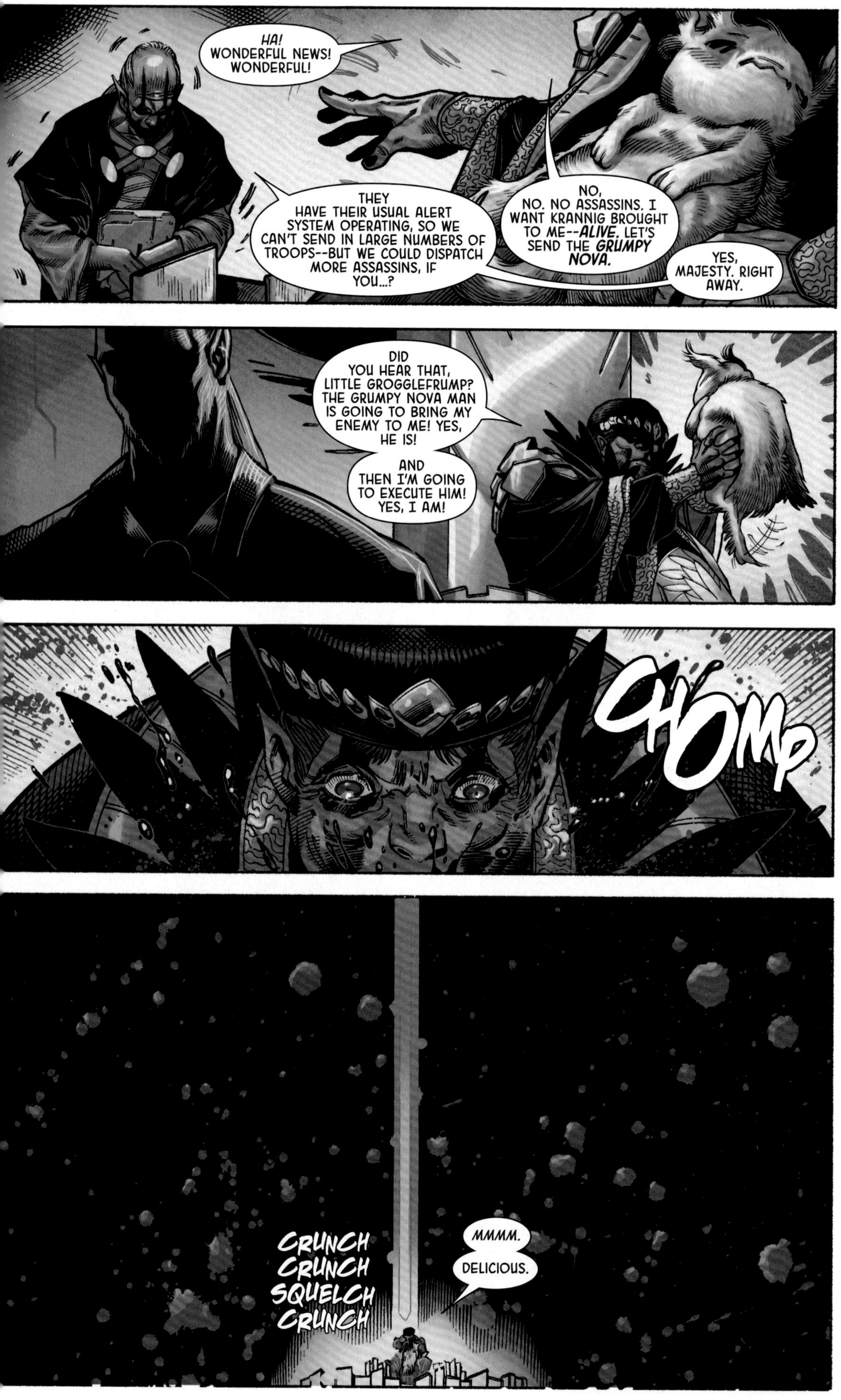
HA! WONDERFUL NEWS! WONDERFUL!
THEY HAVE THEIR USUAL ALERT SYSTEM OPERATING, SO WE CAN'T SEND IN LARGE NUMBERS OF TROOPS--BUT WE COULD DISPATCH MORE ASSASSINS, IF YOU...?
NO, NO. NO ASSASSINS. I WANT KRANNIG BROUGHT TO ME--ALIVE. LET'S SEND THE GRUMPY NOVA.
YES, MAJESTY. RIGHT AWAY.
DID YOU HEAR THAT, LITTLE GROGGLEFRUMP? THE GRUMPY NOVA MAN IS GOING TO BRING MY ENEMY TO ME! YES, HE IS!
AND THEN I'M GOING TO EXECUTE HIM! YES, I AM!
CHOMP
CRUNCH
CRUNCH
SQUELCH
CRUNCH
MMMM.
DELICIOUS.

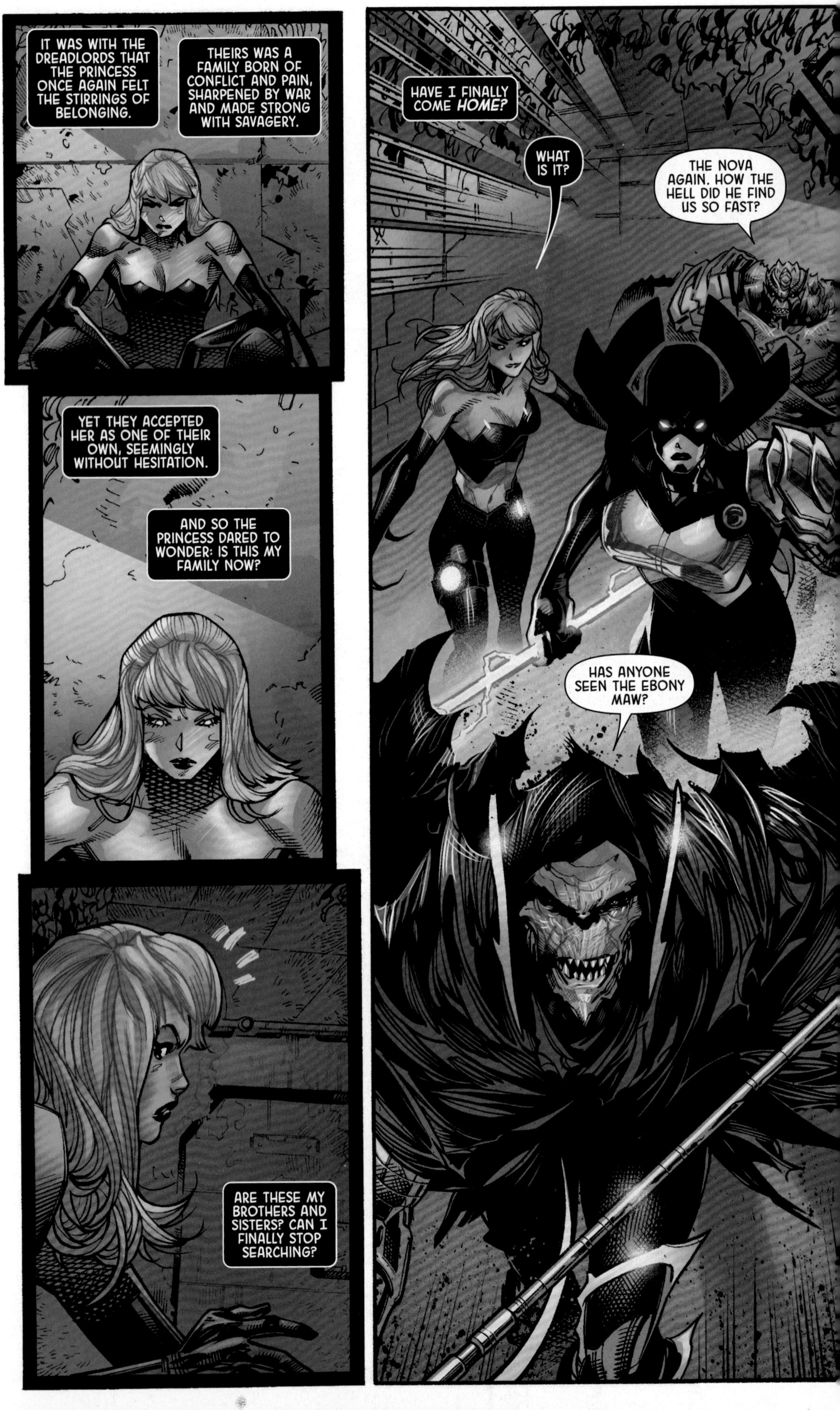
IT WAS WITH THE DREADLORDS THAT THE PRINCESS ONCE AGAIN FELT THE STIRRINGS OF BELONGING.
THEIRS WAS A FAMILY BORN OF CONFLICT AND PAIN, SHARPENED BY WAR AND MADE STRONG WITH SAVAGERY.
YET THEY ACCEPTED HER AS ONE OF THEIR OWN, SEEMINGLY WITHOUT HESITATION.
AND SO THE PRINCESS DARED TO WONDER: IS THIS MY FAMILY NOW?
ARE THESE MY BROTHERS AND SISTERS? CAN I FINALLY STOP SEARCHING?
HAVE I FINALLY COME *HOME?*
WHAT IS IT?
THE NOVA AGAIN. HOW THE HELL DID HE FIND US SO FAST?
HAS ANYONE SEEN THE EBONY MAW?

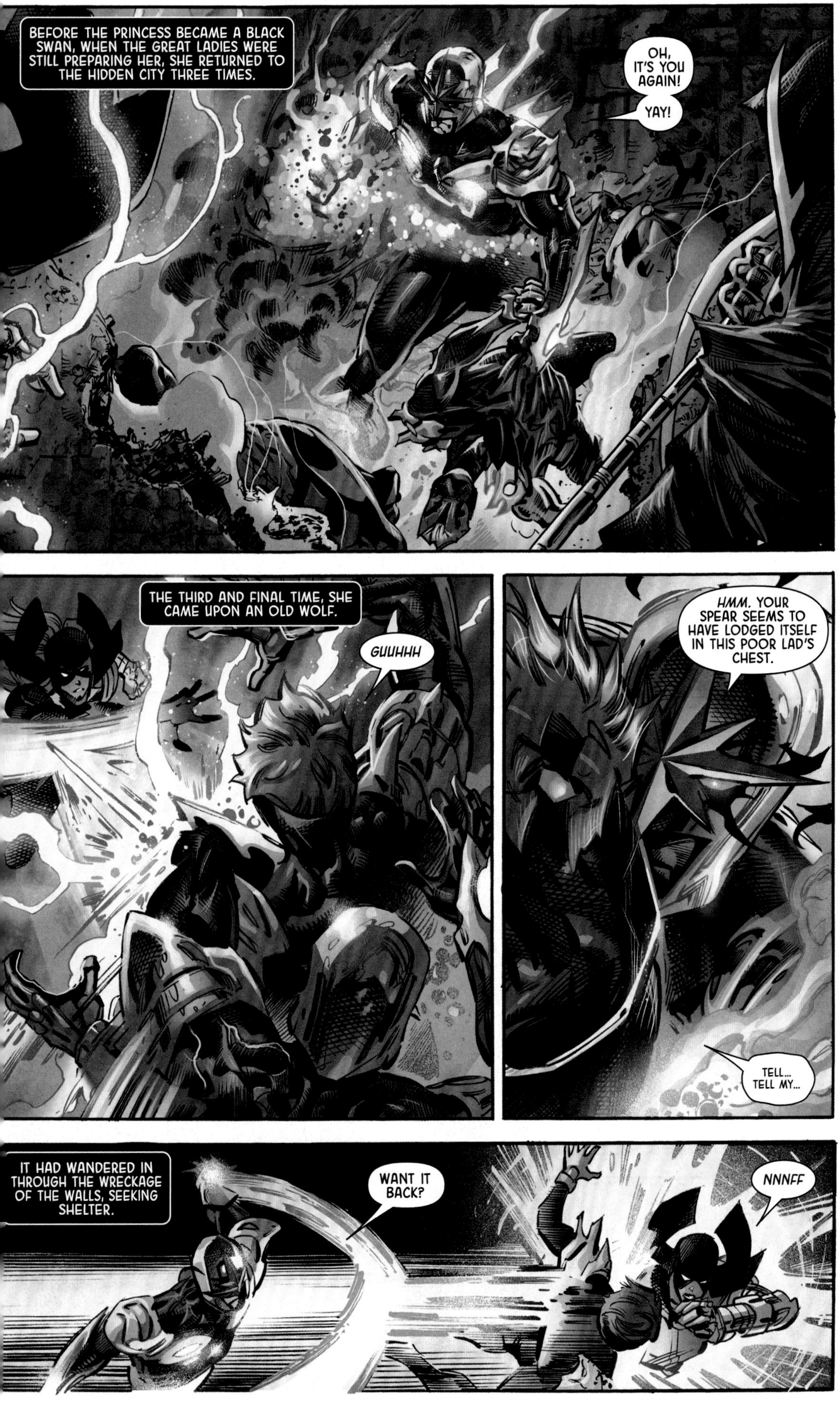

BEFORE THE PRINCESS BECAME A BLACK SWAN, WHEN THE GREAT LADIES WERE STILL PREPARING HER, SHE RETURNED TO THE HIDDEN CITY THREE TIMES.
OH, IT'S YOU AGAIN!
YAY!
THE THIRD AND FINAL TIME, SHE CAME UPON AN OLD WOLF.
GUUHHH
HMM. YOUR SPEAR SEEMS TO HAVE LODGED ITSELF IN THIS POOR LAD'S CHEST.
TELL... TELL MY...
IT HAD WANDERED IN THROUGH THE WRECKAGE OF THE WALLS, SEEKING SHELTER.
WANT IT BACK?
NNNFF

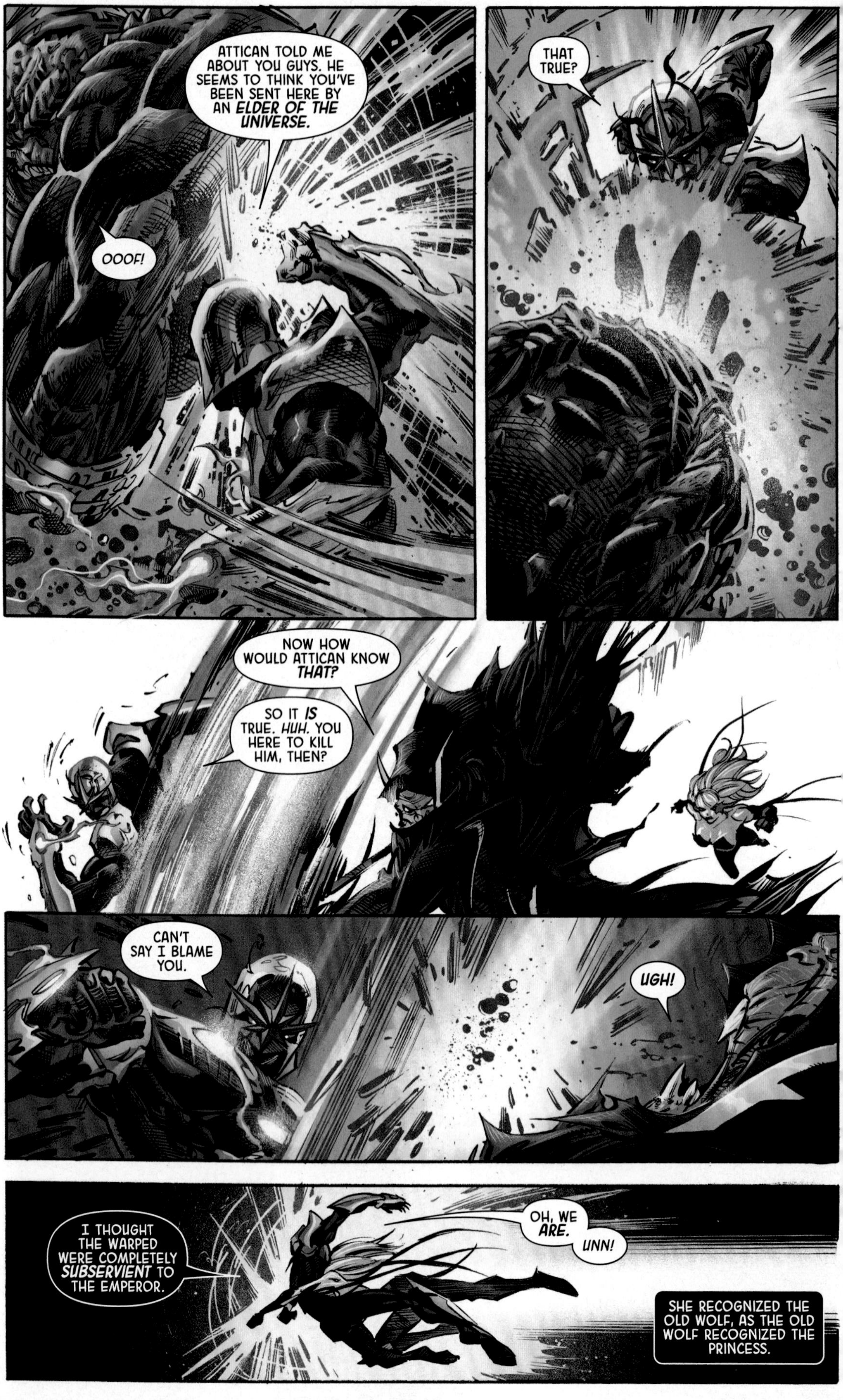
ATTICAN TOLD ME ABOUT YOU GUYS. HE SEEMS TO THINK YOU'VE BEEN SENT HERE BY AN ELDER OF THE UNIVERSE.
OOOF!
THAT TRUE?
NOW HOW WOULD ATTICAN KNOW THAT?
SO IT IS TRUE. HUH. YOU HERE TO KILL HIM, THEN?
CAN'T SAY I BLAME YOU.
UGH!
I THOUGHT THE WARPED WERE COMPLETELY SUBSERVIENT TO THE EMPEROR.
OH, WE ARE.
UNN!
SHE RECOGNIZED THE OLD WOLF, AS THE OLD WOLF RECOGNIZED THE PRINCESS.

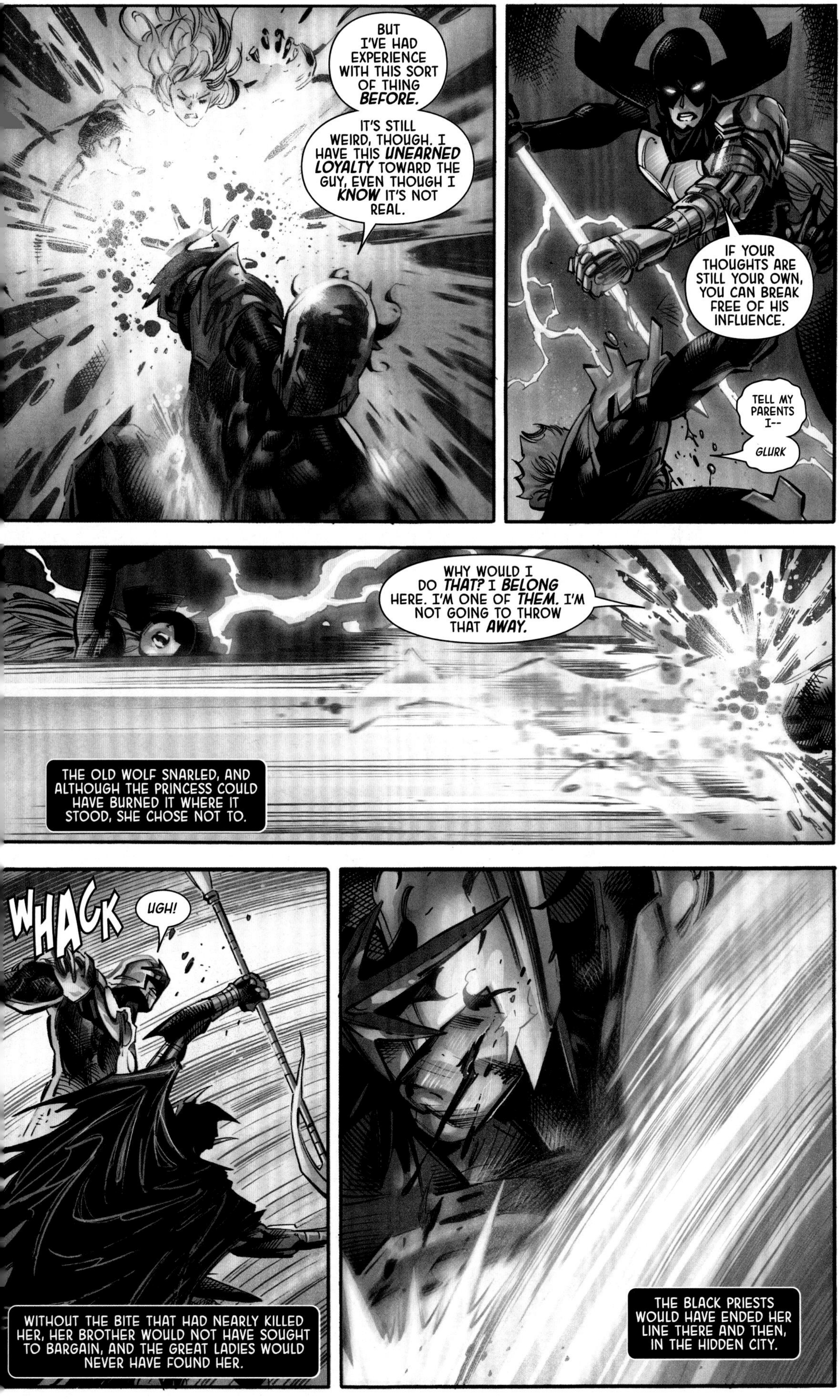

BUT I'VE HAD EXPERIENCE WITH THIS SORT OF THING BEFORE.
IT'S STILL WEIRD, THOUGH. I HAVE THIS UNEARNED LOYALTY TOWARD THE GUY, EVEN THOUGH I KNOW IT'S NOT REAL.
IF YOUR THOUGHTS ARE STILL YOUR OWN, YOU CAN BREAK FREE OF HIS INFLUENCE.
TELL MY PARENTS I--
GLURK
WHY WOULD I DO THAT? I BELONG HERE. I'M ONE OF THEM. I'M NOT GOING TO THROW THAT AWAY.
THE OLD WOLF SNARLED, AND ALTHOUGH THE PRINCESS COULD HAVE BURNED IT WHERE IT STOOD, SHE CHOSE NOT TO.
WHACK
UGH!
WITHOUT THE BITE THAT HAD NEARLY KILLED HER, HER BROTHER WOULD NOT HAVE SOUGHT TO BARGAIN, AND THE GREAT LADIES WOULD NEVER HAVE FOUND HER.
THE BLACK PRIESTS WOULD HAVE ENDED HER LINE THERE AND THEN, IN THE HIDDEN CITY.

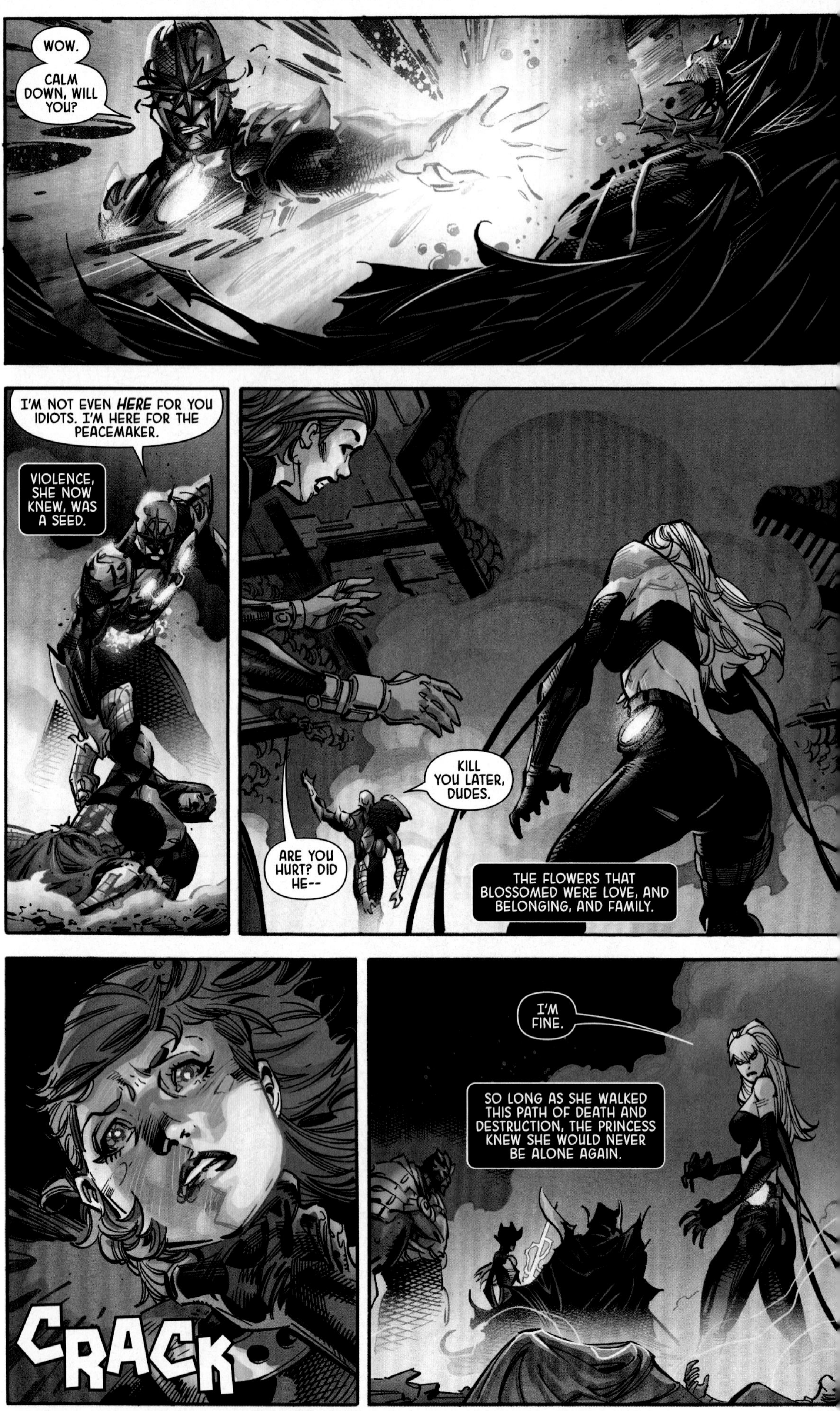
WOW.
CALM DOWN, WILL YOU?
I'M NOT EVEN HERE FOR YOU IDIOTS. I'M HERE FOR THE PEACEMAKER.
VIOLENCE, SHE NOW KNEW, WAS A SEED.
ARE YOU HURT? DID HE--
KILL YOU LATER, DUDES.
THE FLOWERS THAT BLOSSOMED WERE LOVE, AND BELONGING, AND FAMILY.
CRACK
I'M FINE.
SO LONG AS SHE WALKED THIS PATH OF DEATH AND DESTRUCTION, THE PRINCESS KNEW SHE WOULD NEVER BE ALONE AGAIN.

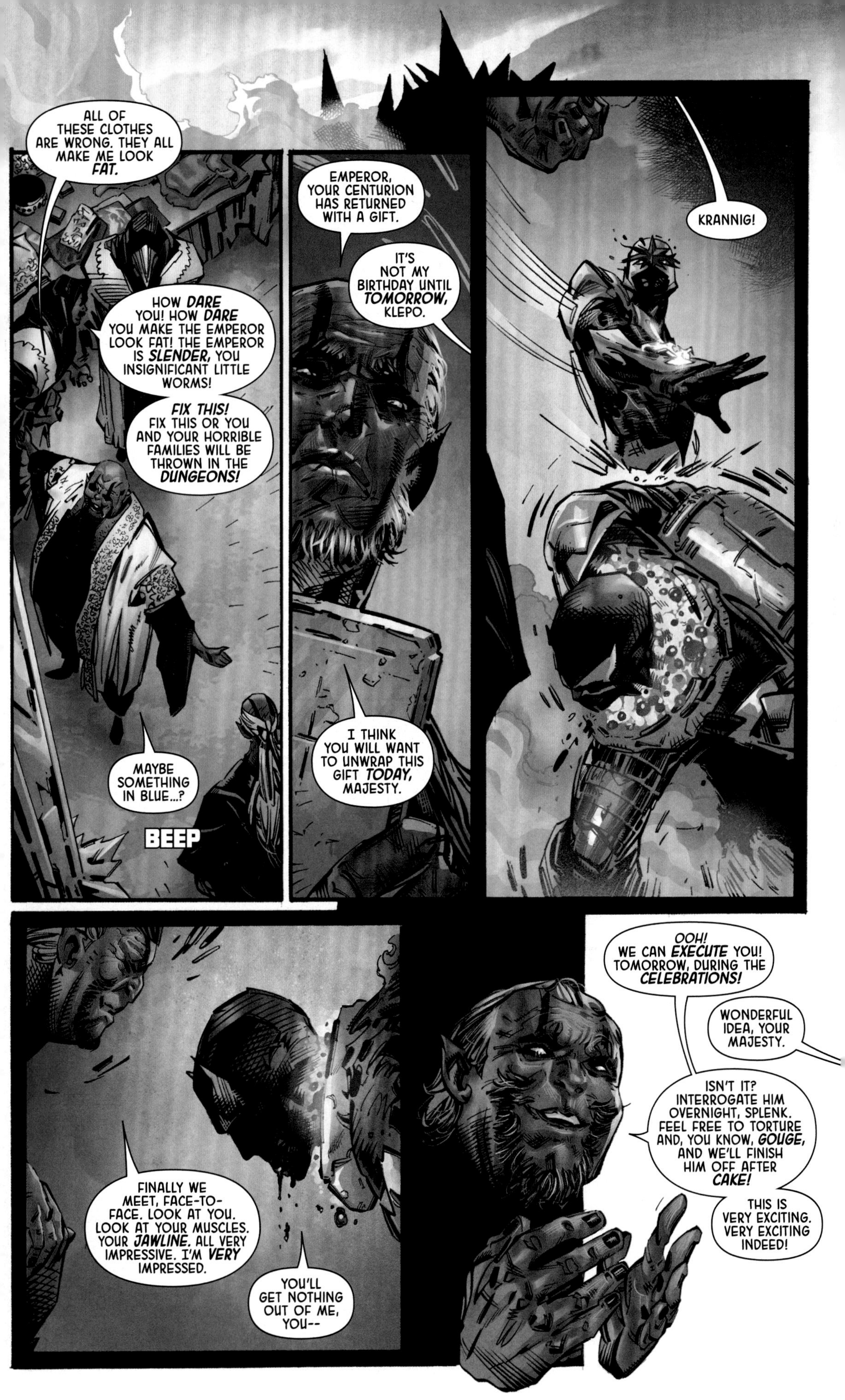
ALL OF THESE CLOTHES ARE WRONG. THEY ALL MAKE ME LOOK FAT.
HOW DARE YOU! HOW DARE YOU MAKE THE EMPEROR LOOK FAT! THE EMPEROR IS SLENDER, YOU INSIGNIFICANT LITTLE WORMS!
FIX THIS! FIX THIS OR YOU AND YOUR HORRIBLE FAMILIES WILL BE THROWN IN THE DUNGEONS!
MAYBE SOMETHING IN BLUE...?
BEEP
EMPEROR, YOUR CENTURION HAS RETURNED WITH A GIFT.
IT'S NOT MY BIRTHDAY UNTIL TOMORROW, KLEPO.
I THINK YOU WILL WANT TO UNWRAP THIS GIFT TODAY, MAJESTY.
KRANNIG!
FINALLY WE MEET, FACE-TO-FACE. LOOK AT YOU. LOOK AT YOUR MUSCLES. YOUR JAWLINE. ALL VERY IMPRESSIVE. I'M VERY IMPRESSED.
YOU'LL GET NOTHING OUT OF ME, YOU--
OOH! WE CAN EXECUTE YOU! TOMORROW, DURING THE CELEBRATIONS!
WONDERFUL IDEA, YOUR MAJESTY.
ISN'T IT? INTERROGATE HIM OVERNIGHT, SPLENK. FEEL FREE TO TORTURE AND, YOU KNOW, GOUGE, AND WE'LL FINISH HIM OFF AFTER CAKE!
THIS IS VERY EXCITING. VERY EXCITING INDEED!

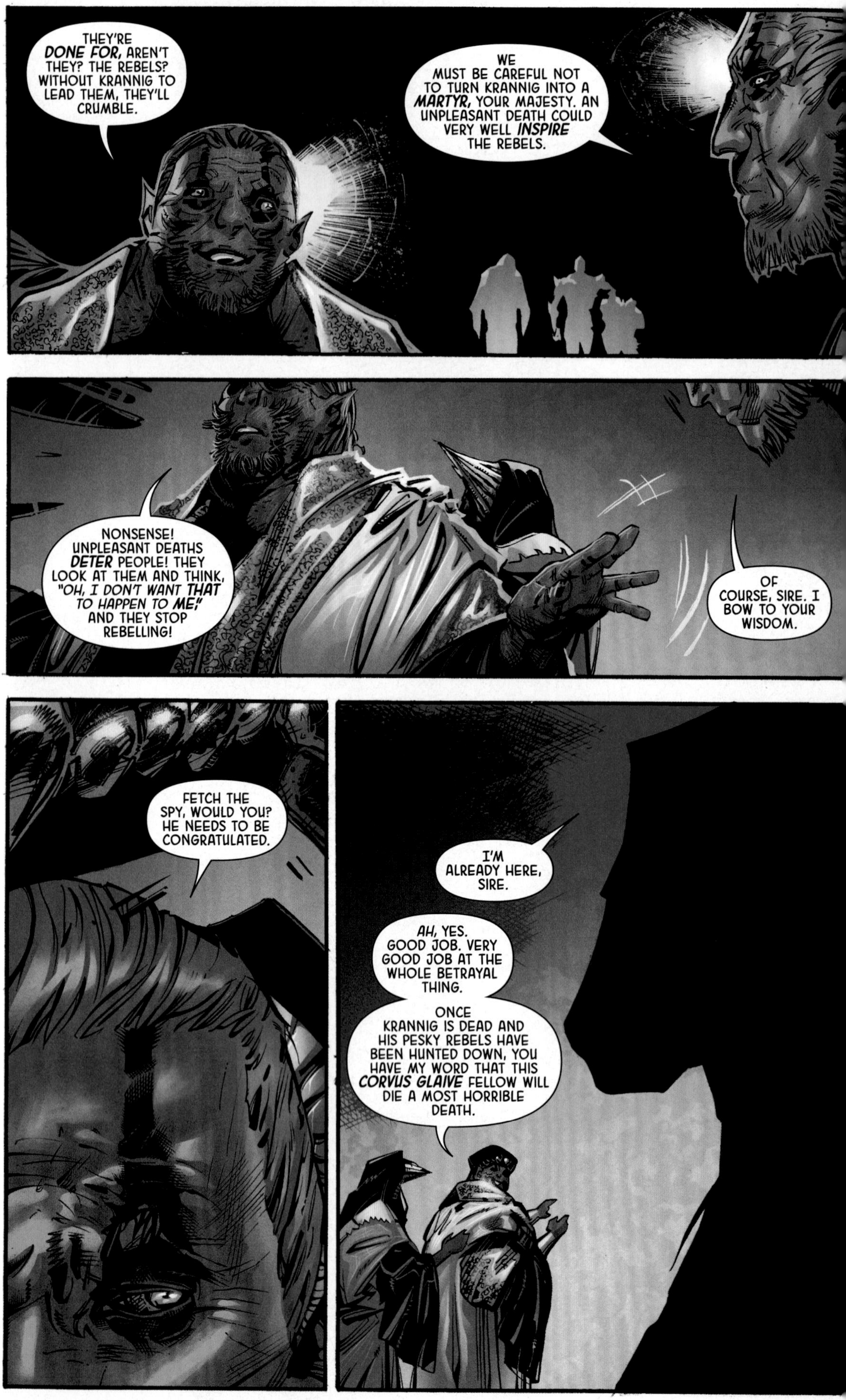
THEY'RE *DONE FOR,* AREN'T THEY? THE REBELS? WITHOUT KRANNIG TO LEAD THEM, THEY'LL CRUMBLE.
WE MUST BE CAREFUL NOT TO TURN KRANNIG INTO A *MARTYR,* YOUR MAJESTY. AN UNPLEASANT DEATH COULD VERY WELL *INSPIRE* THE REBELS.
NONSENSE! UNPLEASANT DEATHS *DETER* PEOPLE! THEY LOOK AT THEM AND THINK, *"OH, I DON'T WANT THAT TO HAPPEN TO ME,"* AND THEY STOP REBELLING!
OF COURSE, SIRE. I BOW TO YOUR WISDOM.
FETCH THE SPY, WOULD YOU? HE NEEDS TO BE CONGRATULATED.
I'M ALREADY HERE, SIRE.
AH, YES. GOOD JOB. VERY GOOD JOB AT THE WHOLE BETRAYAL THING.
ONCE KRANNIG IS DEAD AND HIS PESKY REBELS HAVE BEEN HUNTED DOWN, YOU HAVE MY WORD THAT THIS *CORVUS GLAIVE* FELLOW WILL DIE A MOST HORRIBLE DEATH.

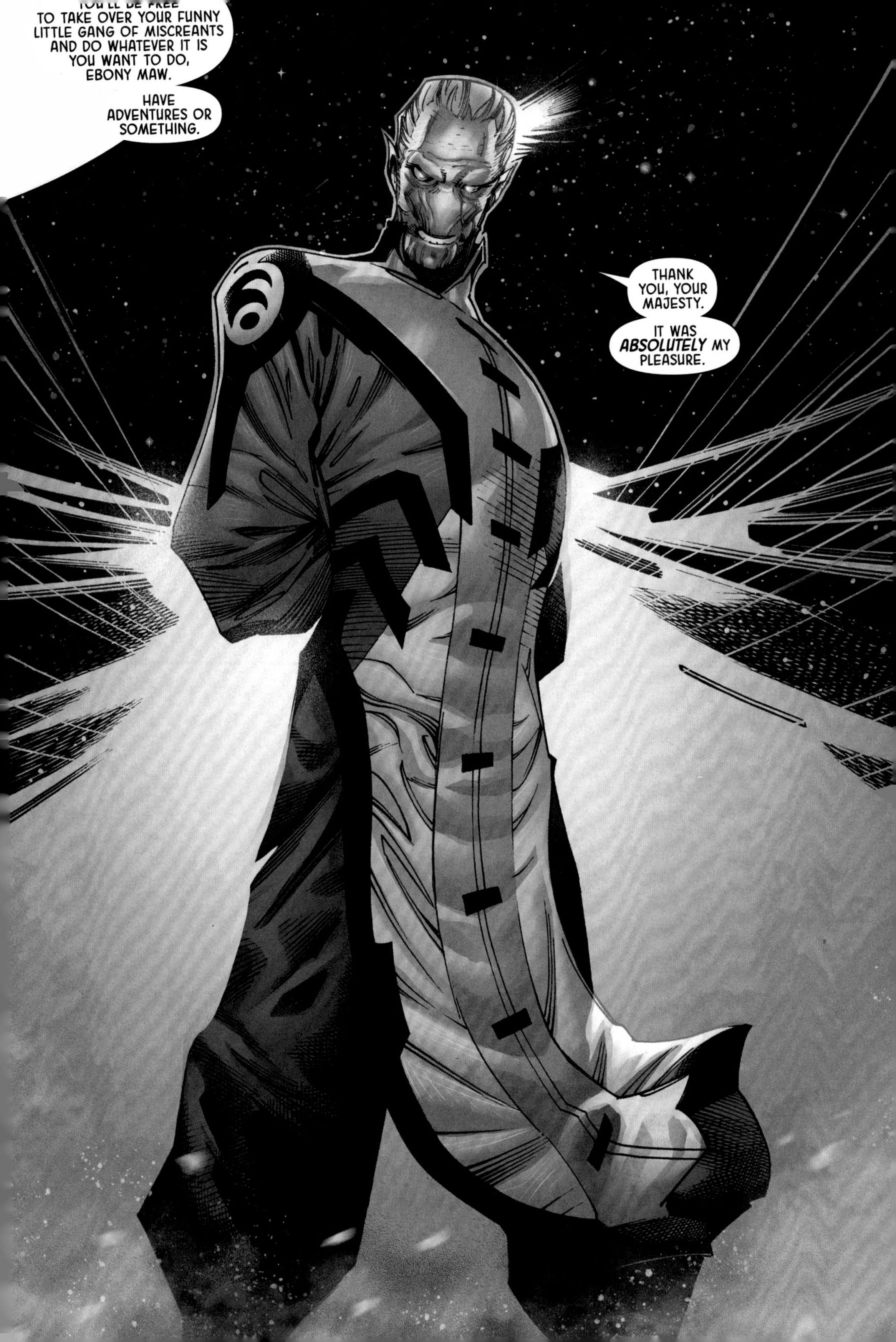
TO TAKE OVER YOUR FUNNY LITTLE GANG OF MISCREANTS AND DO WHATEVER IT IS YOU WANT TO DO, EBONY MAW.
HAVE ADVENTURES OR SOMETHING.
THANK YOU, YOUR MAJESTY.
IT WAS ABSOLUTELY MY PLEASURE.

5

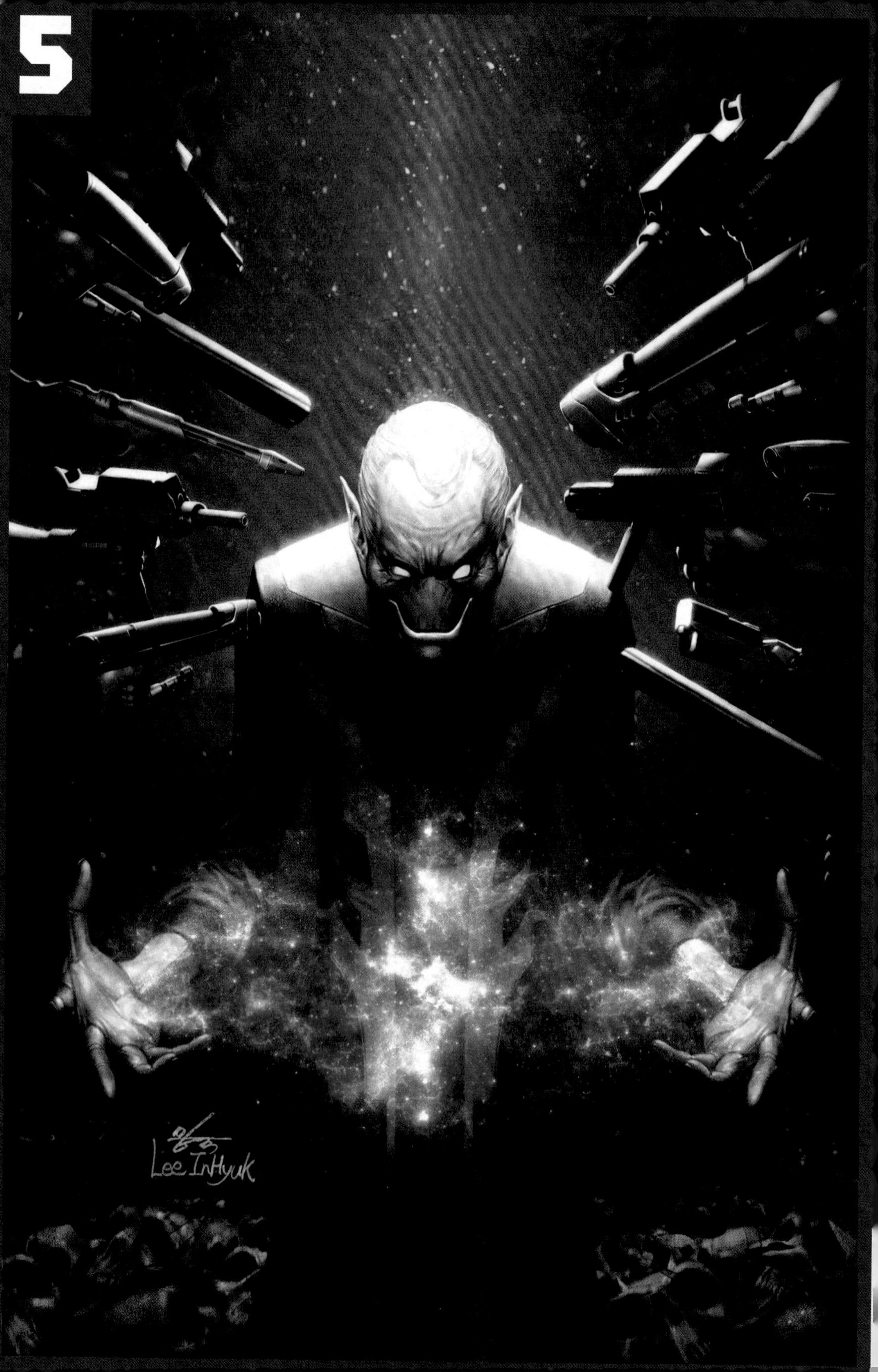
Lee InHyuk

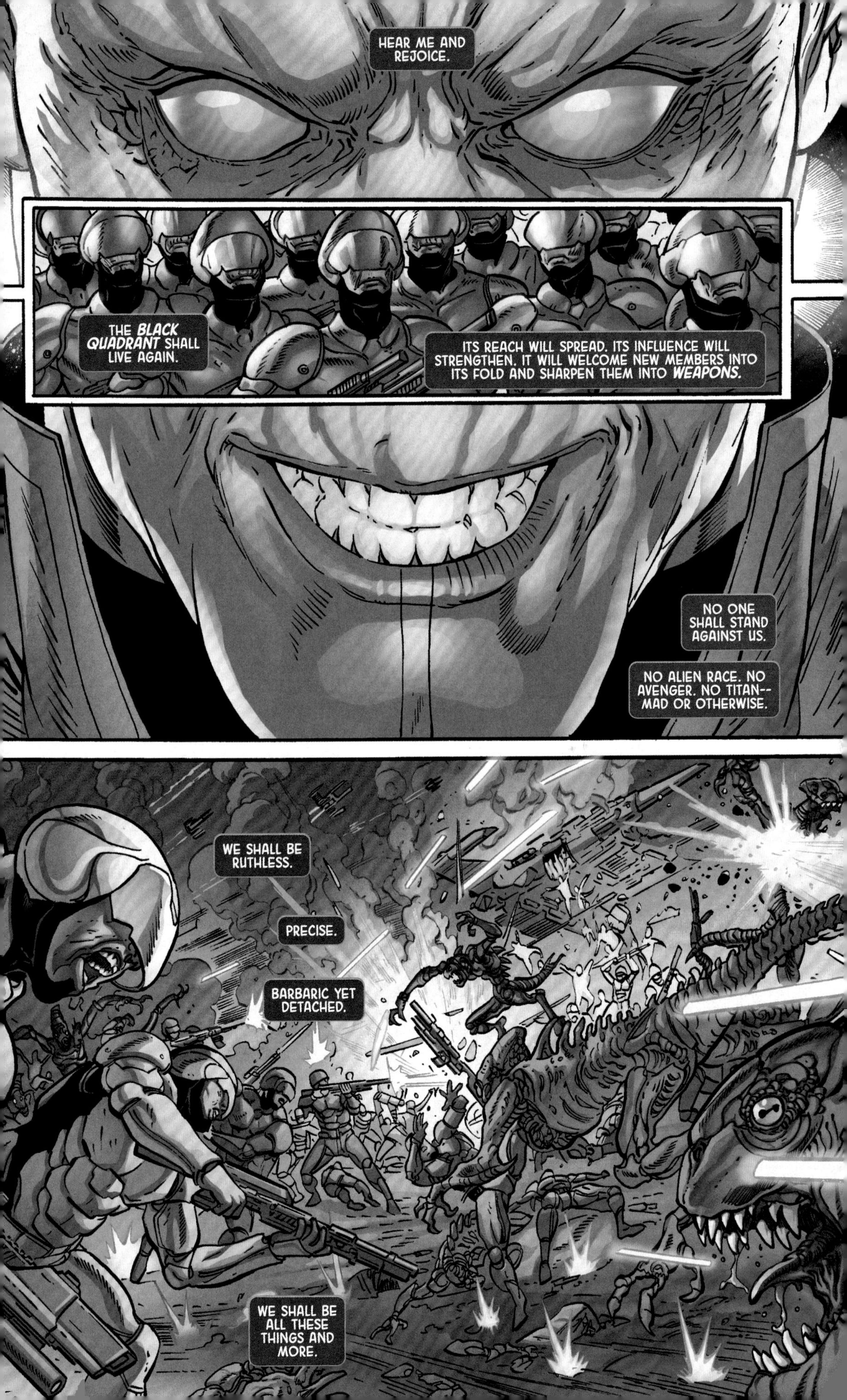
HEAR ME AND REJOICE.
THE BLACK QUADRANT SHALL LIVE AGAIN.
ITS REACH WILL SPREAD. ITS INFLUENCE WILL STRENGTHEN. IT WILL WELCOME NEW MEMBERS INTO ITS FOLD AND SHARPEN THEM INTO WEAPONS.
NO ONE SHALL STAND AGAINST US.
NO ALIEN RACE. NO AVENGER. NO TITAN-- MAD OR OTHERWISE.
WE SHALL BE RUTHLESS.
PRECISE.
BARBARIC YET DETACHED.
WE SHALL BE ALL THESE THINGS AND MORE.

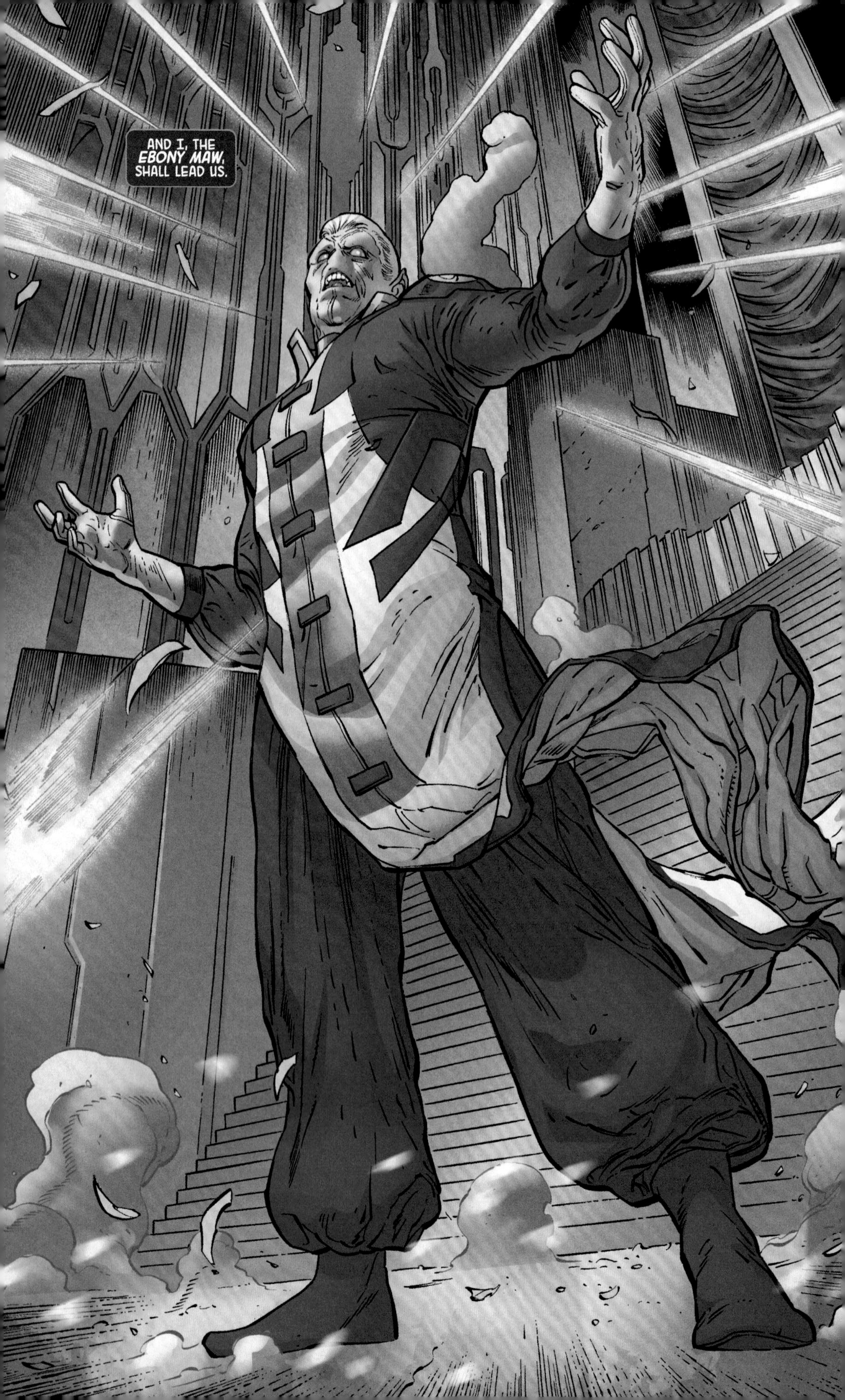
AND I, THE EBONY MAW, SHALL LEAD US.

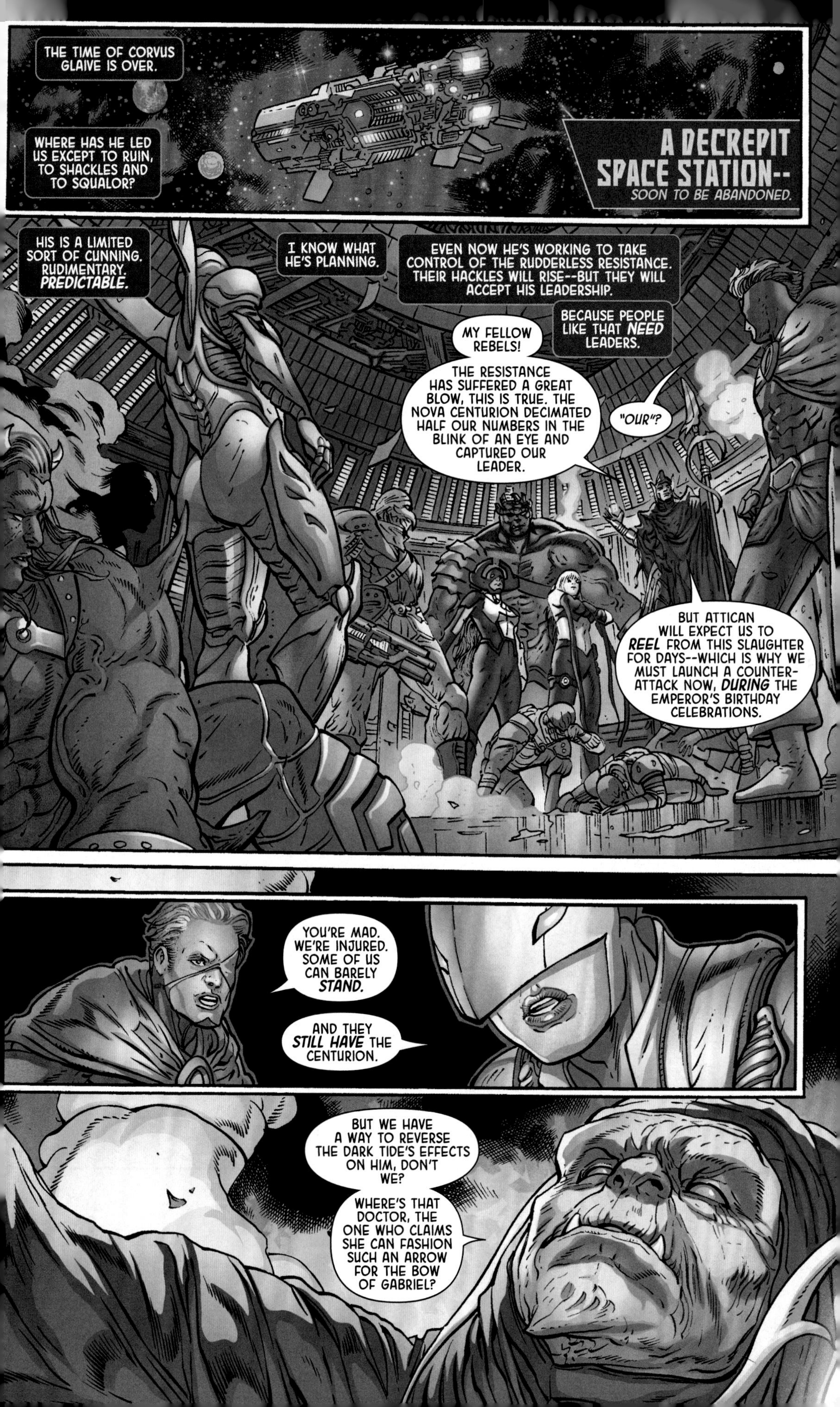

THE TIME OF CORVUS GLAIVE IS OVER.
WHERE HAS HE LED US EXCEPT TO RUIN, TO SHACKLES AND TO SQUALOR?
A DECREPIT SPACE STATION-- SOON TO BE ABANDONED.
HIS IS A LIMITED SORT OF CUNNING. RUDIMENTARY. PREDICTABLE.
I KNOW WHAT HE'S PLANNING.
EVEN NOW HE'S WORKING TO TAKE CONTROL OF THE RUDDERLESS RESISTANCE. THEIR HACKLES WILL RISE--BUT THEY WILL ACCEPT HIS LEADERSHIP.
BECAUSE PEOPLE LIKE THAT NEED LEADERS.
MY FELLOW REBELS!
THE RESISTANCE HAS SUFFERED A GREAT BLOW, THIS IS TRUE. THE NOVA CENTURION DECIMATED HALF OUR NUMBERS IN THE BLINK OF AN EYE AND CAPTURED OUR LEADER.
"OUR"?
BUT ATTICAN WILL EXPECT US TO REEL FROM THIS SLAUGHTER FOR DAYS--WHICH IS WHY WE MUST LAUNCH A COUNTER-ATTACK NOW, DURING THE EMPEROR'S BIRTHDAY CELEBRATIONS.
YOU'RE MAD. WE'RE INJURED. SOME OF US CAN BARELY STAND.
AND THEY STILL HAVE THE CENTURION.
BUT WE HAVE A WAY TO REVERSE THE DARK TIDE'S EFFECTS ON HIM, DON'T WE?
WHERE'S THAT DOCTOR, THE ONE WHO CLAIMS SHE CAN FASHION SUCH AN ARROW FOR THE BOW OF GABRIEL?

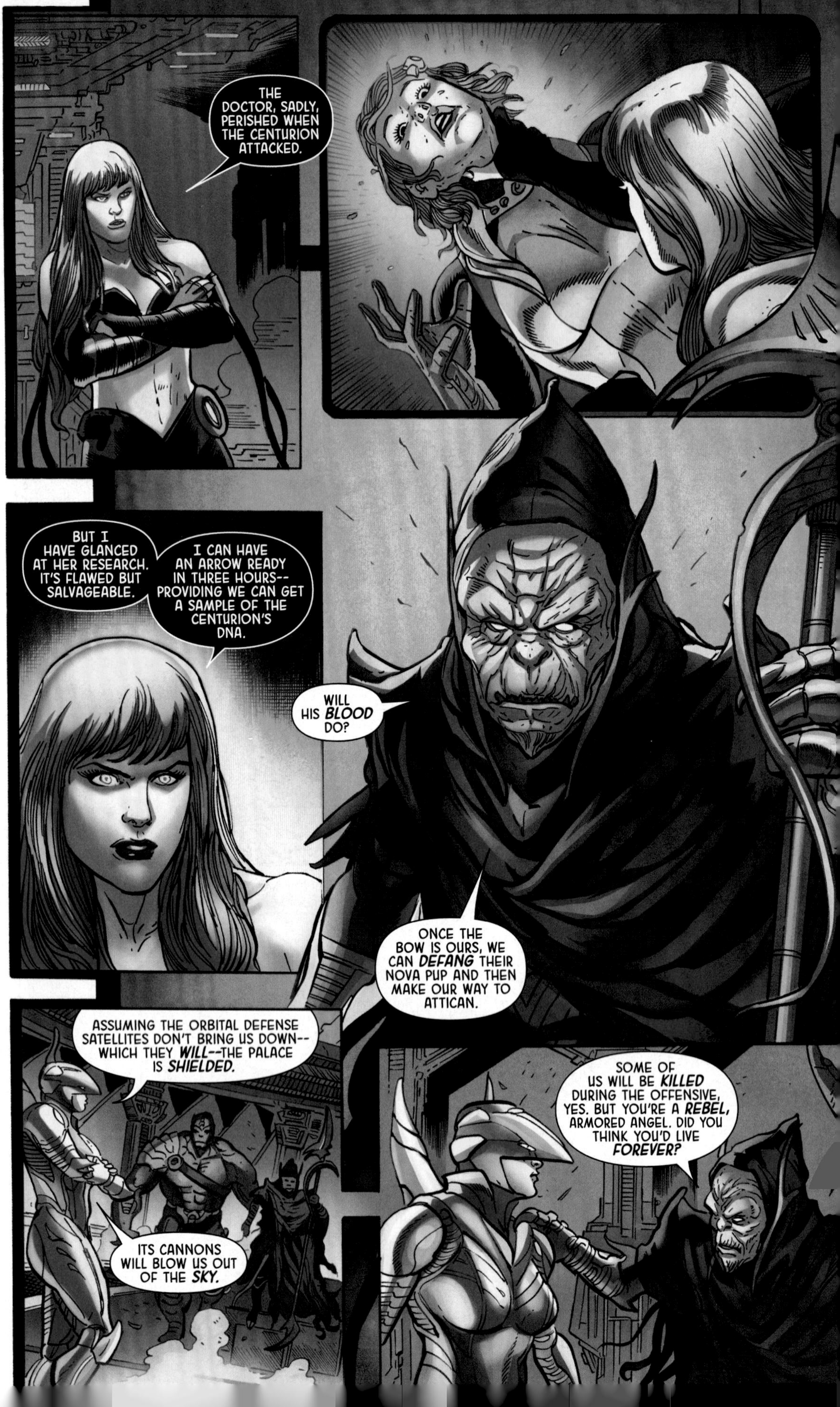
THE DOCTOR, SADLY, PERISHED WHEN THE CENTURION ATTACKED.
BUT I HAVE GLANCED AT HER RESEARCH. IT'S FLAWED BUT SALVAGEABLE.
I CAN HAVE AN ARROW READY IN THREE HOURS-- PROVIDING WE CAN GET A SAMPLE OF THE CENTURION'S DNA.
WILL HIS *BLOOD* DO?
ONCE THE BOW IS OURS, WE CAN *DEFANG* THEIR NOVA PUP AND THEN MAKE OUR WAY TO ATTICAN.
ASSUMING THE ORBITAL DEFENSE SATELLITES DON'T BRING US DOWN-- WHICH THEY *WILL*--THE PALACE IS *SHIELDED.*
ITS CANNONS WILL BLOW US OUT OF THE *SKY.*
SOME OF US WILL BE *KILLED* DURING THE OFFENSIVE, YES. BUT YOU'RE A *REBEL,* ARMORED ANGEL. DID YOU THINK YOU'D LIVE *FOREVER?*

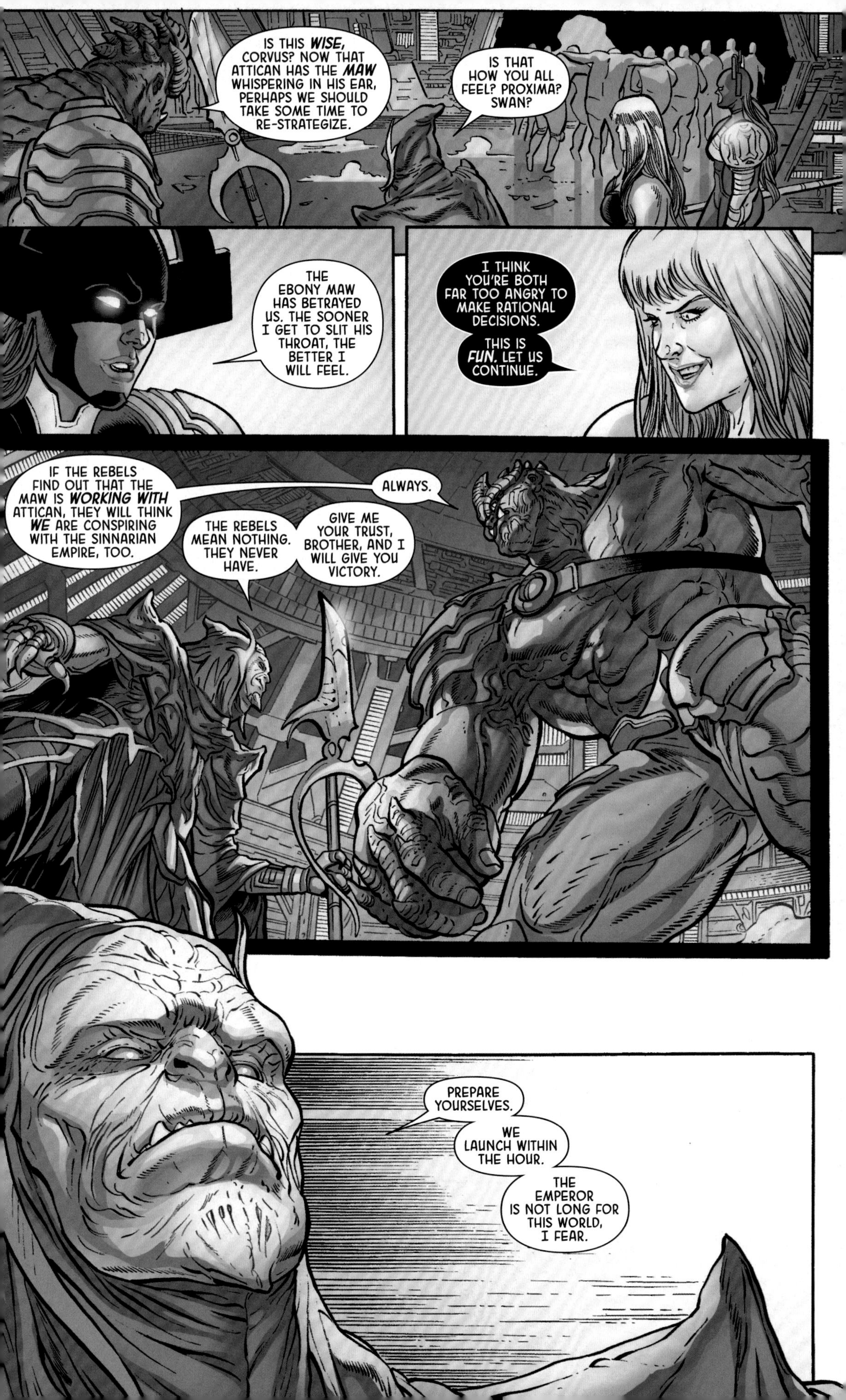
IS THIS WISE, CORVUS? NOW THAT ATTICAN HAS THE MAW WHISPERING IN HIS EAR, PERHAPS WE SHOULD TAKE SOME TIME TO RE-STRATEGIZE.
IS THAT HOW YOU ALL FEEL? PROXIMA? SWAN?
THE EBONY MAW HAS BETRAYED US. THE SOONER I GET TO SLIT HIS THROAT, THE BETTER I WILL FEEL.
I THINK YOU'RE BOTH FAR TOO ANGRY TO MAKE RATIONAL DECISIONS.
THIS IS FUN. LET US CONTINUE.
IF THE REBELS FIND OUT THAT THE MAW IS WORKING WITH ATTICAN, THEY WILL THINK WE ARE CONSPIRING WITH THE SINNARIAN EMPIRE, TOO.
ALWAYS.
THE REBELS MEAN NOTHING. THEY NEVER HAVE.
GIVE ME YOUR TRUST, BROTHER, AND I WILL GIVE YOU VICTORY.
PREPARE YOURSELVES.
WE LAUNCH WITHIN THE HOUR.
THE EMPEROR IS NOT LONG FOR THIS WORLD, I FEAR.

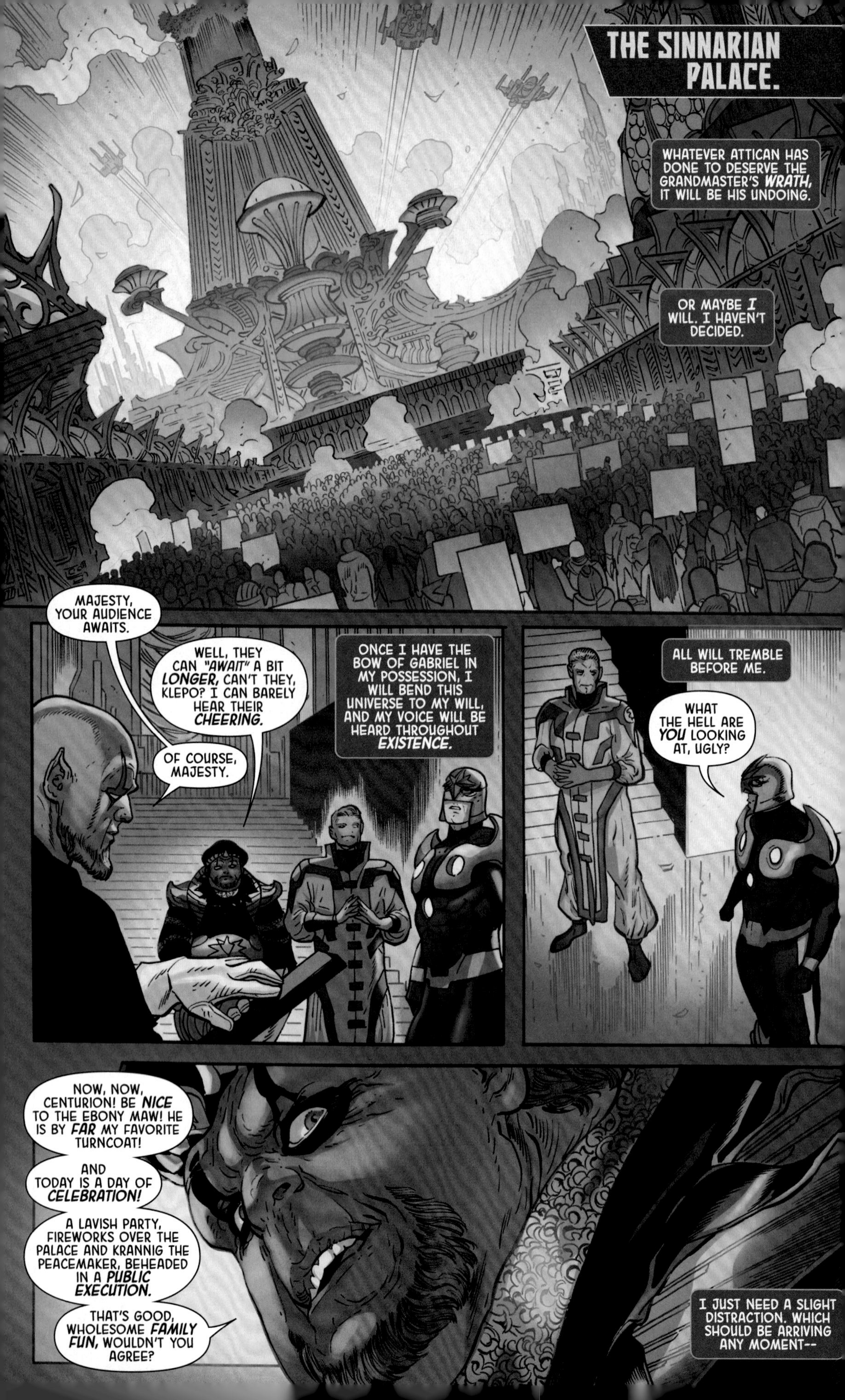
THE SINNARIAN PALACE.
WHATEVER ATTICAN HAS DONE TO DESERVE THE GRANDMASTER'S WRATH, IT WILL BE HIS UNDOING.
OR MAYBE I WILL. I HAVEN'T DECIDED.
MAJESTY, YOUR AUDIENCE AWAITS.
WELL, THEY CAN "AWAIT" A BIT LONGER, CAN'T THEY, KLEPO? I CAN BARELY HEAR THEIR CHEERING.
OF COURSE, MAJESTY.
ONCE I HAVE THE BOW OF GABRIEL IN MY POSSESSION, I WILL BEND THIS UNIVERSE TO MY WILL, AND MY VOICE WILL BE HEARD THROUGHOUT EXISTENCE.
ALL WILL TREMBLE BEFORE ME.
WHAT THE HELL ARE YOU LOOKING AT, UGLY?
NOW, NOW, CENTURION! BE NICE TO THE EBONY MAW! HE IS BY FAR MY FAVORITE TURNCOAT!
AND TODAY IS A DAY OF CELEBRATION!
A LAVISH PARTY, FIREWORKS OVER THE PALACE AND KRANNIG THE PEACEMAKER, BEHEADED IN A PUBLIC EXECUTION.
THAT'S GOOD, WHOLESOME FAMILY FUN, WOULDN'T YOU AGREE?
I JUST NEED A SLIGHT DISTRACTION. WHICH SHOULD BE ARRIVING ANY MOMENT--

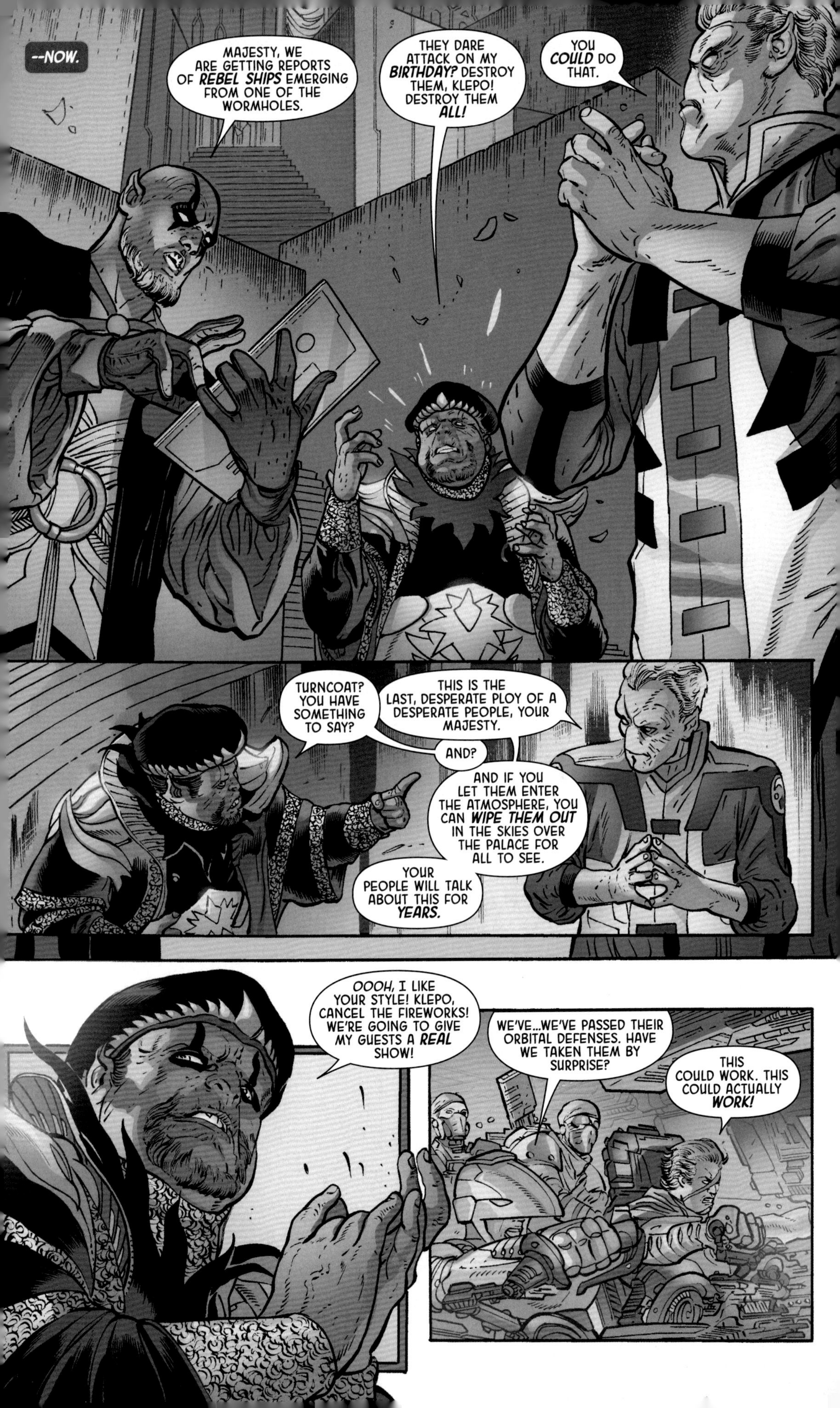

--NOW.
MAJESTY, WE ARE GETTING REPORTS OF REBEL SHIPS EMERGING FROM ONE OF THE WORMHOLES.
THEY DARE ATTACK ON MY BIRTHDAY? DESTROY THEM, KLEPO! DESTROY THEM ALL!
YOU COULD DO THAT.
TURNCOAT? YOU HAVE SOMETHING TO SAY?
THIS IS THE LAST, DESPERATE PLOY OF A DESPERATE PEOPLE, YOUR MAJESTY.
AND?
AND IF YOU LET THEM ENTER THE ATMOSPHERE, YOU CAN WIPE THEM OUT IN THE SKIES OVER THE PALACE FOR ALL TO SEE.
YOUR PEOPLE WILL TALK ABOUT THIS FOR YEARS.
OOOH, I LIKE YOUR STYLE! KLEPO, CANCEL THE FIREWORKS! WE'RE GOING TO GIVE MY GUESTS A REAL SHOW!
WE'VE...WE'VE PASSED THEIR ORBITAL DEFENSES. HAVE WE TAKEN THEM BY SURPRISE?
THIS COULD WORK. THIS COULD ACTUALLY WORK!

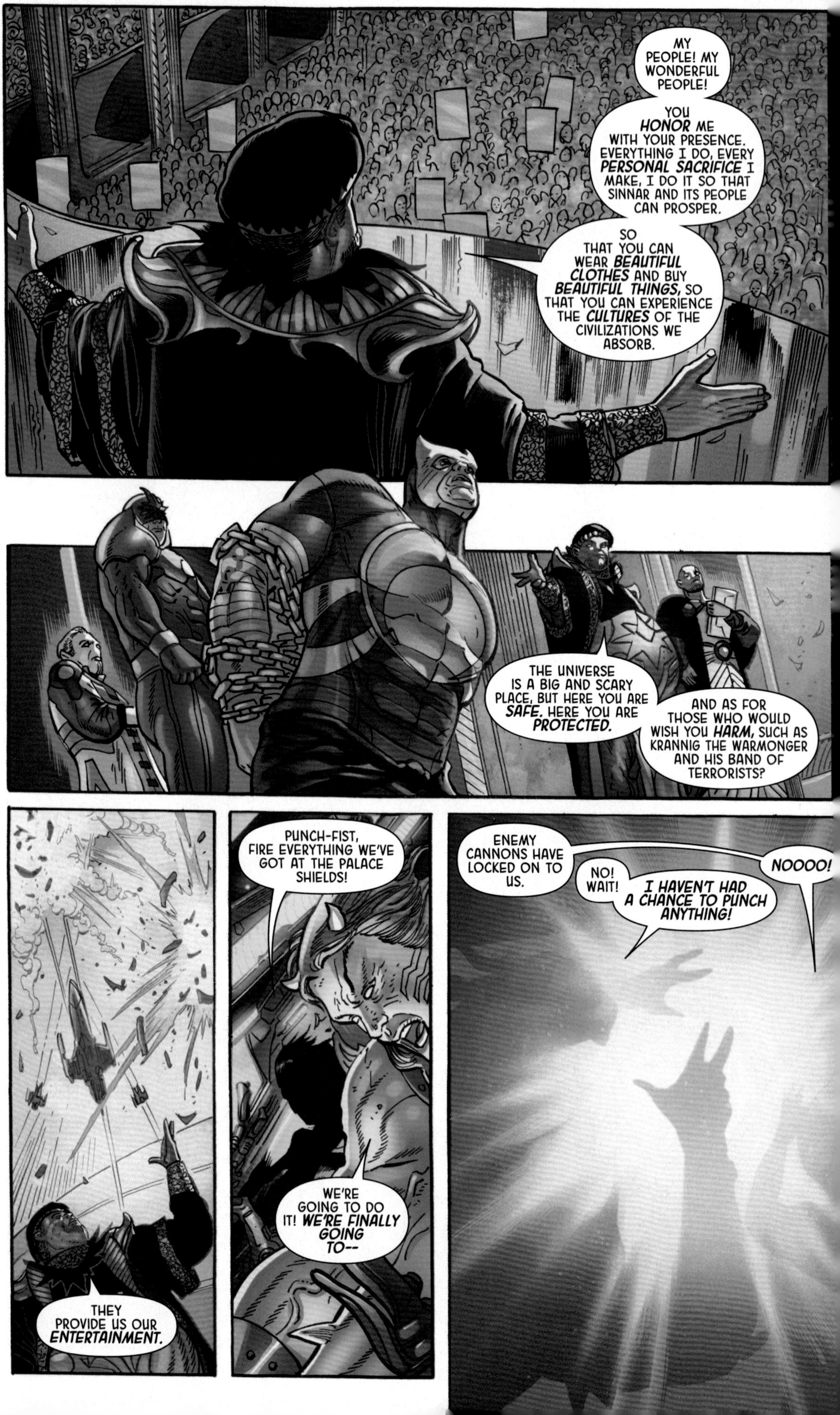
MY PEOPLE! MY WONDERFUL PEOPLE!
YOU HONOR ME WITH YOUR PRESENCE. EVERYTHING I DO, EVERY PERSONAL SACRIFICE I MAKE, I DO IT SO THAT SINNAR AND ITS PEOPLE CAN PROSPER.
SO THAT YOU CAN WEAR BEAUTIFUL CLOTHES AND BUY BEAUTIFUL THINGS, SO THAT YOU CAN EXPERIENCE THE CULTURES OF THE CIVILIZATIONS WE ABSORB.
THE UNIVERSE IS A BIG AND SCARY PLACE, BUT HERE YOU ARE SAFE. HERE YOU ARE PROTECTED.
AND AS FOR THOSE WHO WOULD WISH YOU HARM, SUCH AS KRANNIG THE WARMONGER AND HIS BAND OF TERRORISTS?
THEY PROVIDE US OUR ENTERTAINMENT.
PUNCH-FIST, FIRE EVERYTHING WE'VE GOT AT THE PALACE SHIELDS!
WE'RE GOING TO DO IT! WE'RE FINALLY GOING TO--
ENEMY CANNONS HAVE LOCKED ON TO US.
NO! WAIT!
I HAVEN'T HAD A CHANCE TO PUNCH ANYTHING!
NOOOO!

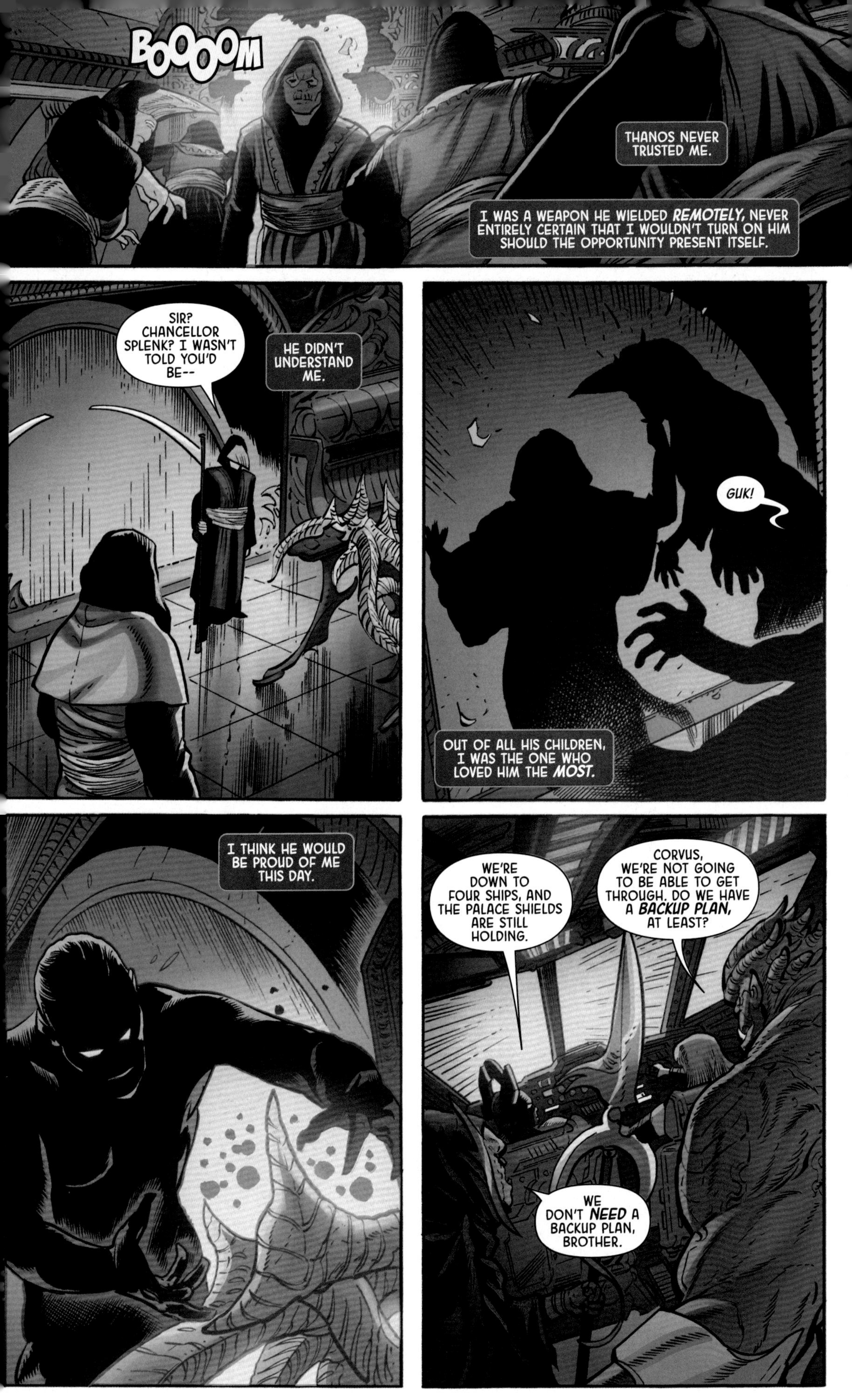
BOOOOM
THANOS NEVER TRUSTED ME.
I WAS A WEAPON HE WIELDED *REMOTELY,* NEVER ENTIRELY CERTAIN THAT I WOULDN'T TURN ON HIM SHOULD THE OPPORTUNITY PRESENT ITSELF.
SIR? CHANCELLOR SPLENK? I WASN'T TOLD YOU'D BE--
HE DIDN'T UNDERSTAND ME.
GUK!
OUT OF ALL HIS CHILDREN, I WAS THE ONE WHO LOVED HIM THE *MOST.*
I THINK HE WOULD BE PROUD OF ME THIS DAY.
WE'RE DOWN TO FOUR SHIPS, AND THE PALACE SHIELDS ARE STILL HOLDING.
CORVUS, WE'RE NOT GOING TO BE ABLE TO GET THROUGH. DO WE HAVE A *BACKUP PLAN,* AT LEAST?
WE DON'T *NEED* A BACKUP PLAN, BROTHER.

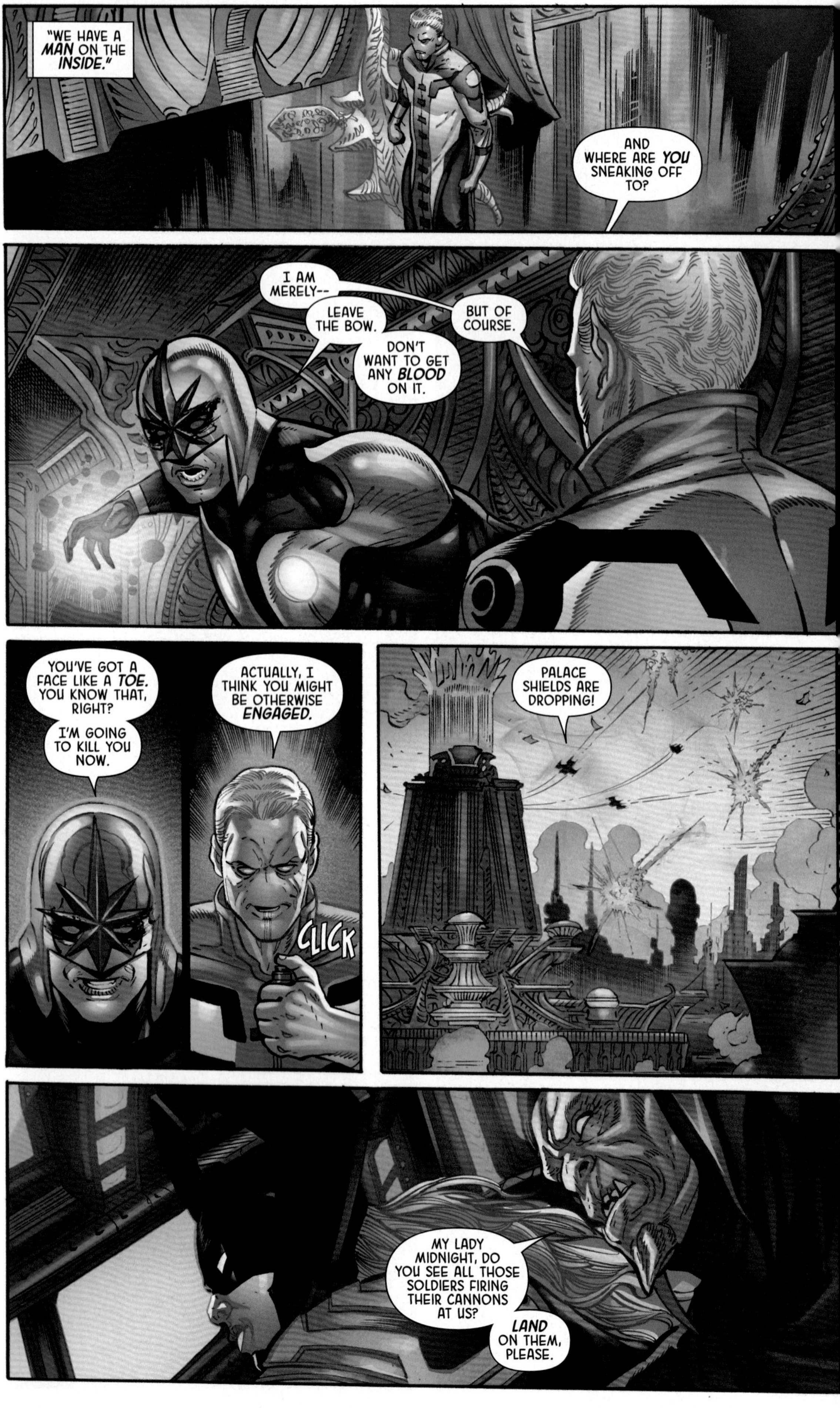
"WE HAVE A MAN ON THE INSIDE."
AND WHERE ARE YOU SNEAKING OFF TO?
I AM MERELY--
BUT OF COURSE.
LEAVE THE BOW.
DON'T WANT TO GET ANY BLOOD ON IT.
YOU'VE GOT A FACE LIKE A TOE. YOU KNOW THAT, RIGHT?
I'M GOING TO KILL YOU NOW.
ACTUALLY, I THINK YOU MIGHT BE OTHERWISE ENGAGED.
CLICK
PALACE SHIELDS ARE DROPPING!
MY LADY MIDNIGHT, DO YOU SEE ALL THOSE SOLDIERS FIRING THEIR CANNONS AT US?
LAND ON THEM, PLEASE.

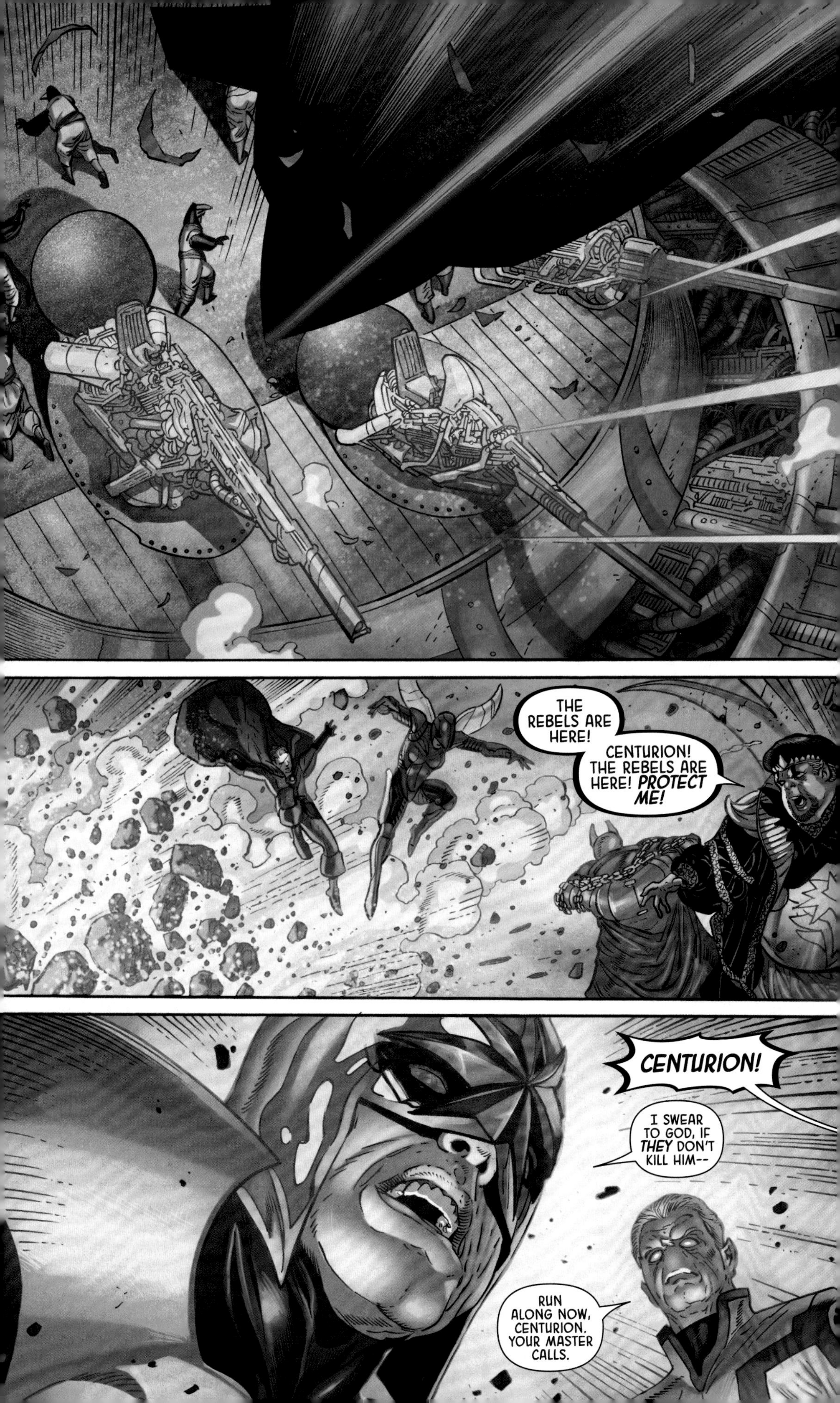

THE REBELS ARE HERE!
CENTURION! THE REBELS ARE HERE! PROTECT ME!
CENTURION!
I SWEAR TO GOD, IF THEY DON'T KILL HIM--
RUN ALONG NOW, CENTURION. YOUR MASTER CALLS.

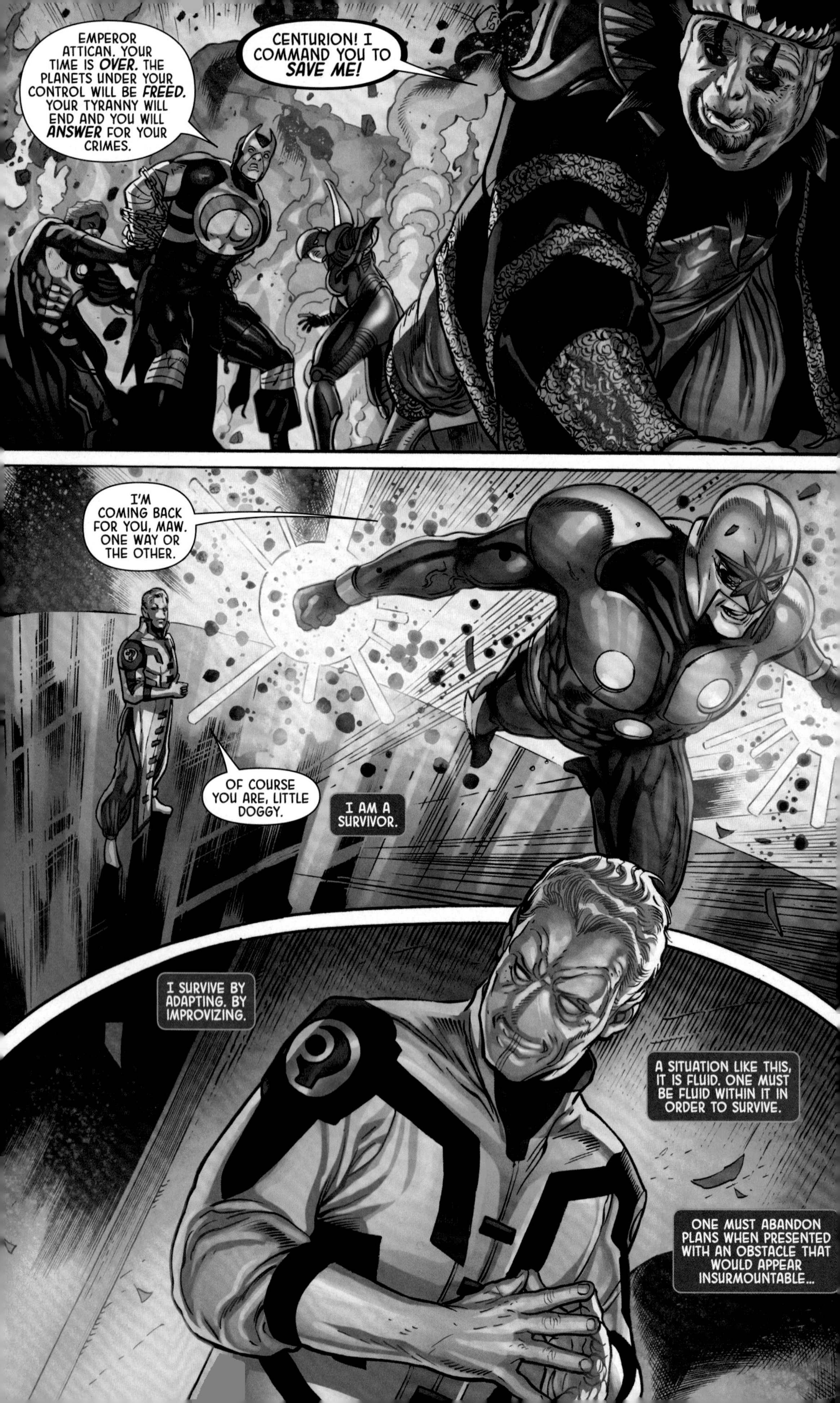
EMPEROR ATTICAN. YOUR TIME IS OVER. THE PLANETS UNDER YOUR CONTROL WILL BE FREED. YOUR TYRANNY WILL END AND YOU WILL ANSWER FOR YOUR CRIMES.
CENTURION! I COMMAND YOU TO SAVE ME!
I'M COMING BACK FOR YOU, MAW. ONE WAY OR THE OTHER.
OF COURSE YOU ARE, LITTLE DOGGY.
I AM A SURVIVOR.
I SURVIVE BY ADAPTING. BY IMPROVIZING.
A SITUATION LIKE THIS, IT IS FLUID. ONE MUST BE FLUID WITHIN IT IN ORDER TO SURVIVE.
ONE MUST ABANDON PLANS WHEN PRESENTED WITH AN OBSTACLE THAT WOULD APPEAR INSURMOUNTABLE...

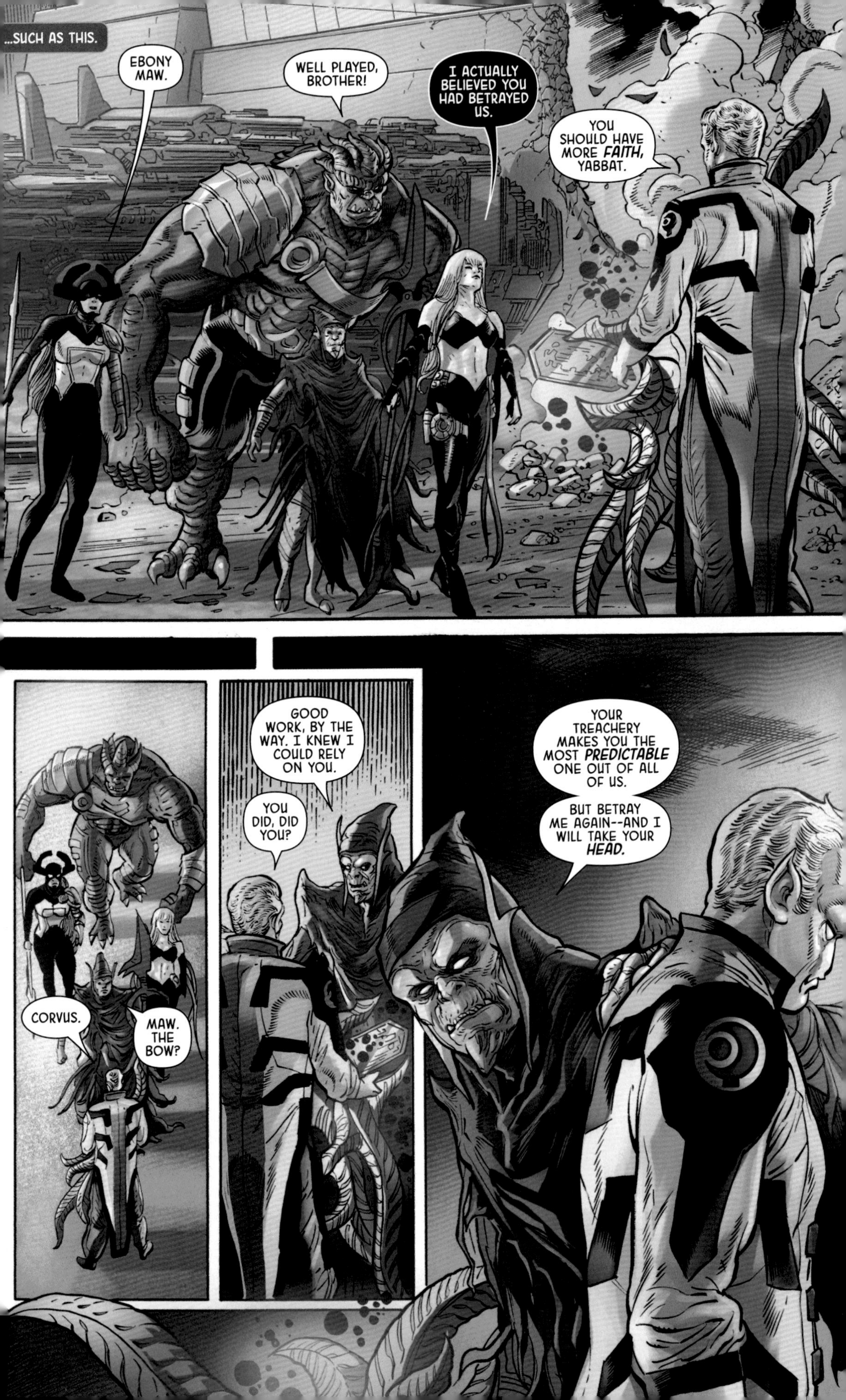
...SUCH AS THIS.
EBONY MAW.
WELL PLAYED, BROTHER!
I ACTUALLY BELIEVED YOU HAD BETRAYED US.
YOU SHOULD HAVE MORE FAITH, YABBAT.
CORVUS.
MAW. THE BOW?
GOOD WORK, BY THE WAY. I KNEW I COULD RELY ON YOU.
YOU DID, DID YOU?
YOUR TREACHERY MAKES YOU THE MOST PREDICTABLE ONE OUT OF ALL OF US.
BUT BETRAY ME AGAIN--AND I WILL TAKE YOUR HEAD.

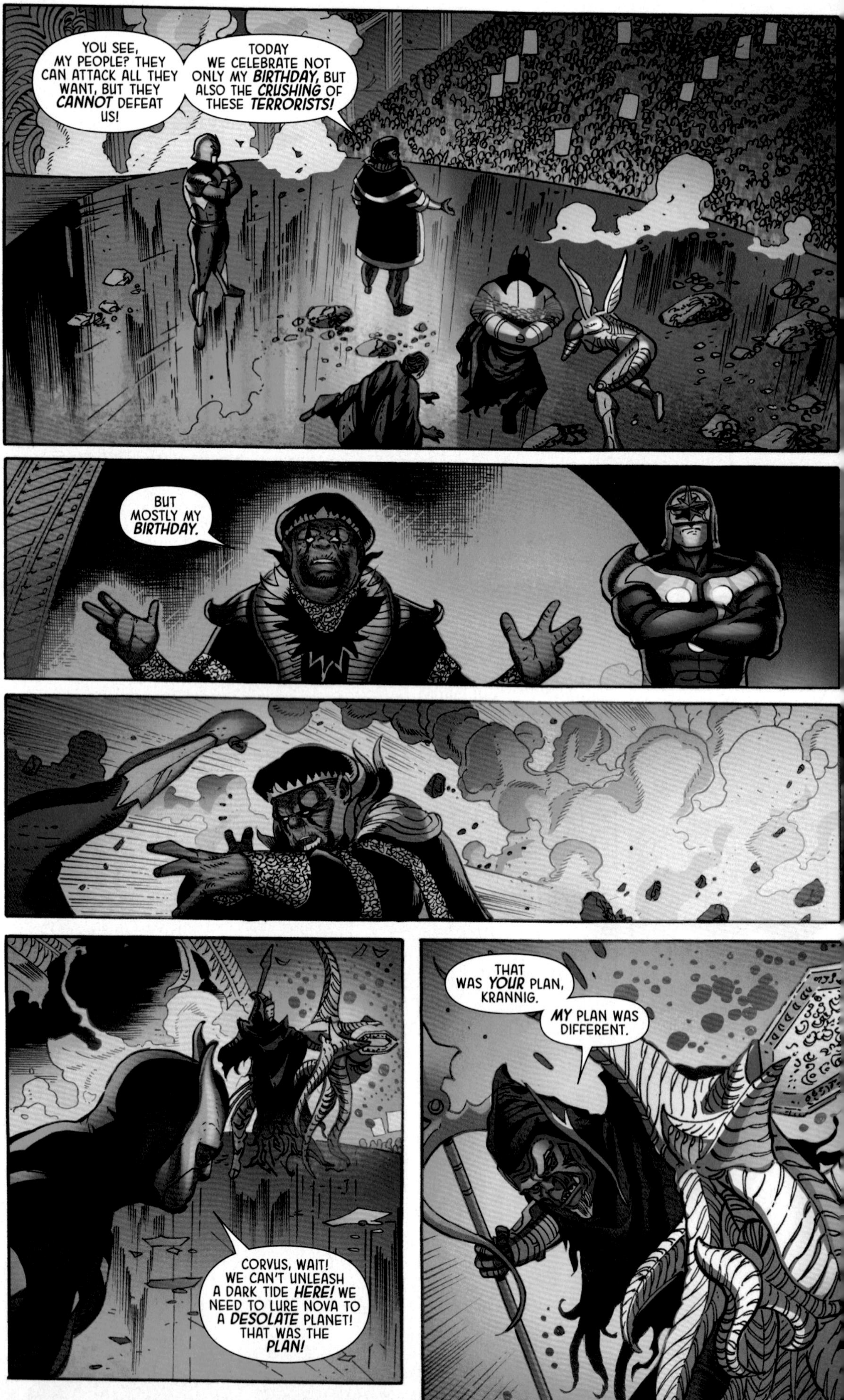
YOU SEE, MY PEOPLE? THEY CAN ATTACK ALL THEY WANT, BUT THEY CANNOT DEFEAT US!
TODAY WE CELEBRATE NOT ONLY MY BIRTHDAY, BUT ALSO THE CRUSHING OF THESE TERRORISTS!
BUT MOSTLY MY BIRTHDAY.
CORVUS, WAIT! WE CAN'T UNLEASH A DARK TIDE HERE! WE NEED TO LURE NOVA TO A DESOLATE PLANET! THAT WAS THE PLAN!
THAT WAS YOUR PLAN, KRANNIG.
MY PLAN WAS DIFFERENT.

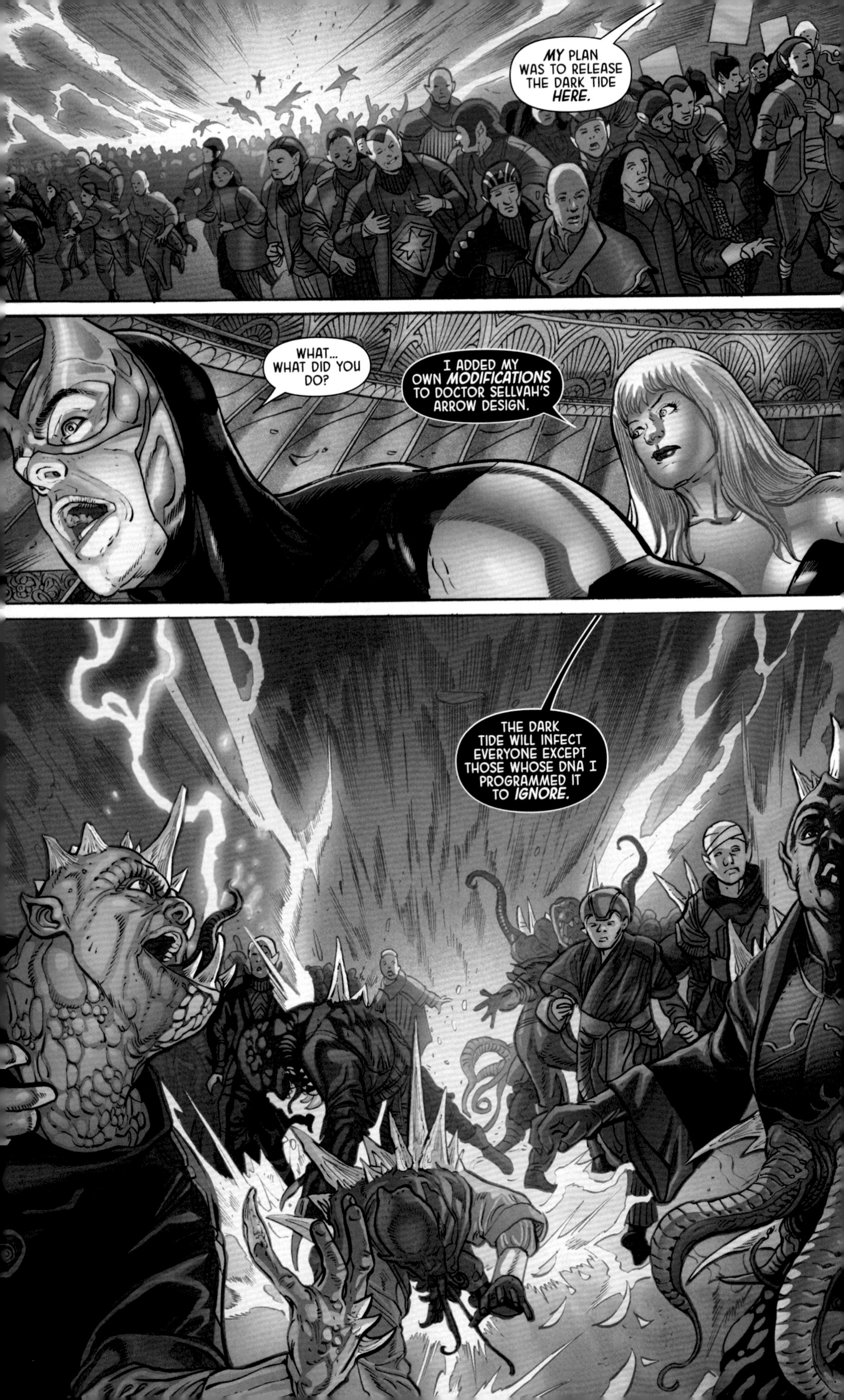
MY PLAN WAS TO RELEASE THE DARK TIDE HERE.
WHAT... WHAT DID YOU DO?
I ADDED MY OWN MODIFICATIONS TO DOCTOR SELLVAH'S ARROW DESIGN.
THE DARK TIDE WILL INFECT EVERYONE EXCEPT THOSE WHOSE DNA I PROGRAMMED IT TO IGNORE.

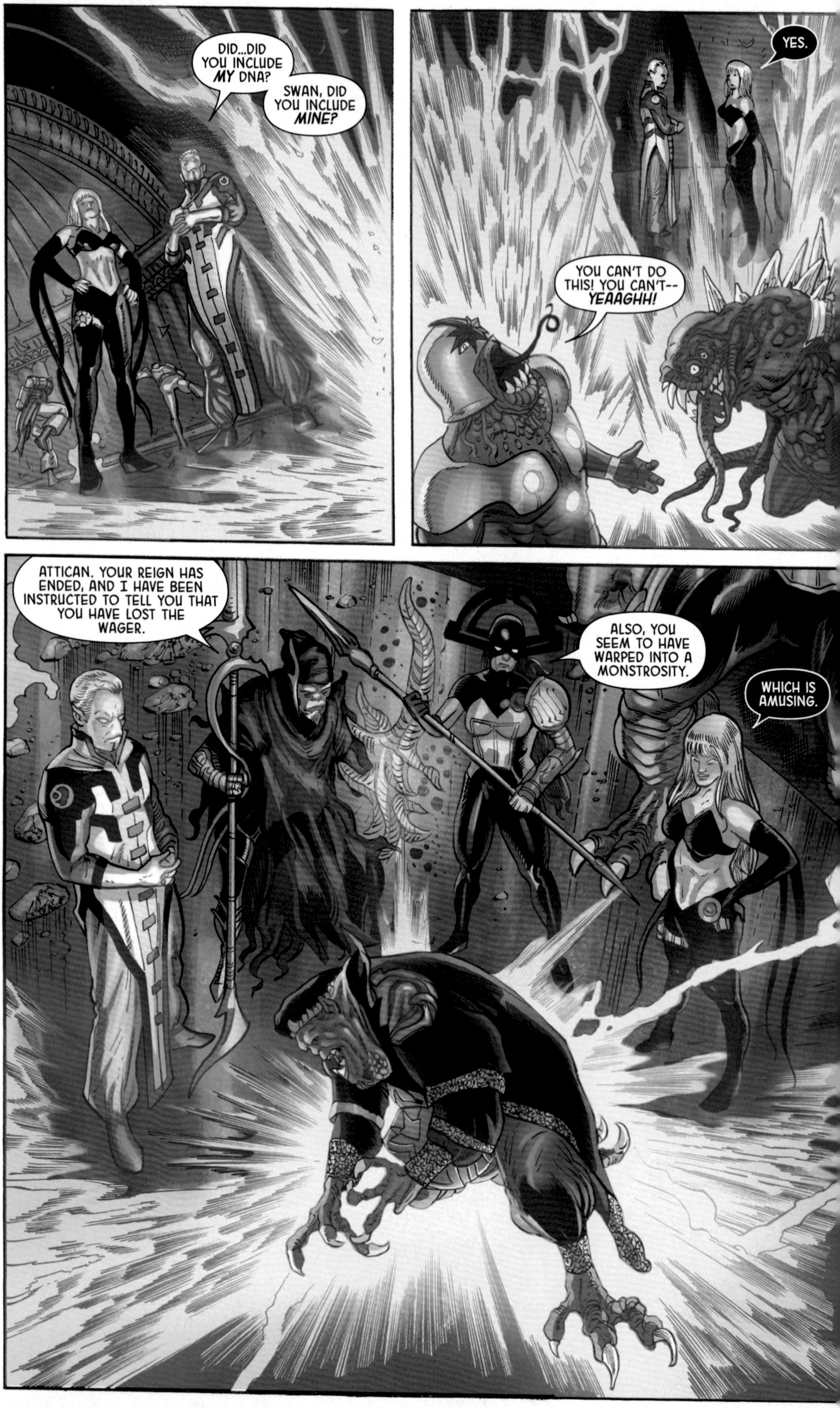
DID...DID YOU INCLUDE MY DNA?
SWAN, DID YOU INCLUDE MINE?
YES.
YOU CAN'T DO THIS! YOU CAN'T-- YEAAGHH!
ATTICAN. YOUR REIGN HAS ENDED, AND I HAVE BEEN INSTRUCTED TO TELL YOU THAT YOU HAVE LOST THE WAGER.
ALSO, YOU SEEM TO HAVE WARPED INTO A MONSTROSITY.
WHICH IS AMUSING.

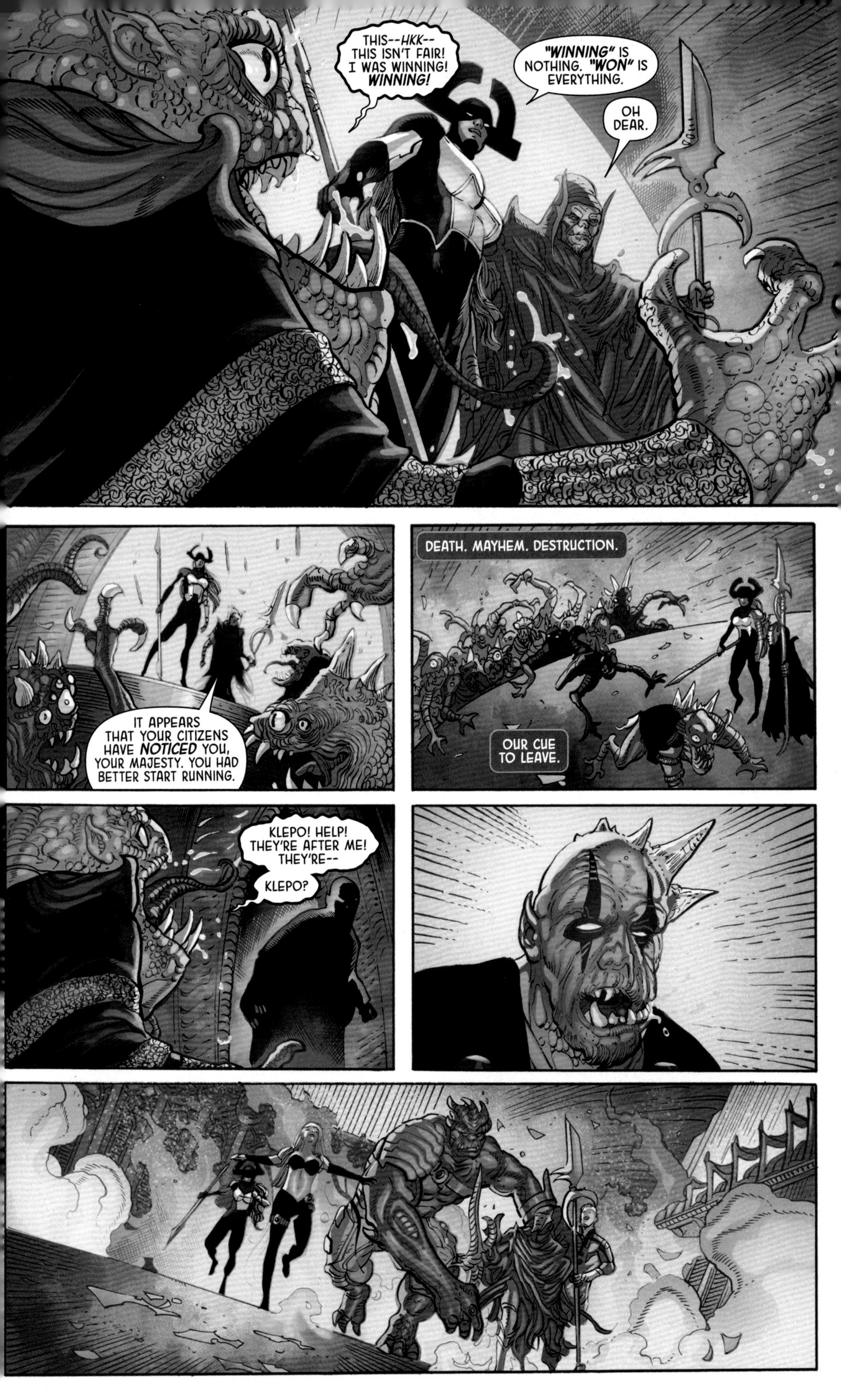
THIS--HKK-- THIS ISN'T FAIR! I WAS WINNING! WINNING!
"WINNING" IS NOTHING. "WON" IS EVERYTHING.
OH DEAR.
IT APPEARS THAT YOUR CITIZENS HAVE NOTICED YOU, YOUR MAJESTY. YOU HAD BETTER START RUNNING.
DEATH. MAYHEM. DESTRUCTION.
OUR CUE TO LEAVE.
KLEPO! HELP! THEY'RE AFTER ME! THEY'RE--
KLEPO?

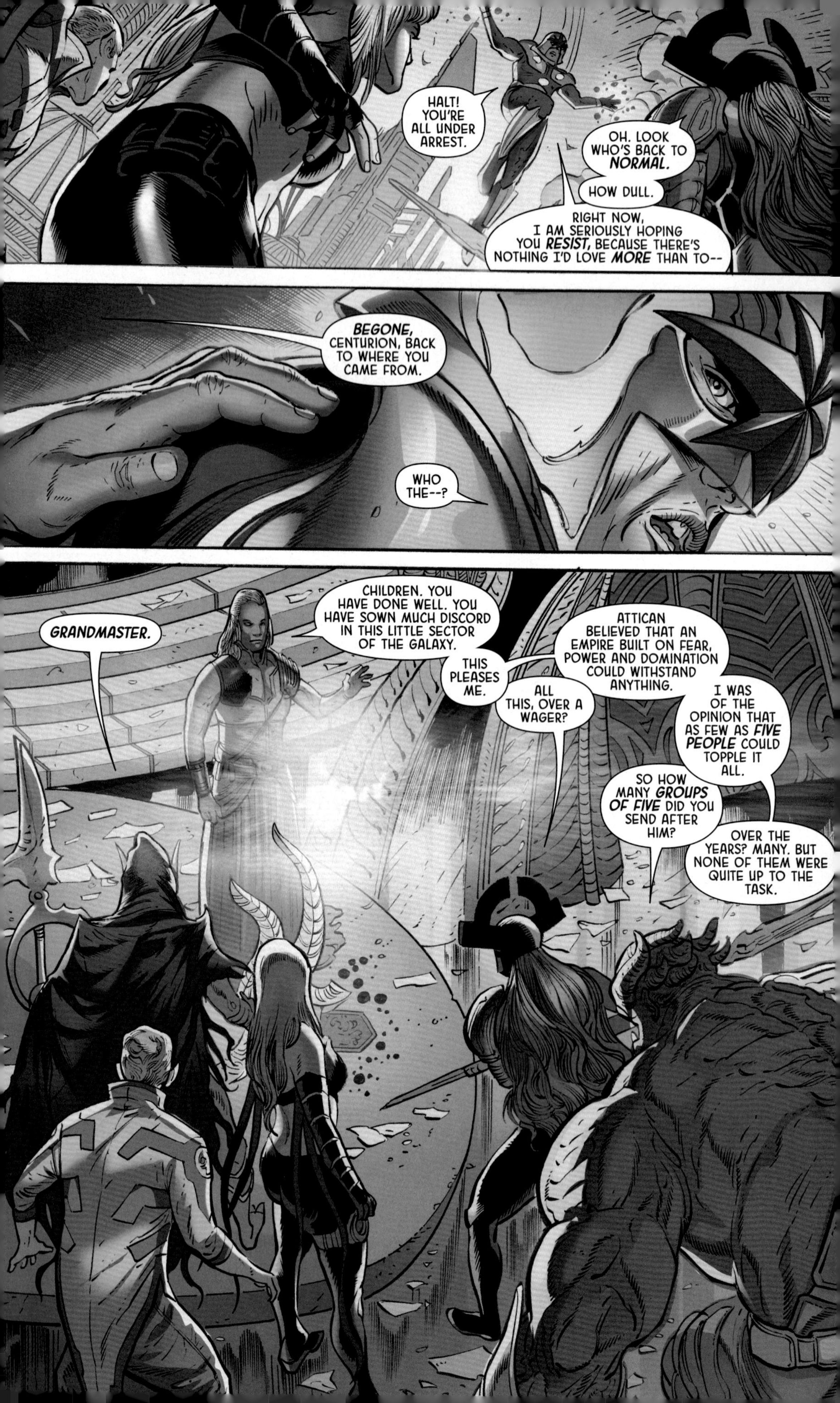
HALT! YOU'RE ALL UNDER ARREST.
OH. LOOK WHO'S BACK TO NORMAL.
HOW DULL.
RIGHT NOW, I AM SERIOUSLY HOPING YOU RESIST, BECAUSE THERE'S NOTHING I'D LOVE MORE THAN TO--
BEGONE, CENTURION, BACK TO WHERE YOU CAME FROM.
WHO THE--?
GRANDMASTER.
CHILDREN. YOU HAVE DONE WELL. YOU HAVE SOWN MUCH DISCORD IN THIS LITTLE SECTOR OF THE GALAXY.
THIS PLEASES ME.
ALL THIS, OVER A WAGER?
ATTICAN BELIEVED THAT AN EMPIRE BUILT ON FEAR, POWER AND DOMINATION COULD WITHSTAND ANYTHING.
I WAS OF THE OPINION THAT AS FEW AS FIVE PEOPLE COULD TOPPLE IT ALL.
SO HOW MANY GROUPS OF FIVE DID YOU SEND AFTER HIM?
OVER THE YEARS? MANY. BUT NONE OF THEM WERE QUITE UP TO THE TASK.

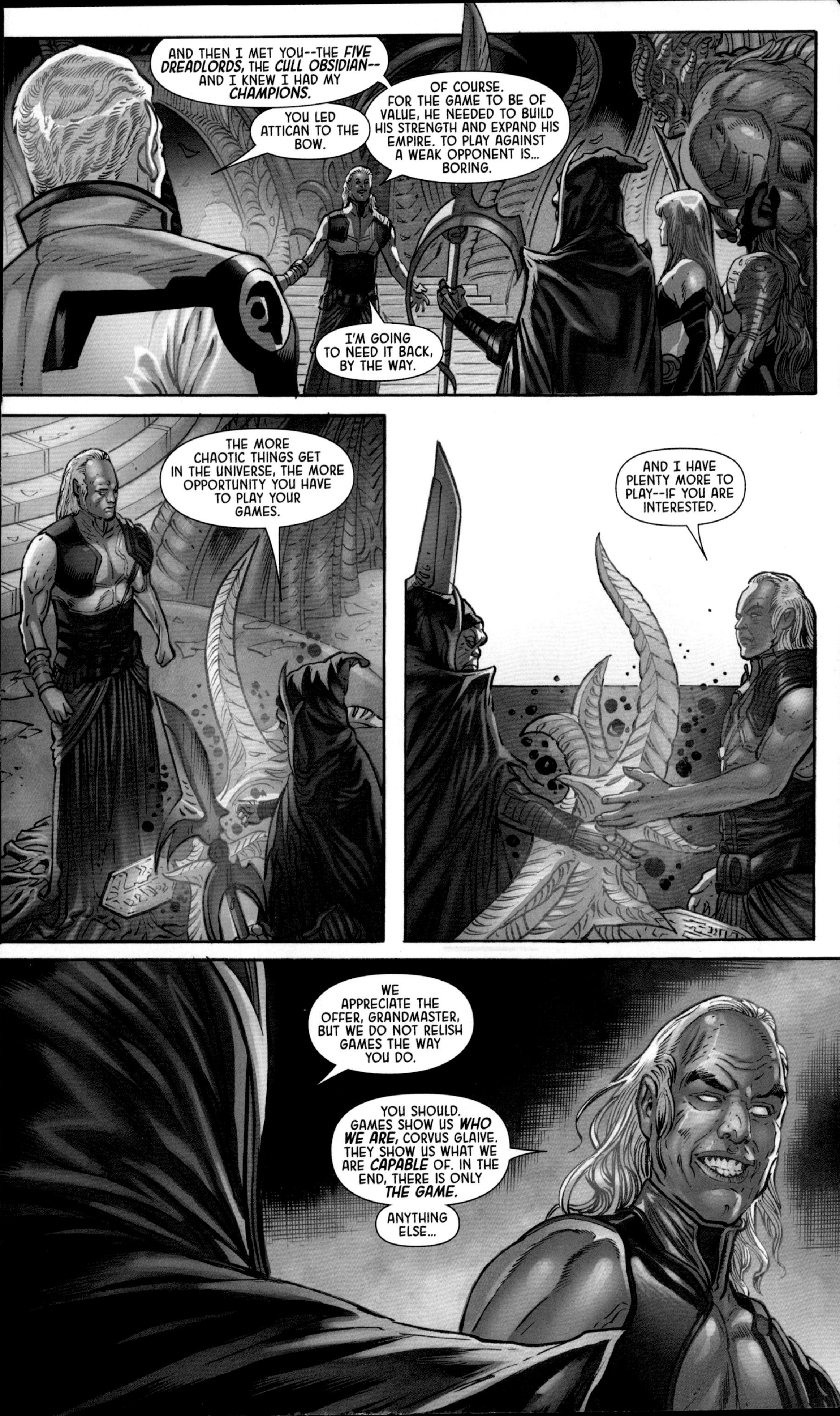

AND THEN I MET YOU--THE FIVE DREADLORDS, THE CULL OBSIDIAN--AND I KNEW I HAD MY CHAMPIONS.
YOU LED ATTICAN TO THE BOW.
OF COURSE. FOR THE GAME TO BE OF VALUE, HE NEEDED TO BUILD HIS STRENGTH AND EXPAND HIS EMPIRE. TO PLAY AGAINST A WEAK OPPONENT IS... BORING.
I'M GOING TO NEED IT BACK, BY THE WAY.
THE MORE CHAOTIC THINGS GET IN THE UNIVERSE, THE MORE OPPORTUNITY YOU HAVE TO PLAY YOUR GAMES.
AND I HAVE PLENTY MORE TO PLAY--IF YOU ARE INTERESTED.
WE APPRECIATE THE OFFER, GRANDMASTER, BUT WE DO NOT RELISH GAMES THE WAY YOU DO.
YOU SHOULD. GAMES SHOW US WHO WE ARE, CORVUS GLAIVE. THEY SHOW US WHAT WE ARE CAPABLE OF. IN THE END, THERE IS ONLY THE GAME.
ANYTHING ELSE...

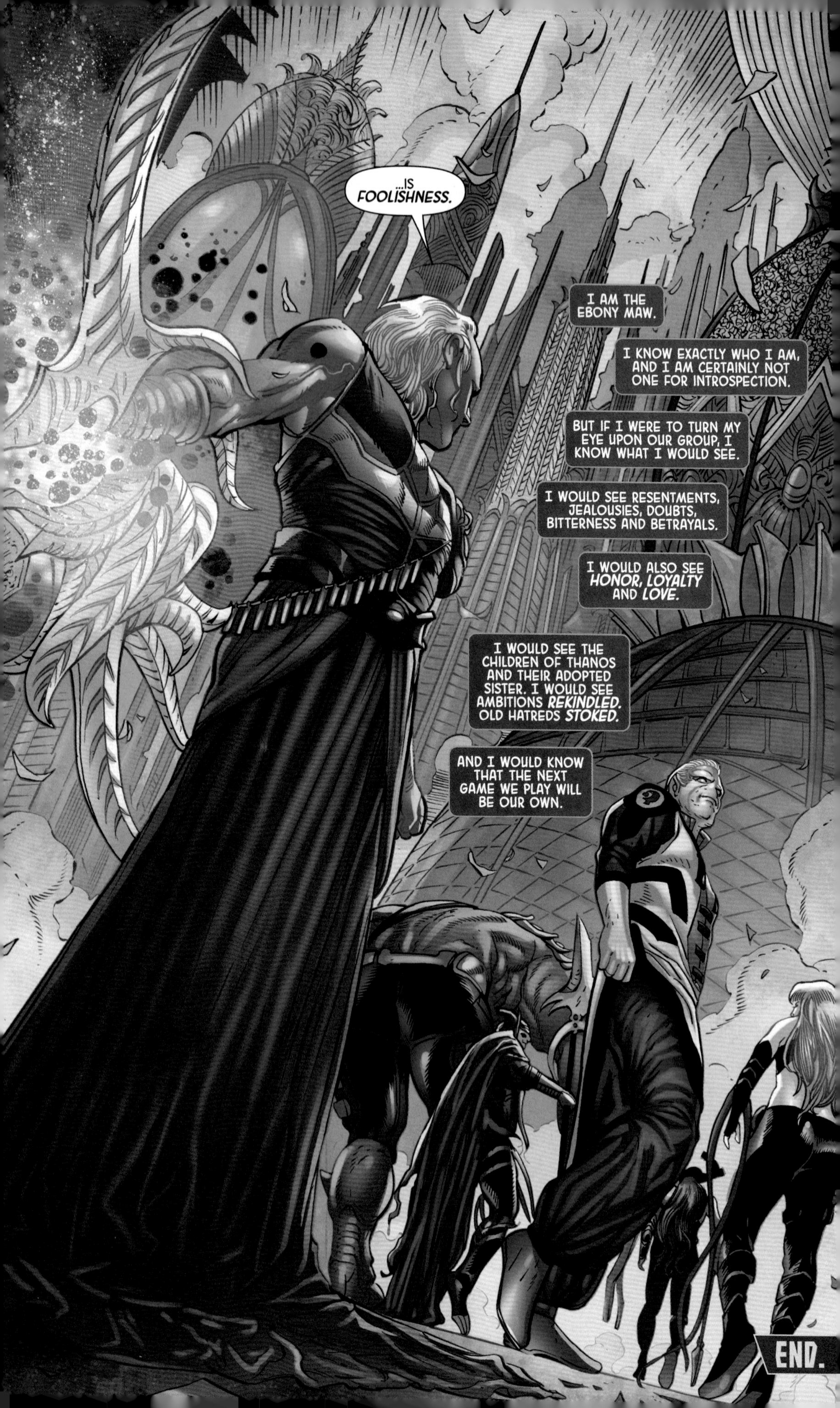
...IS FOOLISHNESS.
I AM THE EBONY MAW.
I KNOW EXACTLY WHO I AM, AND I AM CERTAINLY NOT ONE FOR INTROSPECTION.
BUT IF I WERE TO TURN MY EYE UPON OUR GROUP, I KNOW WHAT I WOULD SEE.
I WOULD SEE RESENTMENTS, JEALOUSIES, DOUBTS, BITTERNESS AND BETRAYALS.
I WOULD ALSO SEE HONOR, LOYALTY AND LOVE.
I WOULD SEE THE CHILDREN OF THANOS AND THEIR ADOPTED SISTER. I WOULD SEE AMBITIONS REKINDLED. OLD HATREDS STOKED.
AND I WOULD KNOW THAT THE NEXT GAME WE PLAY WILL BE OUR OWN.
END.

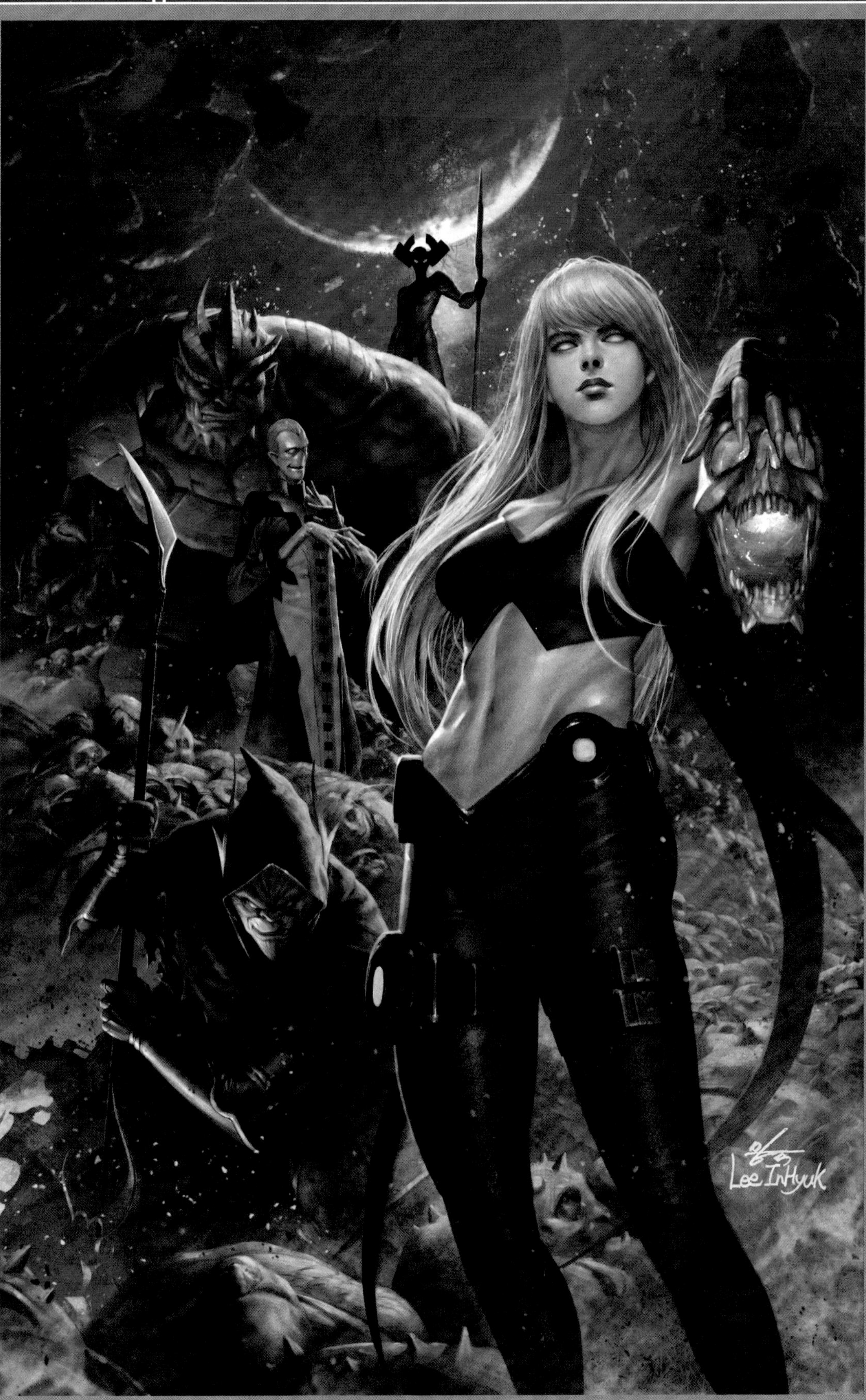
Lee InHyuk

#1 VARIANT
BY **INHYUK LEE**

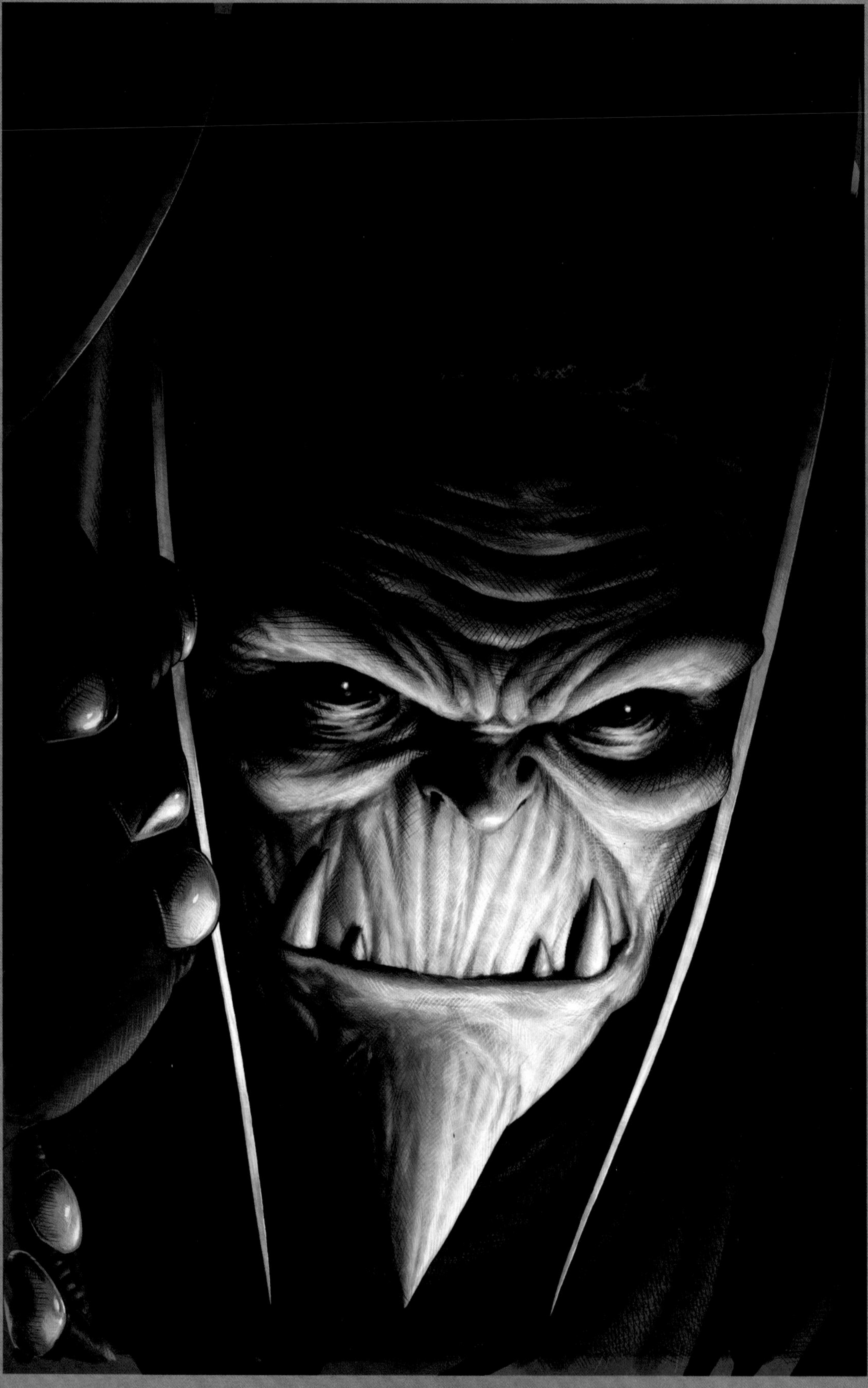

#1 VARIANT
BY **JOHN TYLER CHRISTOPHER**

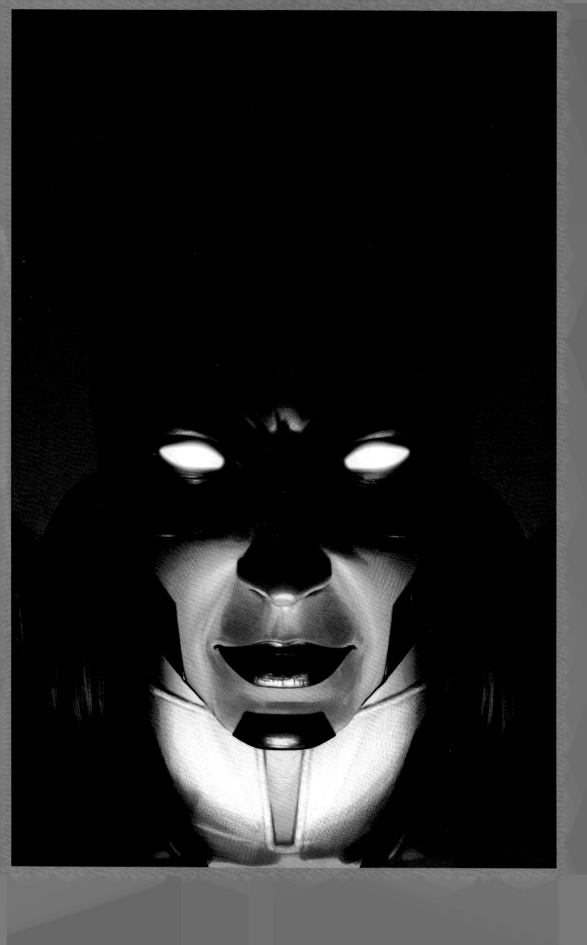

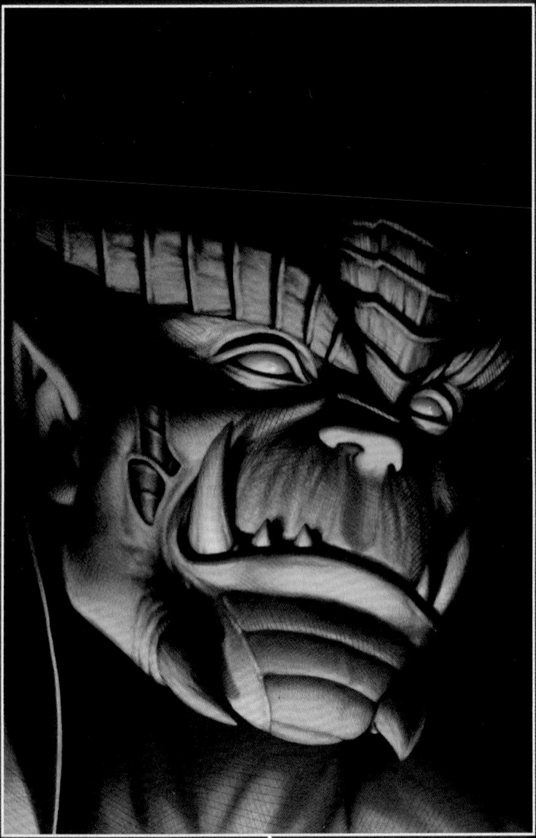

#3 VARIANT
BY **JOHN TYLER CHRISTOPHER**

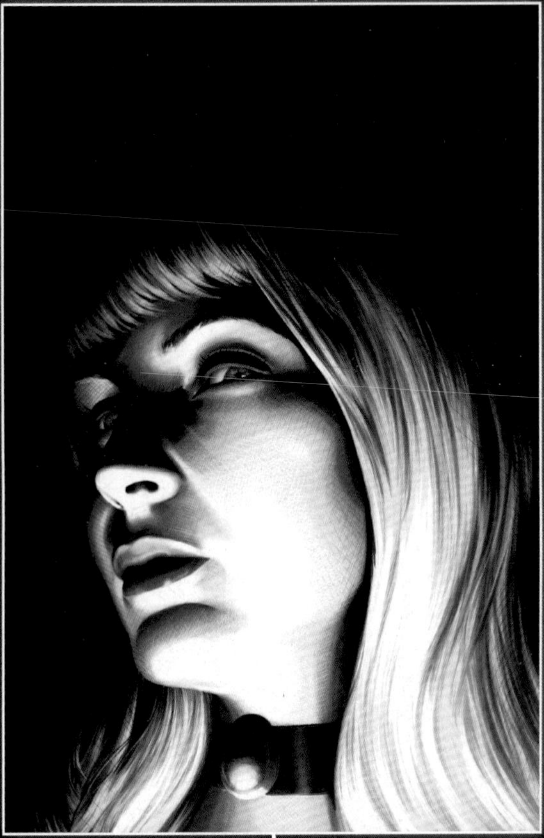

#4 VARIANT
BY **JOHN TYLER CHRISTOPHER**

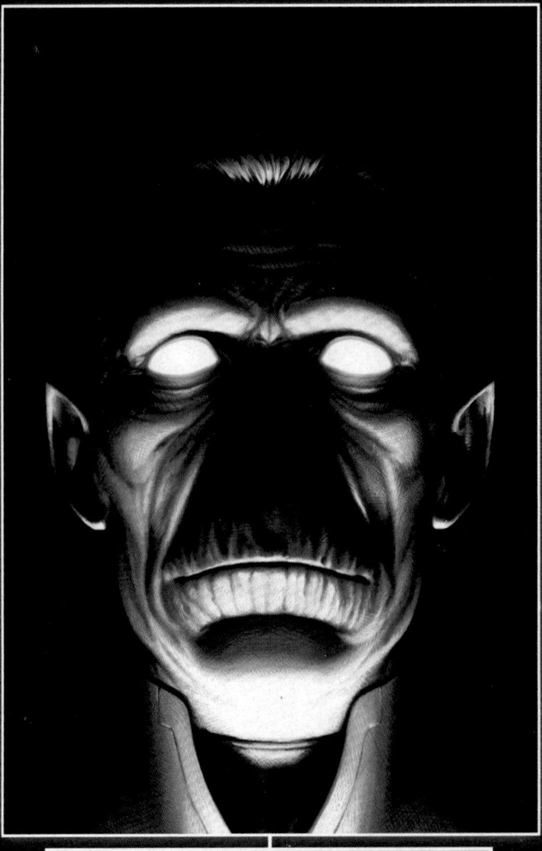

#5 VARIANT
BY **JOHN TYLER CHRISTOPHER**